TRAINING THE STREET℠

Preparing Financial Professionals for Success
www.trainingthestreet.com

123115.2

INTRODUCTION
How To Use This Guidebook

This guidebook discusses the primary valuation methods most commonly employed by valuation practitioners—from investment bankers and financial analysts to corporate managers and stock market investors. To gain the most from it, it is recommended that you review the basics of financial statements and financial statement analysis before you begin.

Please check our website at **www.trainingthestreet.com** for future potential products regarding accounting and financial statement analysis.

Chances are that the corporate finance and accounting principles you learned in the classroom had a theoretical twist. They probably lacked the practical emphasis that professionals give these concepts as they use them every day. At Training The Street (TTS), we have had years of experience in not only teaching the principles of valuation, but also using them as tools in a broad spectrum of real-world valuation situations and transactions. This guidebook is essentially a compact distillation of everything that we know. It provides you with the information you need and nothing more. Each chapter is clearly divided into four to seven topics, each beginning with an overview that offers a big picture of the central themes you will encounter in the chapter. Our aim is to teach valuation methods as if you were working for a Wall Street firm or in an investment house. In a lucid, practical way, we lay out the applied components of what you were taught in class, without shortchanging you on any of their most important conceptual underpinnings.

As you go through this practical material, however, bear in mind that learning is not about formula memorization, computational manipulation, or mechanical success in reaching the right answer. It is about understanding the underlying concepts, and why you are doing what you are doing. This book presents you with a box of razor-sharp tools, but it also sets them up within the contexts in which they are typically used.

Chapter 1: Investment banking and mergers and acquisitions (M&A)

Chapter 2: Corporate valuation and its techniques

Chapter 3: Public comparables analysis and how it works

Chapter 4: Acquisition comparables analysis and how it works

Chapter 5: Discounted cash flow analysis

Chapter 6: Merger consequences analysis

Chapter 7: Leveraged buyout analysis

Appendix: Real World Case Study

SPECIAL FEATURES

 Hotwords You will also come across ◀**hotwords**▶ throughout the book. These words, bolded and bracketed in solid arrowheads, are terms widely used in corporate finance and M&A work. They can be looked up in the Hotword Glossary at the end of the book.

 Key Formulas To accelerate learning, we have also identified key formulas we regard as especially critical to performing company valuations. You will recognize them by the "key" icon next to them.

 Mastery Quizzes At the end of each chapter, we've designed a set of questions to test your knowledge on the key topics covered throughout the chapter. Once you've answered the questions, check and see if you got the correct answers! We've provided you with not only an answer key, but also an explanation of the correct answer and the intuition behind our logic. Reading the explanations of any questions you miss will provide an additional learning opportunity, and show you the insight that a seasoned valuation professional uses when performing valuation analysis.

Text Boxes Finally, throughout the book there are sidebars, mini-case studies, and text boxes that address commonly asked questions, explain unfamiliar phrases, and offer you useful tips and fill-ins. Throughout the chapters, you will find the following:

> *Ask the Finance Guru* boxes present questions to which we have invited TTS experts to respond and share their thoughts. Because we train thousands of finance professionals every year, we have an experienced viewpoint in addressing the finance and valuation questions that puzzle students and practitioners alike. We have drawn on this reservoir of experience to frame and answer some of the most commonly posed questions.

> *Tips of the Trade* and *Rules of Thumb* boxes provide you with practical suggestions, calculation assistance, shortcut tools, how-to tips, and commonly encountered pitfalls and errors you should watch out for.

Financial Factoids and *Did You Know?* boxes present interesting, relevant facts that will help fill out your contextual knowledge of valuation, valuation analysis, and the industries in which they are employed.

A Word on Terminology and *Words to Know* boxes offer you quick definitions of difficult or arcane terms.

A final word of advice before we jump into the thick of things: try to view this book not as a "textbook" but rather as a practical guide that offers you a framework for the kinds of analyses finance professionals perform when they value businesses. Above all, we hope it will help demystify the whole topic of financial analysis by laying out in a truly clear, down-to-earth way the types of analytics finance professionals use every day when they go to work.

Have fun!

CHAPTER 1
Introduction to Investment Banking and M&A

TOPIC 1: WHAT IS AN INVESTMENT BANK?

Investment banks typically turn profits in three ways: assisting their clients in the buying and selling of securities or companies; raising capital for their clients; or making proprietary investments on their own behalf. Under these three broad categories, investment banks offer a multitude of products and services to their clients, which range from individual retail investors to large corporations.

When you are finished with this chapter, you should be able to:

- *have a general understanding of the functions and departments of an investment bank*

- *have a general understanding of the competitive landscape of financial institutions*

I. The Investment Banking Group

There are two main arms in an investment bank: the investment banking group, and the sales, trading and research group.

The investment banking group is the traditional arm. Its usual clients are corporations, government entities, and private equity firms seeking to raise capital, to buy another company, or to sell themselves. The investment banking group provides the advice and support capabilities necessary to complete the intended transaction. This may range from helping a private company complete an initial public offering ◀(IPO)▶, to arranging debt (for example, in the form of a bond) for a government municipality that needs to borrow money, to advising a large firm on a complicated merger.

But what exactly does the investment banking group do? As the traditional arm of an investment bank, much of its work is that of ◀underwriting▶ transactions. In short, underwriting means taking on the risk of raising capital for a client,

1

in exchange for fees. To assist a client that wants to raise money, the investment banking group assumes the risk of finding interested investors and the responsibility of placing the new stocks or bonds with them.

In a typical debt or equity underwriting, the investment banking group examines ways to create an optimal capital structure for the client through the offering. The group then structures the deal, draws in potential investors, helps the client's management to "pitch" the offering to the investors, and prices the deal.

 In an **◄M&A►** (mergers and acquisitions) transaction, the role of the investment banking group varies, depending on whether it is representing a prospective seller of a company or a buyer. In a "sell-side" transaction, the investment bank represents a client that wants to sell itself—hence the name. The group will identify and analyze potential buyers, manage the negotiation and sale process, and provide an opinion as to how much the client should sell for and to whom.

When the bank represents a buyer in a "buy-side" engagement, it analyzes prospective candidate targets that the client may wish to acquire. It also provides advice on how best to approach the most attractive target, guides the negotiations and provides an opinion regarding how much the client should pay for the target.

Striking the right price in an acquisition is, needless to say, hugely important. This book will examine some of the valuation tools that investment banks use when they value businesses both for sale and for purchase.

Within the investment banking division, there are often dozens of smaller groups that fall into one of two clusters: **industry groups** or **product groups**.

A. **Industry groups** are the investment bank's client managers. They establish and maintain relationships with the bank's clients and are involved in a transaction from the initial pitch to its close. An example of an industry group might be the consumer & retail industry group. Industry groups need to understand not only the particular issues each of their clients is facing, but also the broader industry in which that client does business—a challenge given the large differences and needs of companies in different industries.

FINANCIAL FACTOID:
SOME CONTRASTS TO NOTE

Generally, investment banks are made up of two super-groups: **investment banking and sales, trading, and research.** Bankers in the investment banking group work with **corporations**—in other words, with clients who need capital. Professionals in sales & trading or in research typically do not work with corporations but with **investors**—clients who have capital to invest. In a sense, the former work on the **demand** side, the latter on the **supply** side. The investment banking group advises clients, executes M&A and other major restructuring transactions, and raises capital using **confidential** information as one of its tools. Sales, trading, and research executes trades and provides research using **publicly** available information.

B. **Product groups** are different. Each one focuses on a particular kind of transaction. Although each bank organizes its product groups differently, there is usually an **M&A** group that specializes in buy-and-sell-side transactions, a **corporate finance** group that assists clients in finding an optimal capital structure for their particular transaction or security offering, a **product development** group that works on tailoring new securities, and a **capital markets** group that helps in the pricing, structuring, and sale of the securities.

Do the two kinds of groups work together? Yes, and increasingly so. For example, in the context of a deal, the industry groups coordinate the efforts of the product groups that are involved in the transaction. Generally, depending on the type of deal that comes in, one or two people from a particular industry group will work with a couple of people from a product group. For example, a managing director and an associate from the consumer & retail industry group might temporarily join forces with a vice president and an analyst from a product group such as M&A to assist a client in buying a target company. After the transaction is complete and the client-supporting roles are defined, the collaboration ends.

However, as the investment banking industry has become more competitive and banking services more commoditized, a trend has emerged toward "cross-selling" sophisticated combinations of banking products and services to one client. It is now common to see several groups working together on a deal. For example, the consumer & retail banker might work with an M&A banker on valuing the company, team up with debt capital markets to arrange the debt financing, and then have another group structure a ◀collar▶ on the target's purchase price. Cross-selling enables investment banks to provide clients with greater value, while at the same time generating higher fees per deal.

II. The Sales, Trading, and Research Group

The sales, trading, and research group helps investors buy and sell securities in the secondary market. Its clients include retail investors, high-net-worth individuals, insurance companies, and large institutional investors such as hedge funds, pension funds, and mutual funds. Sales, trading, and research actually consists of three related sub-groups:

A. The sales professionals develop relationships with the bank's clients and provide them with investment advice. Depending on the type of account, they make commissions from the trades (that is, purchases and sales of securities), or they earn fees based on the assets the client has placed with the bank.

B. The traders help the sales people by providing liquidity to the clients. They do this by executing trades requested by the clients, or by buying and selling the bank's own inventory of securities to the clients. Each trade is usually profitable for the trading desk by a small amount called a bid-ask spread, which is the difference between what a client can buy the security for, and what they can sell it for. It is therefore critical for traders to generate large volumes of trades.

C. The research professionals are a bit different from those in sales and trading. They focus on analyzing companies, markets, and products. Their research is then published to benefit clients and the other groups in the bank. For example, their conclusions and insights into companies and markets are often used by the sales team in pitching ideas to the bank's clients in order to generate fresh trading revenue. Professionals from the investment banking group also use the earnings projections of the research staff to help build their projection models.

A Complicated Relationship
There is a complicated relationship between the two arms of an investment bank—the investment banking group and the sales, trading, and research group. They need each other, yet at the same time they are forbidden from collaborating too closely or even appearing to be collaborating. On the one hand, the success of an investment bank's underwriting operations depends on the linkage between the two groups. The investment bankers would have little hope of winning any IPO mandates if they did not have the investor distribution network in which to sell the new issuances, research analysts to provide the investors with some guidance on the company issuing the securities, and traders to support a secondary market in the stock.

On the other hand, there is a significant conflict of interest between the work of the investment banking group and that of the sales, trading, and research group. Investment bankers have access to confidential information from the corporations; yet sales, trading, and research make their clients money by buying and selling in the public market the securities of those very corporations whose confidential information the investment bankers peruse every day. As a result, in recent years the relationship between investment banking and research has become highly regulated, requiring a "Chinese wall" between public and private functions, and specific protocols for any direct interaction between them. The bank's left arm must literally not let the right arm know what it is doing.

TOPIC 2: THE COMPETITIVE LANDSCAPE

Just as an investment bank makes money in several different ways, investment banks also have their own specialties and reputations and fall into a number of different categories.

The following discussion of landscape is as of the date of this original writing. Needless to say, the landscape in this field is constantly changing and will no doubt continue to change. Please feel free to rely on your resources for updated information.

I. The Bulge Bracket

The so-called bulge bracket banks are the largest and most active investment banks as measured by a variety of ◀**league table**▶ standings. Numbering fewer than a dozen, they receive the most media attention and are the most publicly visible. They have dominant underwriting and M&A franchises and are typically involved in the biggest deals, often acting as the main underwriters in new issues of securities.

II. Advisory Boutiques, the Middle Market, and Others

Outside the bulge bracket are firms that sometimes compete directly with the bulge-bracket firms for business, but more often target different markets or undertake specialized work. There are several different types:

- Advisory boutiques which focus on specialty M&A deals.

- Middle-market investment banks which concentrate on serving ◀**middle-market**▶ companies. These banks have their own sales, trading, and research operations and raise capital for their clients in addition to providing them with M&A advice.

- There are even more specialized banks that focus on specific industries or on a specific practice, such as restructuring work.

CHAPTER 2
Introducing Corporate Valuation

QUICK SUMMARY

When you are finished with this chapter, you should be able to:

- *understand which valuation methods finance professionals most commonly use and some basic differences among them;*

- *understand some of the main considerations professionals have in mind, and the key questions they try to answer, when they undertake valuation analyses;*

- *appreciate some of the fundamental limitations inherent in the valuation process;*

- *understand four of the basic building blocks that professionals use in valuation analyses—Equity Value, Enterprise Value, EBIT and EBITDA—and how to measure them.*

The five most commonly used company valuation methods are:

1. Public Comparables Analysis
2. Acquisition Comparables Analysis
3. Discounted Cash Flow (DCF) Analysis
4. Merger Consequences Analysis
5. Leveraged Buyout Analysis (LBO)

There are some broad similarities and differences among these valuation techniques: Public Comparables and Acquisition Comparables both value a company by looking outside—by comparing relevant statistics about the company or transaction to others that are similar. DCF and LBO Analyses value a company by looking inside—by estimating its capacity to generate future cash flows. LBO analysis and Merger Consequences are "affordability" analyses: they try to determine how much a buyer could afford to pay for a company.

Each of the next five chapters in this book is devoted to covering one of these five valuation approaches. In this chapter, you will learn about two different ways of representing a company's value: Equity Value and Enterprise Value. We will use them to calculate Equity Value-based metrics such as the price to earnings (P/E) multiple, and Enterprise Value-based metrics such as EBIT and EBITDA. The P/E ratio is one of the more frequently encountered multiple-based indicators of value. EBIT and EBITDA are also two of the more commonly used measures of financial performance.

Life, of course, is never simple, so we will discuss some common complications in measuring value—such as what to do with non-recurring items in the income statement. The sections, examples, and exercises below are designed to give you a practical grasp of these topics.

TOPIC 1: VALUATION TECHNIQUES: AN OVERVIEW

Purpose of Valuation
Why do we measure a company's value at all? There are many reasons why financial analysts, investors, bankers, and companies undertake valuation analyses. Knowing what ◄strike price► your company should use in issuing ◄options►, whether to advise a company to accept an acquisition offer, whether to hold or sell your 1,000 shares in Apple, or how to price your stock as your company prepares for an ◄IPO►, are all decisions that are made more intelligently when some valuation work has been done ahead of time.

Let's take a closer look at valuation by examining an actual transaction. On May 18, 2014, the following headline and paragraph appeared in a news article.

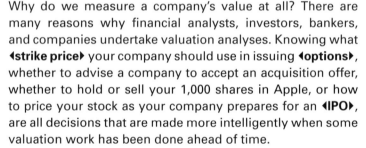

AT&T to Acquire DirecTV in $49 Billion Deal

AT&T, Inc. agreed to acquire DirecTV for $49 billion, a deal that would enable it to be a large player in television and increase is power with media companies at a time when video consumption is going online. The deal shows how the biggest companies in telecommunications are bulking up to face an ever-changing media environment.

$49 billion! How did the acquirer's finance advisory team come up with this figure? Might another team have come up with a different number? Is this an art or a science? If it is at least partly a science, what fundamental principles of valuation drive this kind of calculation? And what exactly does the amount represent? Does the acquirer take on the target's debt, if it has any, or only its equity? Let's look under the hood of this transaction.

Valuing DirecTV

Imagine your supervisor asks you to try valuing DirecTV because AT&T, a long-time client of your bank, is thinking of buying it. There are **two** key questions you must ask right away.

QUESTION ONE:

What is the target actually worth, and how do I go about valuing it?

Seeing no purpose in reinventing the wheel, you go over and ask a seasoned colleague experienced in valuation: "What valuation techniques do *you* use the most?" His or her typical response would be:

Public Comparables, Acquisition Comparables, and Discounted Cash Flow (or, more likely, your colleague would just say "Comps" & "DCF").

These three are the bread-and-butter tools of corporate finance. You will get a chance to master them later on. The first two approaches are *relative* valuation techniques: you value the company by looking outside, at other companies and/or transactions. The third method is an *intrinsic* valuation technique: you value the company by looking at the company itself as a stand-alone entity.

▶ **Public Comparables Analysis**
Here, you are trying to figure out the target's value by looking at the value of comparable firms. You're trying to determine the target's *relative value* based on its *peers*. *(More about this in Chapter 3.)*

▶ **Acquisition Comparables Analysis**
Here, again, you are trying to determine the target's relative value, but this time based on similar past transactions within the same industry. *(More on this in Chapter 4.)*

▶ **Discounted Cash Flow Analysis**
Here, you are not making any comparisons. You are trying to calculate the target's intrinsic value by figuring out how

much free cash flow the company generates. You do this by projecting its **◀unlevered free cash flows▶** out several years into the future, and then calculating what those cash flows are worth today. *(More about this in Chapter 5.)*

QUESTION TWO:

What could or would someone pay for this company? How attractive or affordable is it to potential buyers?

This is the second question you need to ask in your valuation exercise. Valuation experts typically answer this question using "affordability" analyses. Merger Consequences Analysis and Leveraged Buyout Analysis are the two most commonly accepted methods:

▶ Merger Consequences Analysis

What you are evaluating here is this: if an acquirer bought a target company, what impact would the transaction likely have on the acquirer's financial position as a strategic buyer? The answer to this will help determine not only how attractive the target is to the acquirer but also how much the acquirer could afford to pay for it. *(More about this in Chapter 6.)*

> *Example*
> *On March 16, 2015, Valeant Pharmaceuticals raised its M&A takeover price to take out rival bidder Endo International PLC. The per-share price was bumped up to $173 (all in cash), or $11.1 billion in total, up $15 from the $158 price Salix agreed to take from Valeant back in February 2015. As a result, Endo withdrew its cash and stock bid.*

▶ Leveraged Buyout (LBO) Analysis

LBO analysis is similar, but what you are asking here instead is: What could a private equity firm (a financial buyer) afford to pay for the target company? LBOs are acquisitions primarily funded with debt—hence the term "leveraged" buyout. *(More on this in Chapter 7.)*

> *Example*
> *On December 14, 2014, it was announced that PetSmart Inc. has agreed to be bought by a consortium investor group led by BC Partners. The deal was for more than $8.2 billion, making it one of the largest LBO deals of 2014. BC Partners prevailed over other private-equity firms Apollo and KKR that had been vying for the retailer.*

Let's delve a little more into affordability analysis. There are a few core questions you must ask to determine what someone is willing to pay for a company:

QUESTION ONE:

*What type of **buyer** are we talking about?*

The world is made up of two kinds of buyers: ◀**Strategic buyers**▶ tend to be other operating companies interested in the long- term investment prospects of the acquisition. Often times the buyer is in the same industry as the target firm, and perhaps even a competitor of it. The second kind of buyer is a ◀**financial buyer**▶. Financial buyers acquire a company and try to create value by taking on additional debt (leverage) while using the cash flows of the acquired business to pay down the debt in the near term. When you come across phrases such as private equity firm, PE shop, financial sponsor, or buyout fund, they often mean a financial buyer.

QUESTION TWO:

*What is the transactional **context**?*

A transaction can be either a "hostile" or a "friendly" deal. In a ◀**hostile transaction**▶, the target company doesn't want to sell, and its shareholders receive an unsolicited offer for their shares. For example, on January 5, 2014, Pfizer offered 46.61 GBP for AstraZeneca. The original bid was rejected by AstraZeneca. Pfizer then made a revised of 50 GBP on May 2, 2014 and a "final" offer at 55 GBP on May 18, 2014. AstraZeneca had told Pfizer that it would need to offer around 58-59 GBP in order to secure the board's recommendation. By contrast, in a ◀**friendly**▶ deal, the acquirer and the target reach a mutual agreement on the selling price and the structure of the transaction.

QUESTION THREE:

*What are the **market conditions**? What premiums were paid in recent comparable transactions? In short, what kind of period are we currently in, and what is the mood within the industry or on Wall Street?*

Historically, when stock markets perform well, M&A activity tends to be robust. In the late 1990s and early & mid 2000s, and, more recently, 2013 to 2015, stock indices hit all-time highs and M&A activity soared. In mid-2007, there was a liquidity crisis and downturn in the stock market, and M&A activity followed the same trend.

Art or Science?

Finance practitioners will tell you that valuation is both an **art** and a **science**. Why is it an art? Because it requires judgment based on the intuitive, subjective interpretation of data. That is why seasoned professional experience can prove so invaluable when determining what someone will pay in an M&A transaction. Different finance teams can have varying interpretations of the same downward data and therefore arrive at distinct valuations based on their answers to questions such as: Does the target company have a quality management team? How quickly or slowly do you expect the company to grow over the next five years? Or next ten years? Changes in your assumptions about expected growth can generate dramatically different valuations.

Valuation is a subjective process in a second sense: transactions involve human parties. Selling the company's story to buyers and crafting the deal are often critical to completing the transaction.

Yet valuation is also very much a **science**, and that is what a book such as this one can help you to learn. There is a powerful toolkit of methods and techniques to help you create a reasonable analytical justification for a potential transaction. How did you determine your DCF value? What are the current market valuation metrics for the public comparables? A financial advisor's task is to create a reasonable, defensible valuation based on the information available.

In summary, there are both **subjective** and **objective** elements in determining a company's value. The ideal strategy then, is to learn both approaches and to synthesize them.

TOPIC 2: MEASURING COMPANY VALUE

Some basic building blocks

Public Comparables, Acquisition Comparables, DCF, Merger Consequences, and LBO analyses are approaches to, or methods of, corporate valuation that are based upon certain building blocks and foundations. In this section, we will review some of the basic building blocks used in these approaches. DCF analysis, for example, is based on projecting future cash flows. The building blocks there are ◄**unlevered free cash flows**► (UFCF) and ◄**weighted average cost of capital**► (WACC). Public Comparables and Acquisition Comparables, by contrast, are based not on the projection of cash flows but on the calculation of multiples, which are financial ratios built around the foundation of Equity Value, Enterprise Value, EBIT, and EBITDA. The first component we will look at is a measure of company value.

I. Equity Value or Enterprise Value?

Equity Value and Enterprise Value are the two most commonly-used measures of a company's public market value. As we will see, each concept serves a different but useful role. Before we learn how to calculate them, let's define what they are.

A company's ◀**Equity Value**▶ is essentially the value of its shareholders' interest. It is the market value of the company's shares in the stock exchange. Unlike the company's formal ◀**Book Value**▶, the market value tends to fluctuate daily or weekly, reflecting movements in the stock market and the company's share price.

By contrast, a company's ◀**Enterprise Value**▶ represents the value of *both* its equity and its debt capital. Enterprise Value is Equity Value plus Net Debt (technically, any ◀**preferred stock**▶ and ◀**noncontrolling interest**▶ (often called minority interest) should also be included in the calculation of Enterprise Value). It is the company's entire economic value, or the total value to all of its capital holders, not just its shareholders. Put differently, it measures the company's market value from the viewpoint of all of its financing sources.[1]

Think of it this way. Let's say you purchased a condo for $700,000: $150,000 cash down, and a mortgage of $550,000. As your condo's single "shareholder" or equity investor, your equity is worth $150,000. That is how much you personally invested in it. But the condo's total **Enterprise Value**, of course, is more than just the $150,000 down payment. Its Enterprise Value includes the $550,000 you borrowed from the lender. Enterprise Value, in other words, takes account of the condo's value to *all* contributors of capital: equity (from you) and debt (from your creditors or debtholders).

By contrast, **Equity Value** captures only the value that the contributors of equity have put into the entity. In the case of a condo, that is the homeowner. In the case of a publicly-owned company, it is the common stockholders.

---

1 Technically, Enterprise Value also includes the value of all **preferred stock** and **noncontrolling interest**. In this book, however, we will not cover these other two forms of capital because, compared to debt, they are much less common.

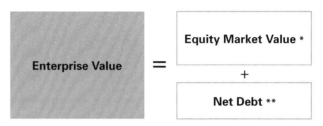

Enterprise Value =	**Equity Market Value** * + **Net Debt** **

*Not to scale, Equity Market Value is usually the largest component
**Any preferred stock and noncontrolling interest should also be included in the Enterprise Value calculation

II. Calculating Equity Value and Enterprise Value

Now, let's walk through the mechanics of calculating Equity Value and then Enterprise Value. Equity Value is simply:

> **Equity Value = Share Price x Diluted Shares Outstanding**

But share prices fluctuate all the time, sometimes literally by the briefest of moments. So to reflect the most up-to-date market valuation, you would typically use the current share price or the latest closing stock price. In addition, most finance professionals use the current ◀**diluted shares**▶ outstanding to reflect potential shares from ◀**options**▶ and ◀**convertible securities**▶.

Exercise

Let's try this with an imaginary public company, Blue Coolite Corporation. Blue Coolite currently trades at $45.76 per share. The company has 99.882 million diluted shares outstanding. What is its Equity Value?

Share Price	$45.76
x Diluted Shares Outstanding	99.882
= Equity Value of Blue Coolite Corp.	⌐ ¬ million

Answer:

Share Price	$45.76
x Diluted Shares Outstanding	99.882
= Equity Value of Blue Coolite Corp.	$4,570.6 million

Now that you have calculated Equity Value, let's take a look at Enterprise Value:

> **Enterprise Value = Equity Value + Net Debt**

There are four practical points to keep in mind when calculating Enterprise Value:

> ◆ **Net Debt = Total Debt – Cash & Equivalents.** We use Net Debt rather than total debt because we are assuming that

---

WHAT IS A DILUTED SHARE?

A diluted share count is a more conservative way of looking at a share count for a company. It not only includes the current shares outstanding for the company, but also any new shares that could arise from the exercise of options and convertible securities.

FINANCIAL FACTOID

Enterprise Value is Equity Value plus Net Debt. Net Debt is total debt minus Cash & Equivalents. So Enterprise Value tends to be **larger** than Equity Value because most companies have more total debt than Cash & Equivalents (i.e., Net Debt is a **positive** number). But some firms—Apple is one example, as are many technology firms—have more Cash & Equivalents than total debt (i.e., Net Debt is a negative number). For such companies, Enterprise Value will actually be smaller than Equity Value.

a company with cash will use that cash to pay down its total debt, dollar-for-dollar. For example, if a company has $100 million of debt, and $10 million of cash, then the company would have $90 million of "net debt".

• Typically, you should use the latest balance sheet to make sure your analysis has the most up-to-date cash and debt numbers. Look again at the formula above. Notice that Equity Value is shown at "Market Value," or derived from a market price. Technically, this means you should use the Market Value of debt and other capital to be consistent. However, not all debt trades in public markets, so determining its Market Value can be quite tedious. As a proxy for Market Value of debt, many professionals use the ◀**Book Value**▶ from the balance sheet. This often works well, but watch out for situations where the market value of debt varies from its book value—for example, in the case of a financially distressed company.

• Debt balances should include all interest-bearing liabilities on the balance sheet.

• Normally, Cash & Equivalents includes any short-term marketable securities that are liquid and easily converted to cash.

Let's try calculating Enterprise Value for Blue Coolite Corp. using its latest balance sheet.

Balance Sheet for Blue Coolite Corp.

Dollars in Millions

Cash	$288.9
Accounts receivables (net)	272.7
Inventories	425.7
Other current assets	42.1
Total Current Assets	**1,029.4**
PP&E (net)	704.2
Intangibles	95.2
Goodwill	417.7
Other long-term assets	287.4
Total Assets	**2,533.9**
Accounts payable	$203.6
Accrued liabilities	103.3
Income taxes payable	141.8
Short-term debt	5.8
Current portion of long-term debt	10.0
Total Current Liabilities	**464.5**
Long-term debt	361.5
Deferred income taxes	257.4
Other long-term liabilities	51.5
Total liabilities	**1,134.9**
Total equity	1,399.0
Total Liabilities and Equity	**2,533.9**

Remember the formula for Enterprise Value = Equity Value + Net Debt. Also, remember that whenever you see the Excel icon on the left, you can use the Excel templates that come with this book to help you solve the problem. The solutions for all the Excel-based problems are also in the Excel file.

Exercise

Equity Value of Blue Coolite Corp.		million
+Short-term Debt		
+Current Portion of Long-term Debt		
+Long-term Debt		
– Cash and Cash Equivalents		
= Enterprise Value of Blue Coolite Corp		million

Answer

Equity Value of Blue Coolite Corp.	$4,570.6	million
+Short-term Debt	5.8	
+Current Portion of Long-term Debt	10.0	
+Long-term Debt	361.5	
– Cash and Cash Equivalents	(288.9)	
= Enterprise Value of Blue Coolite Corp	$4,659.0	million

ASK THE FINANCE GURU

What is the difference between Total Cash and Excess Cash?

Total Cash is all the cash a company has on its balance sheet. Excess Cash is Total Cash minus any required operating or financial cash needs. When calculating Net Debt, Excess Cash is the more accurate measure to use. But Excess Cash is often difficult to estimate and varies from company to company, so finance practitioners often use Total Cash as a simplifying proxy.

TOPIC 3: MEASURING FINANCIAL PERFORMANCE: EBIT AND EBITDA

Now that we have calculated Equity Value and Enterprise Value, we are ready to start looking at the company's financial performance indicators. But before we do that, let's step back and look at the big picture to see where we are. The essential question corporate valuation analysis seeks to answer is, *What would a buyer get for his money?* In other words, valuation analysis and valuation ratios are used to compare:

1. how much a company would cost a buyer, versus
2. how well the company is being run.

Equity Value and Enterprise Value, which we have learned to calculate under Topic 2, address the **first** part of this equation: how much is a company worth? They also potentially give an idea as to how much you have to spend to acquire a company. EBIT and EBITDA address the **second** part of the equation: what you get for your money—that is, how well the company is performing.

EBIT and EBITDA are two key financial performance measures that, in turn, ultimately influence a firm's Equity and Enterprise Values (i.e., how much buyers—or stock investors, for that matter—are willing to pay for it). Let's start with **EBIT**.

EBIT stands for **E**arnings **B**efore **I**nterest and **T**axes. It is essentially a company's earnings before you deduct financing expenses. The *interest* the company pays on money borrowed, and the *taxes* it pays to the IRS, are both items which are not related to the core operations of a business. In other words, EBIT gives you a snapshot of the company's raw profitability from only its operating activities by eliminating the effects of financing and other capital structure decisions that the company has made.

You can think of it this way: a company with "high operating profitability" is a company with a high EBIT. But note that this does not tell us anything about the company's tax and interest expenses, which could be very high as well. Those expenses will affect the company's *Net Income*, but not its EBIT (its operating profitability). To give you a handle on this, take a look at the financial information below.

	Axxiss Corp.	Gotham Co.
Sales	$100.0	$100.0
Cost of goods sold.............................	45.0	45.0
Gross profit.......................................	55.0	55.0
Selling, general & administrative......	25.0	25.0
Depreciation & amortization..............	10.0	10.0
EBIT...	20.0	20.0
Interest expense................................	5.0	10.0
Pretax income	15.0	10.0
Taxes @ 40%.......................................	6.0	4.0
Net Income...	**$9.0**	**$6.0**

On purely an *operating basis*, which company is more profitable, Axxiss or Gotham? Or are they equally profitable? The answer is that on an operating basis, they are equally profitable. Why? Because even though Axxiss has more after-tax, after-interest *Net Income*, before taxes and interest it has the same earnings, or EBIT, as Gotham: $20 million.

The *financing* decisions that determine what a company's capital structure will be—that is, how much debt it will take on versus how much equity capital has been invested—influence how much interest the company pays. This in turn affects its taxable income and hence how much it pays in taxes, which together determine its Net Income. Net Income therefore reflects financing decisions. By contrast, operating profitability (captured by EBIT) is income measured before you include the effects of any financing activities.

EBIT allows you to separate *operating* activities, which are intrinsic to the company itself and not that easily changed, from *financing* activities, which are extrinsic because they depend on whether the company chooses to finance growth with debt vs. equity, which lenders the company went to, and what rates the lenders offered the company. In that sense, EBIT tells you how efficient the operating business is while disregarding the company's financing decisions (or capital structure) inside the company itself.

		Axxiss Corp.	Gotham Co.
	Sales	$100.0	$100.0
	Cost of goods sold.............................	45.0	45.0
	Gross profit.......................................	55.0	55.0
	Selling, general & administrative......	25.0	25.0
"Above the line"	Depreciation & amortization..............	10.0	10.0
Operating	EBIT..	20.0	20.0
Financing	Interest expense.................................	5.0	10.0
"Below the line"	Pretax income	15.0	10.0
	Taxes @ 40%	6.0	4.0
	Net Income...	**$9.0**	**$6.0**

Look at the dotted line above. It neatly separates these two activity groups—operating and financing. Both companies have the same EBIT ($20 million) because EBIT measures income from operations, and the two companies have identical operating activities (those above the dotted line). In fact, EBIT is commonly referred to as "the line"; and anything above "the line" is considered part of core operations. Precisely because EBIT is independent of a company's capital structure, it offers practitioners a useful and ready way of comparing the operations of two companies.

EBITDA

Now that we know what EBIT is, we can calculate EBITDA. **EBITDA** stands for **E**arnings **B**efore **I**nterest, **T**axes, **D**epreciation and **A**mortization. It is basically EBIT with Depreciation and Amortization (D&A) added in. If EBIT is essentially *operating profitability*, EBITDA is essentially a surrogate for *operating cash flow*. EBITDA effectively removes from the analysis the impact of financing, major capital investments, and the resultant depreciation, by eliminating the effects of the company's capital structure and accounting decisions.

Keep in mind, however, that EBITDA is not a formal accounting definition but a rough proxy or stand-in for cash flow, because it takes EBIT and then adds two ◄non-cash► expenses, depreciation and amortization. Cash flow is centrally important when you are valuing a company because it measures the actual cash generated by its operations rather than just the accounting profit on paper.

Let's try to identify EBIT from the income statement on the next page and use it to calculate EBITDA.

Income Statement for Talimara Corporation

Sales	$2,111,830
Cost of sales	1,617,261
Gross profit	494,569
Selling, general & administrative	331,695
Loss on divestiture	–
Operating income	162,874
Interest expense	10,510
Other income (net)	2,633
Pre-tax income	154,997
Income tax expense	58,899
Income before cumulative effect of accounting change	96,098
Cumulative effect of accounting change (net of tax of $17,920)	(59,782)
Net Income	**$36,316**

The very first thing you should do when you are trying to determine EBIT from an income statement is to identify which line items relate to the company's core operations. In the example above, Talimara's core operations are represented by "Sales," "Cost of Sales," and "Selling, General & Administrative." So EBIT is most likely "Operating Income" ($162,874).

ASK THE FINANCE GURU

Why didn't you include "Other income, net" in Talimara's EBIT?

It really depends on the industry and the situation. In the example above, the disclosure that accompanied "Other income, net" showed that this entry consisted mainly of interest income, which is financing-related. Remember that EBIT is income from operations before you bring in the effects of taxes and interest payments from financing. Because Talimara's interest income is financing-related, we excluded this line item from EBIT. But there are situations where items such as interest income could be a part of operations. A financial institution, for example, would count interest income as part of its operating income.

Sample Cash Flow from Talimara's Operations

Cash Flow From Operating Activities

Net Income	$36,316
Adjustments to reconcile Net Income to net cash provided by operating activities	
Cumulative effect of accounting change – net of income taxes	59,782
Loss on divestiture	–
Depreciation and amortization	30,695
Change in receivables	42,376
Change in inventories	(41,028)
Change in payables	9,927
Change in other assets and liabilities	(19,080)
Change in deferred taxes	6,004
Proceeds from insurance recovery	–
Total adjustments	88,676
Net cash provided by operating activities	**$124,992**

After you have calculated EBIT from the income statement ($162,874 in this case), the next step is to search for D&A. Again, the first place to look is on Talimara's cash flow statement—specifically under "Cash flow from Operations." You will notice from the disclosure above that D&A for Talimara is $30,695. This means that EBITDA = $193,569 ($162,874 + $30,695).

TOPIC 4: NORMALIZING FINANCIALS: COMPLICATIONS IN CALCULATING EBIT

When you are examining financial statements, calculating EBIT is not as simple as just finding the firm's reported operating income and utilizing that as EBIT in your analysis. There are a couple of wrinkles you need to know about. Let's look at two examples.

The first is **non-recurring items**. These are items that are not part of the company's normal course of business, and therefore not likely to be replicated in the future. To be able to draw meaningful comparisons between a company's past and future performance, and between the company and other companies, practitioners often adjust for these one-time, out-of-the-blue anomalies.

Examples of non-recurring items include (but are not limited to):

- Restructuring charges
- A gain or loss on the sale of a division

* A gain on the sale of an investment
* Asset impairment charges
  (including the impairment of goodwill)
* Legal settlements

Let's look at the following income statement, from Sprint Nextel:

SPRINT NEXTEL CORPORATION

CONSOLIDATED STATEMENTS OF OPERATIONS

	Year Ended December 31,		
	2007	*2006*	*2005*
	(in millions, except share amounts)		
Net operating revenues	$40,146	$41,003	$28,771
Operating expenses			
Cost of services & products (exclusive of depreciation included below)	17,191	16,763	12,537
Selling, general and administrative	12,673	11,957	8,850
Severance, exit costs and asset impairments	440	207	43
Goodwill impairment	29,729	—	—
Depreciation	5,711	5,738	3,864
Amortization	3,312	3,854	1,336
	69,056	38,519	26,630
Operating income (loss)	(28,910)	2,484	2,141

At first glance, it would appear that Sprint Nextel went from an operating profit of $2.5 billion in 2006 to an operating **loss** of $28.9 billion in 2007! What is going on? The answer lies in the "Goodwill impairment" charge. If you adjust EBIT by excluding this one-time charge, Sprint Nextel's "adjusted" EBIT for 2007 is actually about $0.8 billion, not a loss of $28.9 billion—A big difference!

ASK THE FINANCE GURU

What is a good example of the "story" behind a non-recurring event?

To answer this, let's look at the "goodwill impairment" charge that Sprint Nextel took in 2007. This accounting write-down reflected the fact that, toward the end of 2007, the valuation of the Wireless segment had dramatically fallen from when the Nextel deal closed in 2004. Because the impairment charge was non-cash, however, it did not reduce actual 2007 cash flow. Yet even so, the impairment signals that the company expected to have significantly lower future cash flows and therefore a lower valuation.

Now that we know how to identify non-recurring items, let's try to calculate The Pearson Co.'s *normalized* EBIT below, adjusting for the non-recurring charge. Start by thinking about what the "adjustment" for the restructuring charge is. What would the "normalized" restructuring charge and "normalized" EBIT be? Here is the rule of thumb: To reverse the effect of the charge, treat the non-recurring item *as if it never occurred*.

Exercise

Income Statement
The Pearson Co.

	Reported	Adjustment	Normalized
Sales	$1,248.0		$1,248.0
Cost of goods sold	773.0		773.0
Gross profit	475.0		475.0
SG&A expense	275.0		275.0
Restructuring Charge	48.0	(48.0)	0.0
EBIT	152.0		200.0

> **RULE OF THUMB**
> To reverse the effect of a restructuring charge, treat the non-recurring item as if it never occurred.

You should know about two complications that often arise when you try to adjust for non-recurring items.

Multiple charges   First, companies may have multiple items that are considered non-recurring. So you will need to examine each item individually and make multiple adjustments in order to normalize.

Hidden items   The second potential complication is this: non-recurring items are often buried in other line items, for example, in ◀COGS▶, ◀SG&A▶, other expense/income, and/or in taxes. Seasoned professionals make sure they go beyond the income statement and read the footnotes and ◀MD&A▶ of a company's public filings, looking for any discussion of a potentially buried item. Once you have identified which line item in the income statement contains the non-recurring expense, you can then make the appropriate adjustment.

What does all this tell us? As you can see, good analysis goes beyond making mechanical mathematical adjustments. Making proper adjustments is an art that requires careful judgment so one can draw appropriate comparisons to other reporting periods and companies. Much like most people, companies like to put their best foot forward and to present their income statement story in the best possible light. So in doing valuation analysis, you need to fully understand the impact of a one-time item on the company's financial position. Ask yourself: what is the story behind this non-recurring item? Why did it happen? Is it a particularly telling indicator of overall financial health?

Remember that the goal of adjusting for one-time items is to evaluate a company's normal ongoing earnings and cash flows so you can predict its future performance more accurately. In The Pearson Co. exercise we did earlier, the *normalized* EBIT of $200.0 is probably a better indicator of the company's operating profit capabilities than the reported figure of $152.0.

SUMMARY
Chapter 2

TOPIC 1: VALUATION TECHNIQUES: AN OVERVIEW

Five common methods used to value companies:

- **Public Comparables**
- **Acquisition Comparables**
- **Discounted Cash Flow Analysis (DCF)**
- **Merger Consequences Analysis**
- **Leveraged Buyout (LBO) Analysis**

Public Comparables and Acquisition Comparables analyses measure a company's value relative to similar other companies or transactions. DCF and LBO analyses, by contrast, try to capture a company's *intrinsic value* based on its projected cash flows. LBO and Merger Consequences are "affordability" analyses: They gauge how much a buyer could afford to pay.

Two key questions to ask when trying to value a firm:

1. Looking inward, what is this company worth in itself? (value)
2. Looking outward, what could someone afford to pay for this company? (affordability)

Valuation practitioners use Public Comparables, Acquisition Comparables, and/or DCF to try to answer Question 1. They use Merger Consequences and/or LBO Analyses to answer Question 2.

Other questions to ask:

- What kind of buyer is this: strategic or financial?
- What is the context of the transaction: friendly or hostile?
- What are the market conditions: optimistic or recession-minded?

Valuation is both an *art* and a *science*. It requires both analytic rigor and the subjective interpretation of data, anchored in solid intuitive judgment. Each model you use has its limitations, and you need to make many assumptions. The goal is to reach a reasonable and defensible valuation, and be able to stand behind the assumptions you make.

TOPIC 2: MEASURING COMPANY VALUE

Equity Value vs. Enterprise Value

Equity Value is the market value of the shareholders' interest. It is calculated as:

Equity Value = Share Price x Diluted Shares Outstanding

Remember to use the most recent share price and ◀**diluted shares**▶ outstanding.

Enterprise Value includes the value of both equity and debt capital (along with other forms of capital such as preferred stock and noncontrolling interest). It is the company's total value to all of its capital holders.

Enterprise Value is calculated as:

Enterprise Value = Equity Value + Net Debt

Net Debt for a company is the Total Debt less Cash & Equivalents. Net Debt assumes a company with excess cash will reduce its debt dollar for dollar using Cash & Equivalents.

Technically, Enterprise Value also includes the value of all preferred stock and noncontrolling interest.

TOPIC 3: MEASURING FINANCIAL PERFORMANCE: EBIT AND EBITDA

EBIT (often called operating income) stands for **E**arnings **B**efore **I**nterest and **T**axes. It is essentially income from operations before you include the effects of financing and taxes. It therefore highlights profitability from operating activities and excludes any specific capital structure decisions.

EBITDA stands for **E**arnings **B**efore **I**nterest, **T**axes, **D**epreciation and **A**mortization. EBITDA measures operating profitability before deducting the non-cash expenses of depreciation and amortization (D&A). Typically, D&A are found on the cash flow statement. Although EBITDA is often used as a rough approximation for operating cash flow, it is not actual cash flow. EBITDA does not account for certain cash items, such as working capital needs and capital expenditures.

TOPIC 4: NORMALIZING FINANCIALS: COMPLICATIONS IN CALCULATING EBIT

Practitioners often adjust earnings for non-recurring items. These are unusual one-time items that are not expected to be part of the normal course of a company's future business.

Examples:

- Restructuring charges
- A gain or loss on the sale of a division
- A gain on the sale of an investment
- Asset impairment charges (including the impairment of goodwill)
- Legal settlements

When adjusting for a non-recurring item, reverse its effect by treating it as if it had never occurred. *Add back* to income a non-recurring **charge**, and *subtract* from income a non-recurring **gain**.

Companies sometimes have multiple items considered to be non-recurring, so examine each item individually and make multiple adjustments if necessary.

Remember that non-recurring items that have a negative impact may be buried in other line items (e.g., COGS, SG&A, other expense/income, and/or taxes). Go beyond the income statement and read the footnotes and **MD&A** to look for any discussion of such buried items.

The main goal of adjusting for one-time items is to evaluate a company's "on-going" earnings and cash flows to allow for better comparisons of prior and future financial results and/or comparisons to the results of other companies.

MASTERY QUIZ
Chapter 2

QUESTION #1

Match the description with the correct valuation technique.

— *Can be thought of as "affordability analysis" for a
non-private equity buyer (strategic buyer)*
— *Is used to find the intrinsic value of a company*
— *Can be thought of as "affordability analysis" for a
private equity buyer*
— *Emphasizes relative valuation*

Merger consequences analysis
DCF analysis
LBO analysis
Public / acquisition comparables analysis

QUESTION #2

True or False:

Since valuation means ultimately getting to a quantitative
figure, valuation practitioners tend to focus solely on
calculations, analytics and formulas.

QUESTION #3

When deriving *Enterprise Value* from *Equity Value*,
which of the following balance sheet line items should
be included? (Identify the most relevant answer)

A. All liabilities
B. Only long term debt
C. Cash and equivalents and total debt
D. Cash and equivalents, total debt, preferred stock and
   noncontrolling interest

QUESTION #4

Assume that Equity Value for a company is $100 million,
debt is $10 million and cash and equivalents is $10 million
(there is no preferred stock or noncontrolling interest).
Which of the following would be the Enterprise Value?

A. $90 million
B. $100 million
C. $110 million
D. $120 million

QUESTION #5

A company has the following reported information: operating income is $100 million, cost of goods sold is $45 million, depreciation is $10 million and amortization is $15 million. Please calculate EBITDA

QUESTION #6

Which of the following would NOT be a typical non-recurring item?

A. Restructuring charge
B. Gain/(loss) on sale of divisions
C. Interest expense
D. Legal settlements

QUESTION #7

If you are normalizing an income statement for a gain on the sale of a division (located above operating income), which of the following would describe the relationship between normalized EBIT versus reported EBIT?

A. Normalized EBIT would be lower than reported EBIT
B. Normalized EBIT would be the same as reported EBIT
C. Normalized EBIT would be higher than reported EBIT

QUESTION #8

A company has the following reported information ($ in millions):

Income Statement

	Reported
Sales	$436.8
Cost of goods sold	270.6
Gross profit	166.3
SG&A expense	96.3
Loss on sale of division	16.8
EBIT	53.2

Assume there are no hidden non-recurring items. Please calculate normalized EBIT.

ANSWER KEY
Chapter 2

ANSWER #1

Merger consequences analysis examines the impact of a possible transaction on the financial position of a potential buyer. This determines what the buyer can afford to pay for a target company. Since **DCF (discounted cash flow) analysis** is based on projections of free cash flow of the company, it provides the intrinsic value. **LBO (leveraged buyout) analysis** examines what a private equity firm can afford to pay for a target in an acquisition funded primarily with debt. Relative valuation techniques such as **comparables analysis** (specifically, public comparables and acquisition comparables) see how a company compares to others in the industry.

ANSWER #2

False   Valuation is both art and science. Valuation can be viewed as art because it requires judgment and interpretation of data. Different parties can have differing interpretations of the same data and therefore very distinct valuations. The science of valuation is creating reasonable analytical justification for the proposed transaction.

ANSWER #3

D — Cash and equivalents, total debt, preferred stock and noncontrolling interest.   Enterprise Value should include all forms of capital, which include Net Debt (total debt less cash), preferred stock and noncontrolling interest.

ANSWER #4

B — $100 million   Enterprise Value in this situation would be Equity Value plus Net Debt (assuming no preferred stock or noncontrolling interest). The Enterprise Value would equal $100 million of Equity Value plus $10 million of debt less $10 million of cash and equivalents.

ANSWER #5

$125 million   EBITDA is a proxy for operating cash flow. To calculate EBITDA, start off with operating income (often equal to EBIT) and add back non-cash charges (such as depreciation and amortization). EBITDA = $100 million (operating income) + $10 million (depreciation) + $15 million (amortization). Cost of goods sold is already factored into operating income and contains many cash expenses.

ANSWER #6

C — Interest expense   Non-recurring items are not expected to be part of the normal course of business in the future (such as restructuring charges, gain/loss on sale of business or investments, legal settlements and asset impairments). **Interest expense** is usually part of on-going operations for a company that has debt financing.

ANSWER #7

A — Normalized EBIT would be lower than reported EBIT Normalized EBIT means that you are adjusting for non-recurring items. In order to reverse the effect of the item, treat the item as if it never occurred. If you are reversing a gain on the sale of a division, you are removing that source of income. That would mean that normalized EBIT would be lower than reported EBIT.

ANSWER #8

$70.0 million   **Normalized EBIT** = reported EBIT +/- any non-recurring item adjustments. Assuming that there are no hidden non-recurring items, the only non-recurring item is the $16.8 million "Loss on Sale of Division." This is a loss so it would be added back to reported EBIT to obtain normalized EBIT. **Normalized EBIT** = $53.2 million + $16.8 million = $70.0 million.

CHAPTER 3
Public Comparables Analysis

QUICK SUMMARY

Public Comparables Analysis, also called Comparable Company Analysis, is a valuation approach used by finance professionals to determine the relative value of a company by comparing it to other similar companies. It is one of the two primary comparison-based approaches to valuation, in contrast to intrinsic methods. The other is Acquisition Comparables Analysis (covered in Chapter 4).

Both approaches involve assessing the value of your target company by calculating a set of key financial ratios called multiples and applying them to the company. In Public Comparables Analysis, however, you determine the target company's value by creating a peer group of similar companies, using their current market valuations to calculate multiples for each company in the peer group, and then applying the relevant multiples you just worked out to your target, so that you can draw conclusions about what its value should be.

Once you have gone through this chapter, you should be able to

- *Perform the mechanics of public comparables analysis. In essence, this comprises three steps:*
  1. Determining the comparable companies you will use as a peer group;
  2. Finding relevant documented public information about them;
  3. Calculating multiples for each company in your peer group.

A WORD ON TERMINOLOGY

Besides Comparable Company Analysis, other names you may come across for Public Comparables Analysis are:

• Analysis of Selected
  Publicly Traded
  Companies
• Trading Comparables
• Trading Multiples
• Comp Co.'s
• Equity Comps
• Common Stock
  Comparisons (CSCs)

• *Understand how to analyze and interpret the multiples you just calculated. This will enable you to draw meaningful comparisons among the companies in your peer group, and between them and your target company. This is sometimes referred to as synthesizing a public comparables analysis.*

• *Derive an implied valuation range for the target company, based on your analyses.*

TOPIC 1: CREATING A PEER GROUP OF COMPANIES

Public Comparables Analysis is a comparison-based, relative valuation technique. Therefore, the first step in determining your target company's value is identifying a group of comparable companies, called a peer group. Typically, finance professionals examine two kinds of features to determine if a firm is comparable to the company they are trying to value —**operational characteristics** and **financial attributes**. Some of the most common ones:

Operational characteristics
   • Industry
   • Products/services
   • Markets
   • Distribution channels
   • Customers
   • Seasonality
   • Cyclicality

Financial attributes
   • Size
   • Leverage
   • Margins
   • Growth prospects
   • Liquidity

It can be harder than it looks
Finding a comparable group for the company you are valuing can be challenging for a number of reasons. The ideal comparable company would have the same operational and financial characteristics as the company under evaluation. It would, for example, be of the same size, be in the same industry, offer the same products and services, sell into the same markets, appeal to the same types of customers, have the same kind of capital structure composition, and so on.

But in reality all companies differ. The question is, how different can a candidate "comparable company" be and still be called comparable? How much does a variance in these metrics among companies make a difference? And if a fair number of variances exist between the two companies, how much will you have to adjust the peer to make it sufficiently comparable to the one you are valuing? The truth is that, although the operational and financial criteria listed here may look objective, choosing comparables is a considerably subjective process. There can be multiple factors to consider. Here are some complications that can make determining a comp set fairly challenging:

1. Companies sometimes have multiple divisions.

Suppose you want to value Callaway Golf Co., a public company that specializes in manufacturing just golf equipment (as of the date of the original writing of this book). The challenge in finding comparable companies for Callaway is that not many publicly traded sports-related companies manufacture only golf equipment. Most golf brands are divisions of large, diversified sports equipment companies that make other things as well. For example, Nike Golf is a division of Nike, and Nike's stock price reflects more than just the assets, growth prospects, and level of profitability of Nike Golf. Similarly, Taylor-Made is an adidas AG division. So who are Callaway's comparables? You may be compelled to include those aforementioned companies as the closest comparables while noting their operational differences.

2. Brand equity and management expertise can be hard to assess.

Imagine you are trying to value PepsiCo Inc. relative to Cola-Cola Co., another beverage company. How do you assess the differences in brand equity or management skill, since they are intangible factors that are not clearly reflected in quantifiable market numbers such as the stock price.

3. Companies can be of substantially different sizes.

Although all the parameters listed above matter, it can be particularly important to try to find companies of roughly comparable size. Why? For one thing, bigger companies tend to take advantage of economies of scale that can possibly lower their production costs, allow them to buy inputs at lower prices, and boost their profitability. Additionally, larger companies may enjoy a degree of market penetration that gives them potential control of a market. Finally, more sizable firms tend to be more liquid, with higher daily stock trading volumes. The greater liquidity of a large company makes it more likely that its stock price will accurately reflect the market's view of it. So to really know how one company compares to its competitors, it is helpful to choose those of comparable size.

4. The number of comparables to include may not be clear.

There is no "right" number of comparable companies to include in a peer group. In practice, comp sets commonly range from 5 to 10 companies. The important thing is to try to identify and analyze as many appropriate comparables as possible without becoming overwhelmed. Use your judgment. But when in doubt, it is better to have a smaller set of companies, and be confident that they are genuinely comparable, than to have a larger set that contains a number of questionable comps.

In short, finding a perfectly comparable company— sometimes called a "pure comp" or "pure play"—can take work. Consider PepsiCo and Cola-Cola again. Most investors view them as competitors, and they are. But PepsiCo is much more diversified. With its Frito-Lay division, it is one of the world's largest snack food providers. By contrast, food products form only a small part of Cola-Cola's operations. Are they competitors? Yes, but they are significantly different in their operational composition.

Deciding what the right comparables universe is for your target company is often as much art as it is science. Careful judgment is the key. The chances are that you will need to make adjustments to control for any significant financial and operational differences among them. But bear in mind that too many adjustments will begin to distort your data. These distortions, in turn, will build directly into the ratios and multiples you are calculating. And this will make it hard both to draw sound conclusions from the values you assign the companies in your peer group, and to apply those to the company you are trying to value.

Practically speaking, how many comparables should you include?

As was mentioned earlier, there is no magic number. Include as many as you feel are appropriate and reasonable. If you are in a complex industry or if you are dealing with a company that has diverse products or services, you may need to spread more comparables. In a mature, well-established industry where companies have evolved over time, there may be fewer relevant comparables for your analysis.

Where should you look to help gather a peer group?

There are several sources that can help you construct a peer group:

I. The company that you are analyzing may have its own views, gleaned from public documents.

II. An industry classification system from a major database such as NAICS, the North American Industry Classification System (visit www.naics.com).

III. Analyses from bankers. These can sometimes be found in the details of a ◀**fairness opinion**▶ (which can usually be found in a ◀**merger proxy**▶ or ◀**S-4**▶).

IV. Previous analyses from in-house professionals and other colleagues with whom you work (for example, bankers, consultants and accountants).

V. Standard industry research reports, such as Standard & Poor's (Capital IQ), Value Line, Factset, and Bloomberg.

Are there limitations in using private companies and divisions of larger companies?

Yes. Unless they are publicly traded, there is no share price for a private company or a division. So you cannot calculate Market Value and other subsequent multiples. Also, there can be limited financial information or disclosure. But you can check to see if the company has publicly traded debt, which will require them to file financial statements.

Let's look at these information sources a bit more closely:

I. The company's own views

These often can be gleaned from publicly available documents. We will look at two kinds:

A. Peer group index (this is often found in a ◀**proxy statement**▶)

Example

In its 2014 Proxy, Facebook used a "Peer Group" to determine compensation benchmarking. The criteria for the "Peer Group" were:

1) high technology or media company
2) key talent competitor
3) minimum revenue of $4 billion; *and / or*
4) minimum market capitalization of $50 billion.

Peers included Amazon.com and Google. One can go look at what companies are listed in that index and use that as a starting point. Be cognizant of the fact that companies have their own viewpoint and can ultimately determine who they think their peers are. Also, keep in mind the purpose of this peer group. Ultimately, it is being used to compare stock price performance. Is that list applicable to public comparables valuation?

 B. Competition section (◀**10-K**▶, ◀**20-F**▶, ◀**IPO prospectus**▶, or an ◀**annual report**▶)

Example

Here is an excerpt from retail grocer Sprouts Farmers Market, Inc. December 28, 2014 10-K:

"The $620 billion U.S. supermarket industry is large, intensely competitive and highly fragmented. We compete for customers with a wide array of food retailers, including natural and organic, specialty, conventional, mass and discount and other food retail formats. Our competitors include conventional supermarkets such as Kroger and Safeway, as well as other food retailers such as Whole Foods, Natural Grocers by Vitamin Cottage and Trader Joe's."

But be careful! Sometimes the list of companies provided are private, not public, or they are divisions of larger companies. They are all competitors, yes, but many cannot be used to construct a peer group.

Be thorough and creative throughout this process. Take the initiative and look at the peer group indexes and competition sections of your target company's competitors. See if there are any substantial overlaps between your target company and its competitors in terms of product mix.

II. An industry classification system from an online database
A. For example, NAICS (North American Industry Classification

System) codes. These replaced the US Standard Industrial Classification (SIC) system.

B. Many other countries may use a similar classification system.

III. Analyses from bankers

Banker analyses can sometimes be found in the details of a fairness opinion (which can be contained in a merger proxy or S-4).

Below is an excerpt from an actual fairness opinion that investment bankers used in SoftBank's acquisition of Sprint. It outlines the comparable companies (or "public comparables") used in the analysis:

> Sprint's financial advisors reviewed and compared the purchase prices and EV/OIBDA multiples paid in the proposed transaction between AT&T and T-Mobile (announced March 2011) and the proposed transaction between T-Mobile and MetroPCS (announced October 2012). Sprint's financial advisors selected these transactions in the exercise of their professional judgment and experience because Sprint's financial advisors deemed them to be generally relevant to the SoftBank Merger. Sprint's financial advisors noted the number of comparable transactions was limited, and that the historical transactions that had occurred prior to 2010 in the U.S. wireless carrier industry were not generally relevant to the SoftBank Merger as a result of substantial changes in the industry and markets generally, specifically in light of the financial crisis of 2008.

IV. Previous analyses from in-house professionals

and other colleagues with whom you work—for example, bankers, consultants and accountants. As the saying goes, you never want to recreate the wheel. Leverage off of work that has already been done and save some time and efficiency.

V. Standard industry research reports

such as Standard & Poor's (Capital IQ), Value Line, Factset, and Bloomberg. Some of these firms that provide research reports also produce industry overviews and periodic reports that give color about a company or industry. Be aware that some of these research services are subscription-based, so seek internal resources for accessibility.

ASK THE FINANCE GURU

I am gathering possible comparables from different sources. Do I need to exercise judgment?

You do indeed. When you are gathering possible comparables from any of the above sources, you need to be on the lookout for potentially biased opinions and perspectives. For example, the company may have a certain opinion about who they believe their peers are, and they may want to highlight this to investors. The perspectives of investment bankers may differ depending on which side they are representing in a transaction. **Bottom line:** *cross-check your sources, and, for balance, try to get as many different perspectives as you can.*

After creating a peer group of comparable companies, the next step is to gather a list of public information sources for each company.

For US companies, this typically means:

1. ◄10-K► or ◄annual report► from the most recent fiscal year
2. ◄10-Q► from the most recent quarter
3. News announcements since the most recent filing
4. Research and EPS estimates
5. Share price (and most recent dividend per share)

For non-US companies, this means:

1. Use their annual report (in place of a 10-K) and an interim filing for any of the periods since the fiscal year end.
2. Familiarize yourself with any existing country-specific industry customs or filing standards.
3. Company websites often contain financial information, along with press releases
4. Click on the Investor Relations web pages and look there.
5. Foreign companies that trade on a US stock exchange are required to file under US SEC guidelines, so they would have a published ◄20-F►.

ASK THE FINANCE GURU

What exactly is a PIB?
A PIB, or **P**ublic **I**nformation **B**ook, *is a bound book that has all of the relevant information a practitioner needs to spread a public comparable— such as filings and research—all gathered in one place for convenience. Firms often customize their PIB for a specific purpose or preference.*

TOPIC 2: CALCULATING EQUITY AND ENTERPRISE VALUE FOR EACH COMPANY

Having assembled a peer group of companies, we are now ready to lay the foundation for calculating valuation multiples for each company. This is often referred to as "spreading a comp." Let us briefly summarize where we are going. The first thing we will do is to calculate the Equity Value and Enterprise Value of each of our peer group companies. Next, we will use Equity Value and Enterprise Value to calculate a set of multiples for each company, after having identified the appropriate multiples that are relevant for the particular industry.

Finally, after calculating multiples for each company, we take these multiples and apply them to the company we are trying to value in order to derive an implied valuation range. This will require analysis and contextual interpretation, as we need to "know the story" of each company and whether our peer group companies tend to trade at a premium or a discount to our target company—and if so, why.

In this current topic, we will calculate Equity Value and Enterprise Value.

> **A WORD ON TERMINOLOGY**
> "Spreading the public comps" may sound technical if you have never heard the term. It just means preparing a set of company comparisons by calculating ratios using a spreadsheet application such as Excel. The term "spreading" just comes from the use of spreadsheets. You literally spread the numbers across the rows and columns of your spreadsheet. "Comp" refers to comparable companies.

1. Step One: Calculating Equity Value

Recall the formula for Equity Value from Chapter 2:

Equity Value = Share Price x Diluted Shares Outstanding

As a refresher from our earlier discussion, here are a few things you should know in order to calculate Equity Value:

First, finance professionals typically use the current share price in order to reflect the most up-to-date market valuation. They also use the current ◀**diluted shares**▶ outstanding in order to reflect any and all shares from ◀**options**▶, ◀**warrants**▶ and ◀**convertible securities**▶. (Warrants are treated like options, and convertible securities are beyond the scope of this book, so we will be focusing on options.)

The Treasury Stock Method, or TSM, is a method by which options (and their equivalents) are included in diluted shares. The Treasury Stock Method assumes in theory that the proceeds the company receives from an option exercise will all be used to buy back outstanding shares of common stock. Note that when you are factoring options into the calculation, you use only "in-the-money" options. "In-the-money" is defined as the condition when:

In-the-money option:

> **Option Strike Price or Exercise Price**
> **< Market Price of Stock**

What is the assumption behind the use of "in-the-money" options? The underlying principle is that a rational option holder, free from undue pressure, would pay the exercise price to the company, receive the share underlying the option, and sell it on the open market at the stock price. If you find there are multiple sets of options (also called tranches) at different strike prices, just determine which groups are "in-the-money" and use those.

ASK THE FINANCE GURU

What are exercisable and outstanding options? And which options do finance professionals typically use in the Treasury Stock Method?

An exercisable option just means it is an option that you can currently use or that is vested. Outstanding options are all the options a company gives out. But only some of those options are exercisable at any given moment. A time-period requirement is one of the very common conditions an option must meet before it becomes exercisable. Example: Bluebird Co. gives you 100 options today at $20 each, but tells you that they will not "vest" (meaning they cannot be exercised) for another three years. When those options do become exercisable, you can buy each of those 100 shares at the strike price you were given, $20, and if the share price at that time is higher than $20, pocket the difference. Company employees who have options therefore have an incentive to help the company raise its share price as high as possible.

*So which options should you use when performing TSM calculations: **outstanding** or **exercisable**? Practitioners typically use outstanding options. This is consistent with US GAAP (generally accepted accounting principles) and international accounting standards for diluted share calculations. But some practitioners prefer the approach of using exercisable options, that is, using only those options that can be exercised as of the date the options were recorded. Be careful of change of control issues when spreading comparables or analyzing a situation. In an acquisition, the outstanding options typically become immediately exercisable.*

Option proceeds refer to the total amount of money the company receives from all holders of "in-the-money" options.

As stated previously, the Treasury Stock Method assumes that the company uses the entire option proceeds to buy back stock. To determine the number of shares repurchased, corporate finance professionals typically use the current stock price in order to reflect current market conditions.

In reality, this may not happen at all—although, often enough, the option proceeds are indeed used to buy back shares. By factoring in a hypothetical repurchase practitioners assume that a company will want to minimize share dilution from the original "in-the-money" options that are being converted into shares.

Let's walk through an exercise using TSM:

Example:
Markovv Corporation currently trades at $15.85 per share. The company has 75.100 million basic shares outstanding. Markovv also has 3.520 million outstanding options, with an average option exercise price of $2.50. What are the option proceeds to the company?

In this exercise, you should assume that the in-the-money options will all be exercised, and that the proceeds will result in a cash inflow to the company.

Option Proceeds =
# of Options In-the-money x Average Strike Price

Then calculate the number of shares repurchased at the current stock price:

Exercise Price (strike price)	$2.50
x Options In-the-money	3.520
= Option Proceeds	$8.8 million

Under TSM, how many shares can the company buy back with the proceeds? Effectively, to minimize the effect of share dilution, all option proceeds should be used to repurchase as many shares as possible at the current stock price.

Shares Repurchased =
Option Proceeds / Current Stock Price

Options Proceeds	$8.8 million
/ Current Stock Price	$15.85
= Shares Repurchased	0.555 million

What are the diluted shares outstanding?

Diluted Shares =
Basic Shares + # of Options In-the-money
– Shares Repurchased Under TSM

Basic Shares	75.100	million
+ Options In-the-money	3.520	
– Shares Repurchased under TSM	(0.555)	
= Diluted Shares Outstanding	**78.065**	**million**

What is the Equity Value? And remember, you should be using the diluted share count to get to the Equity Value for the company.

Equity Value = Share Price x Diluted Shares Outstanding

Diluted Shares Outstanding	78.065	million
x Current Stock Price	$15.85	
= Equity Value	**$1,237.3**	**million**

2. Step Two: Calculate Enterprise Value

Now that we have worked out Equity Value, we are ready to calculate Enterprise Value. Remember, Enterprise Value is Equity Value plus Net Debt (assuming there is no ◂**preferred stock▸** or ◂**noncontrolling interest▸**). Refer to Chapter 2 if you need to refresh your memory.

Once you have calculated Equity Value and Enterprise Value, the next step is to gather the historical income statement information. Bear in mind two things: first, the income statement information is typically normalized for non-recurring items. Second, to be able to compare all of your peer group companies on a similar basis, you should examine a similar historical time period for all of them. The latest twelve months (LTM for short) is commonly used as a historical time period benchmark.

3. Step Three: Calculate the latest twelve months

LTM can be calculated two ways: one is to add up the last four quarters of information, or the last two half-year periods of information. The second, more common technique, is to take the latest fiscal year, add the current period, then subtract the last period. A period is defined as the time from the end of the fiscal year to the latest quarter end. The second method is preferable because you need no more than two documents: the 10-K and, if needed, the most recent 10-Q. The first technique requires sourcing four documents for four individual quarters.

Here is an illustration of how LTM works, using the second quarter of 2015:

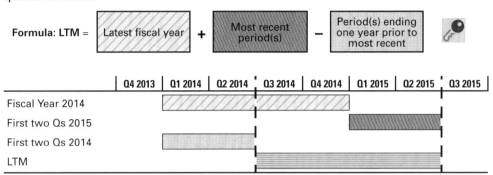

There are three reasons why the LTM time period is so important:

1. It is a more recent 12-month period than the last fiscal year.

2. Stating every company's financials on an LTM basis allows you to compare data across companies that have different fiscal-year ends.

3. Because it utilizes a full 12 months of performance, an LTM calculation controls for seasonality. In other words, it minimizes the analytical effects of season-based, cyclical data such as sales. For example, you would reach inaccurate conclusions if you simply took the last quarter's results and multiplied them by four to get a "12-month period" because, at many companies, revenue streams vary dramatically from period to period depending on the season. Below is an excerpt from the financials of Abercrombie & Fitch, which manufactures apparel for teens and young adults. This excerpt from their 10-K is typical for the disclosure of a company that experiences seasonality.

> "The Company views the retail apparel market as having two principal selling seasons, Spring and Fall. As is generally the case in the apparel industry, the Company experiences its peak sales activity during the Fall season. This seasonal sales pattern results in increased inventory during the back-to-school and Christmas selling periods."

HINT

Remember: re-calculate the LTM margins based on the new LTM financials (rather than using the margins across).

Exercise

Let's try to calculate LTM for a sample company, a similar manufacturer of apparel for teens and young adults. The following is from its 10-K:

Please calculate LTM and Margins
(a margin = $ amount / sales):

Dollars and shares in millions, except for per share data

	Fiscal year ending 12/31/05	1 quarter ending		LTM
		3/31/06	3/31/05	
Net Sales	$224.0	$48.6	$47.3	
EBITDA	$42.4	$10.2	$9.4	
EBIT	$33.8	$8.0	$7.2	
Margins				
EBITDA	18.9%	21.0%	19.9%	
EBIT	15.1%	16.5%	15.2%	

Answer

	Fiscal year ending 12/31/05	1 quarter ending		LTM
		3/31/06	3/31/05	
Net Sales	$224.0	$48.6	$47.3	$225.3
EBITDA	$42.4	$10.2	$9.4	$43.2
EBIT	$33.8	$8.0	$7.2	$34.6
Margins				
EBITDA	18.9%	21.0%	19.9%	19.2%
EBIT	15.1%	16.5%	15.2%	15.4%

TOPIC 3: CALCULATING EQUITY VALUE AND ENTERPRISE VALUE MULTIPLES

Under Topic 2, you learned how to calculate Equity Value, Enterprise Value, and LTM financials. You are now in a position to calculate a set of Equity Value-based and Enterprise Value-based multiples for each company in your peer group. But first, we should understand what a multiple is and why we rely on them so heavily in relative valuation methods such as Public Comparables and Acquisition Comparables Analyses. To see why multiples are so important in determining the value of a company, let's look at a real-life example.

Alibaba's IPO: $68 a Share

Alibaba Group Holding Ltd's shares priced on September 18, 2014 at $68 per share, putting the Chinese company on track for one of the largest initial public offering ever. The price was at the top of the company's expected range of $66 to $68, which was increased from an initial $60 to $66.

QUESTION

Is $68 high or low? As an investor, should you buy it at that price?

The truth is that there is no way to tell. A share price that is merely lower than expected is not necessarily a good deal! In fact, the market price of $68 tells you almost nothing, other than that it is not as high as $120.

As an investor, is there anything you can do to turn Alibaba's share price into an informative piece of data that could move you toward a decision to buy or pass on it? The answer: turn it into a multiple!

A multiple enables you to draw meaningful comparisons between two companies by controlling for some important differences between them. In a sense, a multiple allows you to make an "apples-to-apples" comparison by putting companies on a common platform. The best way to understand this is through an everyday example. Let's pay a quick visit to our local health food store.

Example:
Is it better to buy two small bags of organic Granny Smith apples at $4.50 each, or one big bag for $8?

Answer:
It depends on how much bigger the bigger bag is. What you really want to know is how much each bag costs per pound. In essence, you are implicitly asking for a **weight multiple** that will control for the difference in bag size by standardizing the two bags on one platform: cost per pound.

Suppose the small bags weigh 1.5 lb. each and the large weighs 4 lb. The price of the small bag, in dollars, is **3x** its weight ($3/lb.); but the larger bag costs only **2x** its weight ($2/lb.). Clearly, the larger bag is the better buy. And the weight multiple you just used captures this succinctly. It allowed

> **FINANCIAL FACTOID**
> There are dozens of financial multiples, but each is a ratio that offers us one measure of a company's value in relation to some financial performance indicator, such as earnings or Net Income.

> **In finance, timing is often critical.** Another key fact about public comparables analysis: finance professionals analyze a company's multiples at a specific point in time. Why? Because they change. Typically, they calculate valuations and multiples using the current stock price. For that reason, company valuations tend to reflect the most recent public information. So a question you should ask is: What information is the market currently pricing into the stock? Try to find that information and use it.

you to compare the prices of the two different-sized bags after taking their weight into account.

Every financial multiple has this basic structure. Similarly, in real estate, a price-per-square-foot multiple allows you to compare two differently-sized homes by taking their size difference into account.

Let's return to Alibaba. Alibaba's offer price of $68 a share valued the company at close to $170 billion. This is roughly 25 times its future proxy for operating cash flow. Okay, we are getting warm. But is 25x enticingly low, forbiddingly high, or just about right? One answer is to look at Alibaba's competitor Amazon. At the time, Amazon was valued at $150 billion—about 24x its proxy for operating cash flow, compared to Alibaba's 25x. Conclusion: Alibaba was priced in-line with one of its competitors.

What led us to this key insight? Two things: calculating the valuation multiple, and doing a comparison between Alibaba and Amazon.

This is the core of public comparables analysis: crunch out informative multiples for a carefully chosen set of peer companies, and apply them to your target company to determine its implied valuation range and get a sense of its relative value. The rest of the chapter will unravel how finance professionals go about doing this, and what they look out for.

On March 20, 2015, Apple Inc. closed the trading day at $125.90 a share. Well, is that high or low? Question is, $125.90 relative to what? There is no way to tell. Multiples supply this missing relative-to-what information. For example, the price to earnings multiple (P/E multiple) relates share price to the earnings you get from each of your shares. For instance, on the same day, Apple's estimated earnings per share (or EPS) for calendar year 2015 was $8.74. That gave Apple a P/E multiple of $125.90/$8.74, or 14.4 times earnings. If you are an investor, you will want to compare Apple's multiple relative to other comparables. Let's say you come across a competitor with a P/E multiple of, let's say, 12 times earnings — the only way to compare the two is to examine the multiple, NOT the share price. In this example, we say Apple was "trading at a premium" compared to the second company. Or the second firm was "trading at a discount" to Apple. This next step in the analysis is to try and understand why!

Bottom line: It is not the absolute value of the share price that counts. It is the value of the share relative to some benefit that you receive if you purchase the stock—and multiples capture this information almost graphically.

> **FINANCIAL FACTOID**
> Earnings per share (EPS) is roughly the net profit a company generates divided by the number of shares.

TOPIC 4: OTHER CONSIDERATIONS

There are a few other considerations you should bear in mind when analyzing comparable companies. We will look at four:

I. **The Need for Numerator-Denominator Consistency**
II. **Industry-Specific Statistics**
III. **Forward Multiples**
IV. **Calendarizing**

I. Numerator-Denominator Consistency: Apples to Apples

When you are calculating multiples, you need to know when to use Equity Value and when to use Enterprise Value in the numerator. The rule of thumb: for consistency, the numerator and denominator should usually both refer to the same "slice" of the company. Typically, if the denominator statistic refers to an income or cash flow that belongs to the company's equity holders (its shareholders), so should the numerator. If the denominator is a statistic that belongs

> **FINANCIAL FACTOID**
> The denominator and numerator of a multiple typically should both refer to the same portion of the company—either all the capitol holders, or just the shareholders. But some multiples will utilize different statistics in the denominator. For example, an internet company may be valued off of equity value / webpage hits. We will discuss this in more detail later.

potentially to all of the company's capital holders, not just the shareholders, then the numerator should reflect the same relationship.

Example 1:

EBITDA is a measure of pre-debt, pre-tax earnings that represents the entire company's value (i.e. its Enterprise Value), not just that portion of the company owned by the equity holders. So in calculating an EBITDA multiple (i.e., one with EBITDA in the denominator) you need to use Enterprise Value in the numerator. Putting Equity Value in the numerator would be the financial equivalent of mixing metaphors.

Similarly, Enterprise Value (including debt) is appropriate for an EBIT multiple because EBIT is a financial statistic that is calculated before interest expense is deducted. The interest on the debt has not been "paid out" to debt holders.

Example 2:

Unlike EBIT or EBITDA, the Net Income generated by a company is an after-debt, after-tax measure. Net Income refers to the portion of the company's income that would go to the shareholders after you take out taxes and take out the money needed to make interest payments to the company's debt holders. Net Income is the residual claim that the common shareholders have, or what is left over to be claimed by the equity holders after a company has paid its taxes and serviced its debt. So when calculating a Net Income multiple (one with Net Income as the denominator), you need to use Equity Value in the numerator.

Top and bottom should both relate either to the equity holders only, or to the entire enterprise. In essence, you need to compare like terms.

Here is a quick mini-quiz: You are calculating the Net Income multiple for a company. Should you use Equity Value or Enterprise Value in the numerator?

Answer:

First decide what kind of measure you have in the denominator. Net Income is an equity-based measure because it goes only to the company's equity holders. The answer is that you should use Equity Value in the numerator.

In short, **Equity Value Multiples** are those ratios that apply only to the equity shareholders, after interest expense, preferred dividends and noncontrolling interest expense have been "paid out." The numerator therefore includes

> **TIPS OF THE TRADE**
> Remember that sales, EBIT and EBITDA are Enterprise Value statistics, whereas the multiple of Net Income is simply Equity Value.

only "Equity Value." Common Equity Value multiples are

- ◆ Equity Value / Net Income
- ◆ Price / EPS (also called the Price-to-Earnings or P/E multiple)
- ◆ Equity Value / ◂**Book Value**▸

Enterprise Value Multiples, on the other hand, are those ratios that apply to all of a company's capital holders, including any debt holders. These are statistics before interest expense, preferred dividends or noncontrolling interest expense have been "paid out." The numerator must therefore include debt and all other forms of capital. Common Enterprise Value multiples are

- ◆ Enterprise Value / Sales
- ◆ Enterprise Value / EBITDA
- ◆ Enterprise Value / EBIT

Exercise

Assume the following information for Gotham Co. and calculate the relevant multiples.

Gotham Co. Financial Information

Current Share Price	$12.84
Market Value	$1,785.2
Enterprise Value	$1,909.8

Financial Statistic		**Multiple:**
LTM Net Sales	$855.5	
LTM EBITDA	$164.9	
Next Twelve Months EPS	$0.58	

Answer:

Current Share Price	$12.84
Market Value	$1,785.2
Enterprise Value	$1,909.8

Financial Statistic		**Multiple:**
LTM Net Sales	$855.5	2.23x
LTM EBITDA	$164.9	11.6x
Next Twelve Months EPS	$0.58	22.1x

II. Industry-Specific Statistics

In addition to the multiples we have just discussed, when you are calculating public comparables, you may need to examine certain other financial statistics that are appropriate for companies in a particular industry sector. These statistics depend on the nature of earnings, assets, growth and leverage for those types of companies. Some examples:

- ◆ Subscribers for a cable company
- ◆ Book value for financial institutions
- ◆ Page views for an internet website company
- ◆ Expected growth for a "growth stock"

A good way to uncover the relevant industry-specific statistics is to check sources such as:

- ◆ *Equity Research reports.* Note what statistics the research analyst is focusing on. If the report includes a comparable companies valuation, the report will highlight the statistics used in deriving relative valuations for the target company.

- ◆ *Corporate Press releases.* Check a company's earnings announcements. Besides providing financials, do they highlight other information and metrics?

- ◆ *Company financial reports.* What other supplemental information is provided?

III. Forward Multiples

This chapter has focused on analyzing historical (time-based) results. Specifically, we learned how to calculate the latest twelve months in order to control for seasonality and to be able to compare statistics across companies. Finance professionals analyze historical results: 1) because they are actual results and 2) because they often help in estimating a company's future performance.

But besides looking back to historical results, professionals also look forward. For example, equity research analysts often make projections of future financials. Additionally, certain aggregators of financial information [e.g., Standard & Poor's (Capital IQ)] try to find a "consensus" among equity research estimates. Many investors like to use these "consensus" figures because of the assumption that the market is "pricing in" these forward expectations. Finance professionals also use these projections to calculate a range of forward multiples, including Current Price/Projected EPS and Today's Enterprise Value/Next Year's EBITDA.

Note that when you are calculating forward multiples, the numerators (i.e., Price and Enterprise Value) do not change from the LTM multiple calculations. Below is a summary of some common Equity Value & Enterprise Value Multiples.

Equity Value Multiples	Enterprise Value Multiples
Price / EPS ("PE multiple")	Enterprise Value / Revenues
PE / Earnings growth	Enterprise Value / EBITDA
Price / FCFE per share	Enterprise Value / EBIT
Equity Value / Net Income	Enterprise Value / ◀FCFF▶
Equity Value / After-tax Cash Flow	Enterprise Value / Projected EBITDA
Equity Value / Book Value	Enterprise Value / Projected EBIT

IV. Calendarizing

When you are analyzing forward results, not every company in your peer group universe will have the same fiscal year end. For comparison purposes, we use calendarized results that place them all on a similar basis—typically a December year end.

Calendarizing is more straightforward when a company is already on a December fiscal year end. But you will sometimes need to calendarize results for a company that is not on a December fiscal year end. Let's try that here:

Example:
Assume that Gotham Co., which operates on a June fiscal year end, has the following quarterly EPS estimates:

1Q 2014 (Sept-13) $0.62   1Q 2015 (Sept-14) $0.52
2Q 2014 (Dec-13) $0.63   2Q 2015 (Dec-14) $0.93
3Q 2014 (Mar-14) $0.28   3Q 2015 (Mar-15) $0.60
4Q 2014 (June-14) $0.25   4Q 2015 (June-15) $0.55

What is the EPS estimate for the calendar year December 2014?

Answer:
EPS estimate = $0.28 + $0.25 + $0.52 + $0.93
         = $1.98

If Gotham has a stock price of $35.60, what is the appropriate "2014" EPS multiple?

Using the $1.98 **calendar** year EPS yields 18.0x ($35.60 / $1.98).

By contrast, using the $1.78 ($0.62 + $0.63 + $0.28 + $0.25) **fiscal year** EPS yields 20.0x ($35.60 / $1.78).

For a comparables analysis, the multiples need to be on a comparable basis. The calendarized P/E of 18.0x would be more appropriate in a scenario where you were comparing P/E multiples in a peer group that all had calendarized multiples.

TOPIC 5: INTERPRETING WHAT YOU HAVE: ANALYZING THE MULTIPLES

The Big Picture: Knowing the Story

Now that we have spread the public comparables (that is, calculated multiples for our comp set), the next thing is to take a step back and look at the big picture. This involves knowing each company's "story"—contextually understanding why some trade higher or lower than their peers. Do these companies have a "premium" multiple, or perhaps a "discount" multiple? Does one company have more sound fundamentals than the others?

The final step will be to take the multiples we have prepared and apply them to our target company to determine its implied valuation range. This can be expressed as a range of multiples or values.

When deriving a valuation, why use a **range** rather than a single value? There are several reasons for this. Valuation is rarely just one pinpoint value for a company. A market is a community of buyers and sellers, all with slightly different perceptions, budgets, and agendas. Not only that, but the various assumptions and adjustments you make as you calculate multiples for your universe of comparables will affect the value you impute for your target company. Finally, each valuation technique—Public Comparables Analysis, Acquisition Comparables Analysis, DCF, and so on—will yield a slightly different valuation range. You want to provide a general sense of what the company's value is.

Knowing the Story

What are the primary drivers of a multiple? It is important to understand what makes a multiple high or low—that is, what its primary drivers are. Typically, there are three fundamental company characteristics that affect multiples: *size*, *risk* and *growth*.

Size	Risk	Growth
• Market share and sector dominance • Market Value	• Operational efficiency and productivity (◄**margins**►, ◄**ROIC**►) • Finance risk (credit profile)	Growth in: • Cash flow • EBITDA or other cash flow proxies • Net Income or EPS • Sales

Analyzing multiples is not a perfect science but a subjective process based on many factors. You should, nevertheless, be able to determine the main drivers of the multiples you are calculating. The following is a typical output of public comparables analysis:

Public Comparables Analysis of Selected Food and Beverage Companies

($ in millions, except for share data) Company	Stock Price as of 5/12/02	Market Value of Equity	Enterprise Value (a)	Enterprise Value as a Multiple of: LTM EBITDA	LTM EBITDA Margin	Total Debt/ EBITDA	Proj. 5 Yr EPS Gr. Rate
Cadbury Schweppes plc (b)	$30.55	$15,841	$18,635	11.9x	19.8%	1.9x	8.5%
Campbell Soup Co.	27.67	11,370	15,148	11.3	19.5%	2.8	7.7%
Kraft Foods Inc.	41.21	71,711	87,531	13.0	19.8%	2.4	14.0%
Tootsie Roll Industries, Inc.	47.05	2,431	2,298	20.4	26.4%	0.1	NA
Wm. Wrigley Jr. Company	56.60	12,815	12,504	21.0	24.0%	0.0	11.2%
High				21.0x	26.4%	2.8x	14.0%
Average				15.5	21.9%	1.4	10.4%
Median				13.0	19.8%	1.9	9.9%
Low				11.3	19.5%	0.0	7.7%
Target Company	$68.40	$9,512	$10,177	11.6x	19.3%	1.0x	10.0%

(a) Calculated as Market Value of Equity plus total debt, noncontrolling interest and preferred stock, less cash & equivalents.
(b) Converted to US $ from British pounds at an exchange rate of 1.44 US per British £.

These companies were selected as the peer group because they are all global producers of food and/or confectionary products. Our overall goal is to "know the story" for each company, and then find out why they trade at a "premium" or "discount" relative to their peers. The target company which we are attempting to value is typically listed at the bottom of the page.

To start this process, try to get a sense of each company's **size**, **risk** and **growth**. Let's begin by analyzing Kraft. Remember, public comparables analysis is a relative valuation method. Your objective in examining size, risk and growth is to compare a company to its peers.

You should notice that Kraft is much larger than its peers. In fact, Kraft is a huge company with an extraordinary range of products and a dominant market share. All things being equal, this fact may result in a slight **size** premium.

Leaving out Wrigley and Tootsie Roll for the moment (they will be addressed later) Kraft's LTM EBITDA margins are close to its peers Campbell and Cadbury. Kraft's LTM EBITDA multiple is also equal to the median. All things being equal, we would expect Kraft's multiple to be in line with those of Campbell and Cadbury, based on similar margins.

Let's examine the **risk** factor. Kraft's Debt/EBITDA multiple is on the higher end, compared to its peers. Only Campbell has a higher Debt/EBITDA. A higher proportion of debt in the capitalization structure means the company has taken on greater **financial risk**. This fact may have a negative impact on valuation. On the other hand, Kraft is a large, well-established company that fairly consistently generates cash flow from its strong brand names. This may possibly offset some of the financial risk.

Now let's take a look at Kraft's EPS **growth**. Notice that it is larger than that of its peers. But be careful here, because Kraft is not normally viewed as a "growth stock"! Perhaps the growth stems from a recent acquisition the company made, or it funded this growth in some other way. You need to ask how sustainable this growth is. This will need further investigation.

To summarize: compared to its peers, Kraft is a large player. The company may be getting a size premium on its valuation, or it could be slightly overvalued. From a **risk** perspective, Kraft's margins are in line with Cadbury and Campbell. The company has more credit risk, but this may be acceptable given Kraft's size. Finally, in the area of **growth**, it has a high expected EPS growth rate, but there are some questions as to whether that will be sustainable in the long term.

Let's assume that valuation professionals are analyzing these companies based on Enterprise Value / LTM EBITDA multiples. (You could perform the same exercise with other multiples.) Kraft is trading at 13.0 times Enterprise Value / LTM EBITDA. Even though Kraft has similar margins to Cadbury and Campbell, because of Kraft's size and growth profiles, we would expect it to be trading at a slight premium relative to those companies.

On the other hand, however, you *could* make the argument that Kraft is slightly overvalued. The bottom line: valuation is more art than science, and you need to understand what is driving the valuations.

ASK THE FINANCE GURU

What is the best kind of growth?

*There are different kinds of growth, and they are not equally valued. In the long run, typically, the market values "organic growth" that is **funded through operations** more than it values growth **funded by acquisitions**. Some of Kraft's 14.0% expected EPS growth is driven by acquisition-related factors (for example, its acquisition of Nabisco). Such growth is not sustainable over the long-term.*

SUMMARY
Chapter 3

In this chapter, we covered the following topics:

1. **Creating a Peer Group of Companies**
2. **Calculating Equity and Enterprise Value for Each Company**
3. **Calculating Equity and Enterprise Value Multiples**
4. **Timing and Other Considerations**
5. **Interpreting What You Have: Analyzing the Multiples**

Overview

Public Comparables Analysis is one of two methods commonly used to determine a company's relative value. You compare your target company to a carefully chosen "peer group" and then value the company by calculating and analyzing multiples for that peer group.

A key fact to remember is that the multiples are based off a stock price at a specific point in time. Ideally, this should be the most current price. That way, the valuation will reflect recent market and public information.

Multiples are used to provide valuations related to underlying financial statistics, and allow for comparisons of similar companies as well as similar transactions.

TOPIC 1: CREATING A PEER GROUP OF COMPANIES

The first step in public comparables analysis is to choose the company's peer group. Generally, there are two criteria used to select similar companies: **operational** factors and **financial** factors.

Operational factors include similar industry, products or markets.

Financial factors include size, leverage and margins.

Some financial criteria are used mainly to explain the target company's relative valuation, and not so much to include or exclude companies from the peer group.

It is rare to find a perfect set of comparables. Several complications can arise. A company may have many divisions; how do you assess such a company? Or how do you factor in intangibles such as brand equity and management expertise? And what is the right number of comparable companies in the peer group? It is a subjective, judgment-based process, and you will get better at it with time.

There are many sources of information to help you determine a peer group. They include public filings, research publications, and databases.

TOPIC 2: CALCULATING EQUITY AND ENTERPRISE VALUE FOR EACH COMPANY

After you have finalized your peer group, the next step is to gather the relevant financial information for each company and use this to calculate its Equity Value:

Equity Value = Share Price x Diluted Shares Outstanding

What share price and diluted shares outstanding should you use? Typically, you use the most recent.

Options and warrants are dilutive types of securities because they can be converted to common shares. One way to reflect the potential shares from options and warrants is the Treasury Stock Method. This method assumes a hypothetical repurchase of shares, at the then-current market price, using option proceeds.

To complete the TSM calculation, the first step is to determine the number of options that are "in-the-money," where

Option Strike Price or Exercise Price < Market Price of Stock

Next, calculate the option proceeds:

Option Proceeds = **# of Options In-the-money x Average Strike Price**

Then calculate the number of shares repurchased at the current stock prices, and finally diluted shares outstanding:

Shares Repurchased = **Option Proceeds / Current Stock Price**

Diluted Shares = **Basic Shares + # of Options In-the-money** **– Shares Repurchased under TSM**

After you have calculated Equity Value, derive Enterprise Value by adding Net Debt (assuming there is no preferred stock or noncontrolling interest).

Once you have derived the valuations, gather the historical income statement information needed to calculate multiples and normalized for any non-recurring items. To analyze the income statement, select a benchmark time period. Practitioners commonly analyze the most recent twelve months (LTM).

The formula for LTM is:

Formula: **LTM** =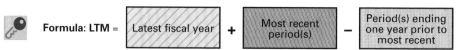

The latest twelve months financial information is important because it is the most recent twelve-month period, it controls for seasonality, and it allows you to make meaningful comparisons across companies that have different fiscal year ends.

TOPIC 3: CALCULATING EQUITY VALUE AND ENTERPRISE VALUE MULTIPLES

When creating a multiple, make sure the numerator is appropriately matched to the underlying financial statistic.

A. *Equity Performance Multiples* are those statistics that apply *only* to equity shareholders.

Common examples include
  • Equity Value / Net Income
  • Price / EPS (often called the P/E multiple)
  • Equity Value / Book Value

B. *Enterprise Performance Multiples* are those statistics that apply to *all* capital holders.

Common examples include
  • Enterprise Value / Sales
  • Enterprise Value / EBITDA
  • Enterprise Value / EBIT

TOPIC 4: OTHER CONSIDERATIONS

There are a few other important considerations to bear in mind when analyzing public comparables:

A. Industry-Specific Multiples
Different industries trade on different metrics. This depends on the nature of earnings, assets and leverage for those types of companies. A good way to find out the relevant industry-specific multiples is to examine research reports, press releases, and company filings.

B. *Forward Multiples*

In addition to multiples based on LTM statistics, finance professionals use forward or estimated results to calculate forward multiples, such as Current Price/Projected EPS.

C. *Calendarizing*

Not every company has the same fiscal year end. To make comparisons easier when analyzing results, finance professionals use calendarized results that place all the companies on a similar basis—typically, a December year end.

TOPIC 5: INTERPRETING WHAT YOU HAVE: ANALYZING THE MULTIPLES

After calculating multiples for each company in the peer group (often called spreading the public comparables), the next step is to know the story for each company and understand why some trade higher or lower than their peers.

Typically, three main factors influence why multiples are high or low: **size**, **risk** and **growth**.

MASTERY QUIZ
Chapter 3

QUESTION #1

Which of the following does not describe Public Comparables Analysis

A. Utilizes multiples in its analysis
B. Utilizes a peer group
C. Is based on precedent transactions
D. Is analyzed at a specific point in time

QUESTION #2

True or false:

The Treasury Stock Method (TSM) is a method of accounting for the number of shares that are currently held as treasury stock by the company.

QUESTION #3

Assume that a company has a group of 10.000 million options with a strike price of $15.00. The company also has another group of 15.000 million options with a strike price of $30.00. The current share price is $25.00. Under the Treasury Stock Method, how many shares are repurchased?

A. 24.000 million
B. 18.000 million
C. 6.000 million
D. None

QUESTION #4

Which of the following is the best reason for calculating the latest twelve months?

A. Controls for seasonality
B. Allows for comparability across companies
C. Includes the most recent financial results
D. All of the above
E. None of the above

QUESTION #5

Assume that a company has 100.000 million shares outstanding with no options. The current share price is $48.00. The company also has Net Debt of $1,000.0

million. LTM Net Income is $250.0 million. What is the multiple of LTM Net Income?

A. 23.2x
B. 19.2x
C. 4.0x
D. 20.0x

QUESTION #6

Assume the following quarterly EPS estimates for FGH Inc., which operates on a September fiscal year end:

1Q 2014 (Dec-13) $0.11   1Q 2015 (Dec-14) $0.08
2Q 2014 (Mar-14) $0.14   2Q 2015 (Mar-15) $0.10
3Q 2014 (June-14) $0.10   3Q 2015 (June-15) $0.10
4Q 2014 (Sept-14) $0.09   4Q 2015 (Sept-15) $0.12

What is the calendar year DECEMBER 2014 EPS estimate?

A. $0.44
B. $0.40
C. $0.39
D. $0.41

QUESTION #7

Which of the following is the most correct statement?

A. Companies in different industries are always valued off of P/E multiples.
B. It is more common to calculate an Equity Value to EBITDA multiple versus an Equity Value to Net Income multiple.
C. Multiples of LTM statistics are comparable to multiples of forward statistics.
D. TSM is hypothetical. There is no actual share repurchase.

ANSWER KEY
Chapter 3

ANSWER #1

C — Is based on precedent transactions.

Only acquisition comparables utilizes precedent transactions. Public comparables utilizes a peer group of companies and analyzes multiples of these companies at a specific point in time.

ANSWER #2

False.

Treasury Stock Method is a popular way to reflect potential shares from options held privately by management, other employees and insiders. TSM assumes a hypothetical repurchase of shares at the current market price with option proceeds.

ANSWER #3

C — 6.000 million

Under Treasury Stock Method, only use in-the-money options. Therefore, only the first group of options would be in-the-money since the strike price of $15.00 is below the current share price $25.00. To calculate TSM, you would find the option proceeds.

Exercise Price (strike price)	$15.00
x Options In-the-money	10.000
= Option Proceeds	**$150.0 million**

After you calculate the option proceeds, you would assume a hypothetical buyback of stock at the current stock price.

Options Proceeds	$150.00 million
/ Current Stock Price	$25.00
= Shares Repurchased	**6.000 million**

ANSWER #4

D — All of the above

Latest twelve months is important because it is the most recent 12-month period, it controls for seasonality, and it allows for comparability across companies with different fiscal year ends.

ANSWER #5

B — 19.2x

The multiple of Net Income is Equity Value / Net Income. Here is the calculation of Equity Value:

Share Price	$48.00
x Shares Outstanding	100.000
= Equity Value	**$4,800.0 million**

To find the multiple of Net Income, divide $4,800 million by $250.0 million. This will be 19.2x.

ANSWER #6

D — $0.41

= $0.14 + $0.10 + $0.09 + $0.08

= $0.41

ANSWER #7

D — TSM is hypothetical. There is no actual share repurchase.

Different industries trade on different metrics. Not all industries trade off of P/E multiples. It is more common to calculate an Equity Value to Net Income multiple because Net Income is a statistic that is associated with common equity shareholders. EBITDA is a statistic that is pre-interest expense, which is relevant to debt holders so you would look at an Enterprise Value to EBITDA multiple. In examining multiples of peers, you must compare companies utilizing the same benchmark. Therefore, choose either LTM multiples or forward multiples as the benchmark for comparability. You cannot compare one company's LTM multiple to another company's forward multiple. TSM assumes a **hypothetical** repurchase of shares at the current market price with option proceeds.

CHAPTER 4
Acquisition Comparables Analysis

QUICK SUMMARY

Acquisition Comparables Analysis, also called Comparable Transaction Analysis, is a valuation approach used by finance professionals to work out the value of a company by comparing it to other transactions in that company's industry sector. It is one of the two primary comparison-based approaches to valuation, in contrast to intrinsic methods. The other is Public Comparables Analysis *(covered in Chapter 3)*.

In both methods, the value of the target company is determined by calculating key financial ratios and applying them to statistics of the target. However; in Acquisition Comparables Analysis, the target is valued using a list of precedent transactions comparable to the one proposed. After this deal list has been compiled, key multiples are then calculated and applied to the target's statistics to arrive at a valuation.

Once you have gone through this chapter, you should be able to:

- Perform the mechanics of Acquisition Comparables Analysis, by:
  - creating a list of comparable precedent transactions, sourcing public information, and calculating a set of transaction multiples and premiums; and
  - analyzing the results of the multiples you have calculated
- Derive an implied valuation range for your target company based on your analysis

TOPIC 1 – OVERVIEW OF ACQUISITION COMPARABLES ANALYSIS

A control premium

Acquisition Comparables Analysis is similar to Public Comparables Analysis in its mechanics. A key difference: Public Comparables Analysis is based on stock prices and thus typically reflects the value of a noncontrolling share in each of the companies in the peer group from which you are drawing comparisons. By contrast, the Acquisition Comparables approach is based on the prices that were paid in transactions that culminated in acquiring control of a company. This price therefore includes a ◀**control premium**▶ the acquiring company paid for the benefit of taking control of the daily operations of the target company.

Synergies

 The premium also reflects the buyer's expectation that the merger will yield positive ◀**synergies**▶ between the two companies. Stated differently, the acquirer pays a bit more on the expectation that the newly merged whole will be greater than the sum of its parts—a kind of "merger" premium, if you like. Because of these two expectations, Acquisition Comparables Analysis typically leads to a higher price for the target than if the value were derived using the Public Comparables approach.

ASK THE FINANCE GURU

When would you expect a very low premium or none at all?

Premiums are often low or non-existent in a "merger of equals," where two companies of similar size come together—typically in a stock-for-stock exchange—to share operating control of the merged entity. Low premiums are also common when a company buys a minority stake in another company, or when it buys out an existing minority shareholder.

Example
On March 9, 2015, Simon Property Group Inc. announced an unsolicited bid for Macerich Co. for $14 billion. The offer represented about a 10% percent premium over Macerich's prior day closing share price. The deal also represented a transaction multiple of about 30 times Macerich's LTM EBITDA.

Tools of the trade

What tools do finance professionals use in analyzing comparable transactions? As in public comparables analysis, practitioners mainly analyze key multiples, financial performance measures, and drivers of value such as growth rates, margins, and credit statistics. Once they have calculated the key multiples, they again try to imply a relative value for the target company, applying those multiples to the target company in order to determine what its value should be. Another tool is analyzing and understanding the premiums paid in similar transactions. In all these analyses, your goal is typically to incorporate into your analysis the information the acquiring and the target companies used in striking the deal.

If there is a material change in a target company's financial results between the date the deal was announced and the date it was closed, what happens?

In general, practitioners focus on the multiples paid on the date of the deal's announcement, and the valuation implied by those multiples. However, they do look out for significant material changes that may negatively impact the terms of the deal. If any are found, the acquirer may try to revise the terms to lower its offer price.

An actual historical example:

In November 2005, Johnson & Johnson and Guidant agreed to a revised offer value of $21.5 billion for Guidant—a full 11 percent lower than the original deal struck in December 2004. The reason? Product recalls had lowered Guidant's sales and financial performance.

TOPIC 2: DETERMINING YOUR GROUP OF PRECEDENT TRANSACTIONS

Step One: Creating a Deal List

The first step in performing Acquisition Comparables Analysis is to identify an appropriate group of similar transactions, often called a **deal list** (analogous to the peer group in Public Comparables Analysis). Your goal is to find transactions where the target deal and the deals you have selected all have similar business and financial characteristics. Some common questions you should ask:

- What are the company's **operations** and lines of business?
- Is the **size** of the transaction comparable?
- Are there similar **financial** aspects (such as growth or margins)?
- Is the **timing** of the transaction appropriate?
- What was the **consideration paid** (cash, stock or both)?
- Were there any important **circumstances** surrounding the deal (for example, ◀hostile▶ vs. ◀friendly▶ transaction, or multiple bidders)?
- Were there any significant industry-wide events occurring at the time (for example, a consolidation wave in the industry)?

♦ What were the **market conditions** when the transaction took place?

Beware, though: valuation can be harder than it looks. As with Public Comparables Analysis, there can be many intangible factors you will need to consider. Challenges and complications often arise. Some typical challenges:

1) Trying to compare companies that have multiple divisions (recall our discussion of Callaway Golf in Chapter 3, Topic 1).

2) Trying to evaluate less tangible aspects like brand equity and management expertise (again, recall our Coca-Cola vs. Pepsi discussion in Chapter 3, Topic 1).

3) Attempting to compare current economic and market conditions with those that prevailed at an earlier date—for example, making comparisons to conditions surrounding a telecommunications transaction in 2000, when that industry was undergoing major market and legislation-driven transformation.

4) Trying to evaluate differences in company operations and financial aspects.

5) Determining how far back you can go and still find transactions you can consider comparable.

6) Choosing the right number of transactions to include.

The answer to the last dilemma is that, as in Public Comparables Analysis, there is no right number of transactions to analyze. In practice, it is common to see 5-10 precedent transactions. That said, try to find and use as many appropriate transactions as you can. For example, if you are doing your analysis in a complex industry sector, you may need to calculate more comparables. But in a mature, well-established industry, there may be fewer comparable acquisitions and thus, fewer deals to use.

Knowing the story

Ultimately, creating and analyzing a deal list of comparable transactions is—as in Public Comparables Analysis—a **subjective** process. For that reason, it is imperative that you **know the story** behind each transaction in your deal list. Reading between the lines and knowing why a deal happened, can be critical in helping you to justify certain multiples and premiums, or to explain certain outliers or anomalies.

The fact that this is a subjective process, fraught with intangibles, limitations, and hard-to-read complications, also means that it is often difficult to find a "perfect deal comp."

Consider, for example, the takeovers of Pharmacyclics and Salix in 2015. The two deals are in the same industry: health-care.

What happened? AbbVie acquired Pharmacyclics for about $21 billion—a transaction multiple of 29 times Pharmacyclics' revenue. Valeant Pharmaceuticals International Inc. paid approximately $11 billion for Salix—a multiple of approximately 10 times Salix's revenue. There are several factors potentially contributing to the discrepancy in the multiples paid: the different size between the two target companies; the different revenue streams and amounts; growth prospects, and potential synergies. Choosing the right deal list, like many aspects of corporate valuation, is often more an art than a science.

Searching information sources

Transaction analysis often requires you to go looking for important documents from the past. The task is frequently time-consuming, and sometimes frustrating, but often critical. The easiest way to find comparable precedent transactions is by performing a database transaction search, either by a classification system or by industry. But be prepared to run into a few dead-ends. Often, there is incomplete information about a transaction, and you need to use judgment, informed hunches, and reasonable assumptions to fill in the missing pieces. Finding appropriate information for acquisition comparables can be very similar to putting together a complex puzzle.

Here are some information sources used by finance professionals to create an Acquisition Comparables deal list:

- Transaction analyses already performed and published by industry experts such as bankers, equity research, etc.
- Widely used databases such as Standard & Poor's (Capital IQ). These can be screened for comparable M&A transactions. These are usually based on industry classification ranges, key words, date ranges and transaction size criteria.

Other sources

To be thorough, check other sources, such as news stories, industry newsletters, M&A journals, and almanacs. They will often give you additional insights into transactions, especially those involving privately-held target companies.

Step Two: Gathering Public Information

The next step after you have created your deal list of precedent transactions is to gather public information you can use to analyze each transaction. You begin by selecting the relevant documents. For companies in the US, some typical documents that professionals gather are:

1) Merger documents
   - ◀Merger Proxy▶/◀S-4▶
   - ◀8-K▶
   - ◀Schedule TO▶
   - ◀14D-9▶
2) Recent financial statements and filings
   - ◀10-K▶ or ◀annual report▶ from the latest fiscal year
   - ◀10-Q▶ from the latest quarter
3) Research reports
4) News reports
5) Summary of the transaction from an M&A database

For non-US companies, documents that professionals gather include:

1) Annual reports (in place of a 10-K)
2) An interim filing for any period since the fiscal year end
3) Tender offer documents (for certain transactions)

In addition, for non-US companies, familiarize yourself with any country-specific customs or filing standards. Company websites often contain financial information, along with press releases within their Investor Relations web pages.

Using LTM

For both US and non-US companies, you ultimately want to find the public documents that will help you calculate LTM figures for the target company as of the announcement date. *For a discussion of LTM, see Chapter 3.*

Privately-held target companies

It can be harder to gather information for a privately held target that does not file public financial statements. The target's historical financials may not be available in the case of small transactions that are not material to the acquirer's financial position. But there are some common places to search for a private company's financials:

- Merger documents such as an ◀S-4▶ or ◀8-K▶ (for a US acquirer)
- Tender offer documents

* Research reports that may disclose some financial details about the target
* A news run

Step Three: Analyzing the information

After gathering the documents related to the transaction, the next step is to search for and analyze the information in each document. As you do this, try to find and use the financial information available to the acquirer at the time of the transaction. Your focus should be on searching for the target's financials, discussions about strategic rationale, and other "color" points regarding the transaction. Through experience—and some trial and error—you will become more efficient.

TOPIC 3: MECHANICS OF SPREADING AN ACQUISITION COMPARABLE

Step One: Calculating Offer Value

The first step in spreading an acquisition comparable is to calculate Offer Value (also called Equity Purchase Price). Offer Value is similar to Equity Value (Market Value), except that Offer Value usually reflects any ◀**control premium**▶ paid.

Equity Value = Share Price x Diluted Shares Outstanding

Offer Value =   Offer Price per Share x Diluted Shares Outstanding

Recall also, from Chapter 3, that under the Treasury Stock Method, the option proceeds are used to repurchase shares.

But Equity Value & Offer Value can also be calculated a second way—using total shares:

Equity Value =   (Share Price x TOTAL Potential Shares Outstanding)   – Option Proceeds

Offer Value =   (Offer Price per Share x TOTAL Potential Shares Outstanding)   – Option Proceeds

Total potential shares outstanding reflects the target company's outstanding shares and potential shares from ◀**options**▶, ◀**warrants**▶ and ◀**convertible securities**▶.

In this second method, instead of using the option proceeds for a share repurchase, you simply deduct option proceeds from the Offer Value for the in-the-money options. Both approaches will lead you to the same answer, but the second method is faster and simpler.

To grasp the difference in mechanics, however, let us go through an example using both approaches.

Assume that Talimara Corporation currently trades at $24.00 per share and has 60.000 million basic shares outstanding, along with 2.000 million outstanding options that have an average option exercise price of $6.00.

1. Under the **Treasury Stock Method**, Equity Value can be calculated as:

Exercise Price	$6.00	
x Options Outstanding	2.000	
= Option Proceeds	**$12.0**	**million**

Option Proceeds	$12.0	million
/ Stock Price	$24.00	
= Shares Repurchased	**0.500**	**million**

Basic Shares	60.000	million
+ Options In-the-money	2.000	
– Shares Repurchased Under TSM	(0.500)	
= Diluted Shares Outstanding	**61.500**	**million**

Diluted Shares Outstanding	61.500	million
x Stock Price	$24.00	
= Equity Value	**$1,476.0**	**million**

2. Now, *deducting* the option proceeds instead, we can calculate Equity Value as:

Basic Shares	60.000	million
+ Options-in-the-money	2.000	
= Total Potential Shares Outstanding	**62.000**	**million**

Exercise Price	$6.00	
x Options Outstanding	2.000	
= Option Proceeds	**$12.0**	**million**

Total Potential Shares Outstanding	62.000	million
x Stock Price	$24.00	
	$1,488.0	million
– Option Proceeds	(12.0)	
= Equity Value	**$1.476.0**	**million**

The two approaches yield the same answer because each uses the same option proceeds to either repurchase shares or deduct from Equity Value.

Remember, Offer Value reflects the **control premium** the acquirer is willing to pay to the target's shareholders.

For speed and simplicity, many practitioners use Method 2 **and simply deduct the option proceeds:**

Offer Value =
(Offer Price per Share x TOTAL Potential Shares Outstanding)
– Option Proceeds

Let us walk through an exercise to calculate the Offer Value of a transaction.

Exercise

Talimara Corp. currently trades at $24.00 per share. The company has 60.000 million basic shares outstanding. Talimara also has 2.000 million outstanding options with an average option exercise price of $6.00. Axxiss Corp. agrees to acquire Talimara for a 25% premium.

What is the offer price of the transaction?

Share Price	$24.00
x (1 + Premium)	125.00%
= Offer Price	**$30.00**

What are the TOTAL potential shares outstanding for Talimara Corp.?

Basic Shares	60.000
+ Options In-the-money	2.000
= Total Potential Shares Outstanding	**62.000 million**

What are the option proceeds to the company?

Exercise Price	$6.00
x Options Outstanding	2.000
= Option Proceeds	**$12.0 million**

What is the Offer Value?

Total Potential Shares Outstanding	62.000 million
x Offer Price	$30.00
	$1,860.0 million
– Option Proceeds	(12.0)
= Offer Value	**$1,848.0 million**

If instead you used the Treasury Stock Method to calculate the offer value, you would arrive at the same solution, as long as you used the same option and offer price assumptions. (See Excel file for solution via TSM.)

ASK THE FINANCE GURU

In comparable transaction analysis, which options are commonly used? Outstanding options or exercisable options?

Options typically vest upon a takeover that is deemed as a "change-of-control event," for example, where a company acquires a majority stake. Because of this, outstanding options are commonly used in comparable transaction analysis.

Typically only in-the-money options are included. In Acquisition Comparables analysis, "in-the-money" is based on the **offer price**, and it is defined as follows:

> **In acquisition comparables analysis, an option is in-the-money when:**
> **Option Strike Price or Exercise Price < Offer Price per Share**

Similar to Public Comparables Analysis, the assumption behind in-the-money options is that a rational option holder would pay the exercise price to the company, receive the share underlying the option, and sell the share to the acquirer at the offer price.

If you find that there are multiple sets of options at different strikes prices, test each set versus the offer price, and use the ones that are in-the-money.

The option proceeds refer to the aggregate amount of money received by the company from all holders of in-the-money options.

ASK THE FINANCE GURU

In an actual M&A transaction, what really happens to options?

The way options are treated varies from deal to deal and can be a negotiating point between the acquirer and target. Until the specifics of the transaction are available, M&A professionals generally start off with the following two assumptions as a rule of thumb:

- *Convert options into new acquirer options in the case of 100% stock consideration.*
- *Cash out in-the-money options if there is any meaningful cash consideration.*

Step Two: Calculating Transaction Value
The next step is to calculate Transaction Value, which is similar to Enterprise Value. Transaction Value equals Offer Value plus Net Debt of the target (assuming no ◄**preferred stock**► or ◄**noncontrolling interest**►). For a more detailed discussion on calculating Enterprise Value, see Chapter 2.

Step Three: Gathering Information
Once you have Offer Value and Transaction Value, your next step is to gather the **historical income statement information**. The income statement is typically normalized for non-recurring items (see Chapter 2). In addition, you will need to examine a relevant historical time period in order to compare all the companies on a similar basis. Although multiples based on projected financial results are ideal, projections are not always available for targets, especially private companies. So the **latest twelve months** (LTM) is commonly used as a historical time period benchmark for Acquisition Comparables. *For a more detailed discussion of LTM, see Chapter 3.*

TOPIC 4: COMPLICATIONS WITH ACQUISITION COMPARABLES ANALYSIS

To ensure the most accurate analysis, make sure you carefully read the facts of each transaction. Below are some common complications that may arise:

1) It is quite common for an acquirer to purchase less than 100% of the target company. And yet when multiples are being analyzed for the transaction, practitioners commonly make the mistake of not "grossing up" the offer value. That is, they incorrectly assume a 100% acquisition.

Exercise
In 2013, Verizon Communications the remaining 45% of the partnership from Vodafone Group for approximately $130 billion. For the purpose of calculating or analyzing multiples, what is the implied offer value? Note: we are using round approximate numbers for illustration purposes. The final bid was around $130 billion.

Purchase Amount	$130 billion
/ Percent Acquired	45.0%
= Implied Offer Value	$289 billion

2) Acquirers frequently use stock as a form of consideration when making a takeover offer. The Offer Price is calculated as:

Offer Price per Share = Acquirer Stock Price x Exchange Ratio

An exchange ratio is the number of acquirer shares issued per target share. It is calculated by dividing the offer price in stock by the acquirer stock price, and then factoring in the % stock consideration:

Exchange Ratio = (Offer Price / Acquirer Stock Price)
x % Stock Consideration

Example
An acquirer with a stock price of $20.00 makes an offer in all stock for 100% of the target company at $30.00 per share. What is the resulting exchange ratio? It is 1.5 ($30/$20 * 100%). That means the acquirer must issue 1.5 of its shares for every share of the target it acquires.

Typically, the acquirer's stock price one day prior to announcement is used. Your objective here is to view the pricing from the acquirer's financial viewpoint.

TOPIC 5: ANALYZING PREMIUMS PAID

As we discussed earlier, an acquirer generally pays a **premium** to the shareholders of the target company. You will need to analyze this premium to develop a fuller picture of the transaction's value. The premium is calculated as

Premium (%) = (Offer Price / Target's Price*) – 1

*Target's share price before the announcement of the transaction

Exercise
Let's assume that Gotham Co.'s stock price was $15.00 based on the closing price yesterday. Blue Coolite Corp. makes an offer for Gotham's stock, and agrees to pay $19.00 per share. What is the implied premium in the transaction?

Premium (%) = ($19.00 / $15.00) – 1 = **26.7%**

Exercise
Once Gotham Co.'s board of directors reviews the offer by Blue Coolite Corp., they go back to the acquirer and demand a 30% premium to sell the company. What is the minimum revised offer price per share that Blue Coolite would have to make to convince the board of directors of Gotham to sell?

(Offer Price / $15.00) – 1 = 30.0%

When solving for offer price, we see that the revised offer would have to be at least $19.50 per share to achieve the 30% premium.

When you are engaged in Acquisition Comparables Analysis, you must try to control for (or make adjustments for) the effect that possible news leaks or speculation about the deal may have on the share price. For example, when there is a buzz in the market about a possible takeover, the target's stock price tends to rise as investors try to anticipate how much the control premium will be.

When calculating the premium, you can partially control for effects such as market anticipation by using the target's stock price taken at different points in the recent past—typically, **1 day**, **1 week**, and **1 month** before the announcement of the deal. Frequently, a more in-depth analysis will also compare the premium to other stock price data, such as the stock's 52-week high or the average share price over a particular time period.

It is also appropriate to use an "unaffected share price" in your premiums paid analysis. This is the share price before a company announces that it is considering a possible merger or evaluating other strategic alternatives. Such an announcement typically raises the share price as investors speculate about the possible premium paid. The following transaction illustrates the point about finding the unaffected share price:

Example
On May 18, 2014, Pfizer made a final offer 55 GBP bid for AstraZeneca. But, as you recall, Pfizer had made two prior bids for AstraZeneca: on January 5, 2014, Pfizer offered 46.61 GBP. The original bid was rejected by AstraZeneca. Pfizer then made a revised of 50 GBP on May 2, 2014. If you were calculating a premium paid off of an unaffected price, you would need to go back to AstraZeneca's closing share price of 35.86 GBP. And, you can get creative and look at the premium to that unaffected price for all three bids. For example, the bid of 46.61 GBP represented a 30% premium to the 35.86 GBP unaffected price. The final 55 GBP bid represented a 53% premium.

Exercise

Let us walk through a calculation of premiums. Let us say that Axxiss Corp. announced it had agreed to buy all the outstanding shares of The Pearson Co. at $67.80 a share. Calculate the appropriate premiums, assuming the following closing prices for The Pearson Co.:

The Pearson Co.'s Share Price Information		Premium
Offer Price per Share	$67.80	
1 day prior to announcement	$58.64	
1 week prior to announcement	$52.78	
1 month prior to announcement	$51.08	

Answer:

The Pearson Co.'s Share Price Information		Premium
Offer Price per Share	$67.80	
1 day prior to announcement	$58.64	15.6%
1 week prior to announcement	$52.78	28.5%
1 month prior to announcement	$51.08	32.7%

As with any corporate valuation analysis, however, you should not just calculate the premiums paid. You have to go beyond that, analyzing precedent transactions to understand the current market conditions and the industry's norms. Ultimately, this is the way to understand whether premiums are high or low, and why.

TOPIC 6: ANALYZING ACQUISITION MULTIPLES

Deriving a valuation range

As in Public Comparables Analysis, after spreading the precedent transactions, the final step is to derive a valuation range for the target company you are analyzing. In order to do that, you need to step back and look at the big picture. This involves **knowing the story** for each deal and understanding why it made sense to do it. If there is a "premium" or "discount" multiple, what drove it? Was one target company fundamentally stronger than the others?

The valuation range can be expressed as a range of multiples or values. Recall *(from Chapter 3)* that, typically, three main company characteristics influence why a transaction's multiples are high or low: **size**, **risk** and **growth**.

Size	Risk	Growth
• Market share and sector dominance • Market value	• Operational efficiency and productivity (margins, ROIC) • Finance risk (credit profile) • Transaction integration risk	Growth in: • Cash flow • EBITDA or other cash flow proxies • Net Income or EPS • Sales

TIPS OF THE TRADE

Remember, analyzing multiples is not a perfect science. It is a somewhat subjective process governed by a wide range of factors. All the same, thorough research should enable you to determine a multiple's primary drivers.

In addition to size, risk and growth, potential **synergies** can profoundly influence the multiples paid for a company. Generally, the larger the expected synergies, the more the acquirer is willing to pay. The following example illustrates this.

Selected Food and Beverage Transactions

($ in millions, except for share data)

Target / Acquiror	Date Announced	Offer Value of Equity	Transaction Value (a)	PRE-SYNERGIES: Transaction Value / LTM Sales	PRE-SYNERGIES: Transaction Value / LTM EBITDA	LTM EBITDA Margin	Announced Synergies	Synergies as % of Target Sales	POST-SYNERGIES: TV / Adjusted EBITDA
Ralston Purina Co. / Nestle S. A.	1/16/01	$10,010	$10,310	3.73x	15.7x	23.8%	$260	9.4%	11.2x
Quaker Oats Co. / PepsiCo.	11/02/00	13,542	14,066	2.82	15.6	18.0%	400	8.0%	10.8
Keebler Foods Co. / Kellogg Co.	10/26/00	3,853	4,553	1.67	11.3	14.8%	170	6.2%	7.9
Pillsbury / General Mills	7/17/00	5,358	10,500	1.73	11.1	15.6%	400	6.6%	7.8
Nabisco Holdings Corp. / Philip Morris	6/25/00	14,934	18,934	2.23	13.6	16.4%	600	7.1%	9.5
Bestfoods / Unilever PLC	06/06/00	20,895	23,535	2.72	14.6	18.6%	750	8.7%	10.0
High				3.73x	15.7x	23.8%		9.4%	11.2x
Average				2.41	13.9	17.2%		7.7%	9.5
Median				2.23	14.6	16.4%		7.5%	9.7
Low				1.67	11.1	13.0%		6.2%	7.8

(a) Calculated as Market Value of Equity plus total debt, noncontrolling interest and preferred stock, less cash & equivalents.

Take a close look at the Table on the previous page. It sets out what you will see in a typical Acquisition Comparables analysis. The overall goal here is to know the story for each transaction and then find out why there was a "premium" or "discount" multiple in that transaction, compared to the other deals.

To start this process, you must get a sense of what is driving the multiple for each deal. What are the **size**, **risk** and **growth** characteristics of the target company? What is the deal's **synergy** potential?

Let us analyze Nestlé's takeover of Ralston Purina to see why the transaction had the highest EBITDA multiple in the list of transactions (15.7 times). Remember, Acquisition Comparables analysis is a relative valuation process. You need to compare one transaction **relative** to other similar deals.

Size

In January 2001 Ralston Purina, a leader in the pet care industry, was the world's largest producer of dry dog foods and dry and soft-moist cat foods. Although more diversified, Nestlé was also a significant global pet care company, with brands such as Friskies, Alpo and Spillers. This transaction would give the combined company an even stronger leadership position in the pet care market.

Risk

Ralston Purina's EBITDA margins are much larger than those of its peers. Typically, such excellent efficiency and productivity numbers—which essentially translate into lower operational risk—result in a higher multiple paid.

Growth

Although it does not appear in the Table above, Nestlé, in an investor relations presentation about the Ralston Purina merger, highlighted Ralston Purina's superior growth potential, pointing to an expected 6-7% annual growth on a stand-alone basis. For the food and beverage industry, this is very high growth indeed.

Synergy potential

Finally, the transaction's relative synergy potential is higher than the other transactions in the list. Remember, comparables is a relative analysis, so you should look at the synergies as a percentage of the target's sales. True, on an absolute dollar basis, some of the other transactions do have higher expected annual synergies (for example, $750 million for Bestfoods and $600 million for Nabisco). But the relative synergy number is highest for Ralston Purina's sales (9.4%). Generally, the greater the potential synergies, the higher the price—and hence multiple—that the acquirer will pay.

Putting it all together, Ralston Purina is a leading player in its industry, with high growth and superior margins, all of which justify a high multiple.

Delving deeper: Adjusted EBITDA

Now, although such a premium multiple will naturally please the target's shareholders, the acquirer's shareholders may be concerned about such a rich valuation. So let us delve deeper into the expected synergies. In certain mergers with large, quantifiable expected synergies, it may be appropriate to adjust the target's EBITDA and recalculate the implied multiple. Here is one way to do this:

$$\frac{\text{Transaction Value}}{\text{Adjusted EBITDA}} = \frac{\text{Transaction Value}}{\text{Target's EBITDA} + \text{synergies}}$$

⇐ *includes the control premium*
⇐ *may justify premium*

From Nestlé's perspective, the **15.7** times EBITDA multiple excludes the benefits of the expected synergies. Adding the $260 million in synergies to Ralston Purina's EBITDA yields an implied multiple of 11.2 times. From Nestlé's point of view, this is a much more reasonable multiple.

Why? In the years just preceding the Nestlé-Ralston merger, in 2000-2001, most large branded food companies traded at around 10-12 times EBITDA. From May 15, 2002 onward, however, they began trading mostly in the 11-12 times EBITDA range. The six transactions in the aforementioned table are all in the 11-16 times EBITDA range, reflecting the control premium paid to the target. But from the acquirers' perspective, the EBITDA multiples, after adjustment, should be more in the 8-11 times range—in line with recent public and market valuations.

ASK THE FINANCE GURU

How often are synergies actually realized after a merger?

Integrating two companies well, and thereby achieving hoped-for synergies, can be a formidable challenge. In fact, when companies fail to meet investor expectations, it is common for them to cite "integration difficulties" and, by implication, some unrealized synergies. When synergies are achieved, it is hard to quantify them because companies typically combine their financial results. They rarely break out the realized synergies separately.

The real question is: do the combined financial results, including any expected synergies, meet investors' expectations?

TOPIC 7: IMPUTING VALUATION RANGES

Implied valuation

Valuation is really an umbrella expression. There are different kinds of valuation, and practitioners speak different languages when they talk about valuation. A company's value can be analyzed or expressed as a price per share, as Equity Value or Enterprise Value, as a multiple of an operating or financial metric, or even as a premium.

It is important that you learn to move skillfully among these different meanings of valuation. That means learning to **infer**—or **imply**—one type of valuation from a second kind of valuation when you are presented only with information about that second kind.

Suppose a research analyst looking at a particular takeover believes it should be within a certain range of EBITDA multiples. From this information, you should be able to (1) calculate the **implied** Equity Value and Equity Value per share, and (2) compare the implied Equity Value per share with the current stock price. Learning how to impute valuation is the key to this.

Exercise

Suppose Axxiss Corp. has agreed to acquire Talimara Corp., below. After analyzing a deal list of similar transactions, we conclude that an appropriate transaction value multiple is 8.0 times LTM EBITDA. Assuming the information below,

    A. What is the implied transaction value and offer value per share? (see 1 & 2)

    B. How does the implied offer price per share compare with the current stock price? (see 3 & 4)

Shares	23.000 million
Net Debt	$180.0 million
LTM EBITDA	$125.0 million
Current Stock Price	$29.83
x LTM Acquisition EBITDA Multiple	8.0

1. Calculating implied transaction value:

LTM EBITDA	$125.0 million
x LTM Acquisition EBITDA Multiple	8.0x
= Implied Transaction Value	**$1,000.0 million**

2. Calculating implied offer value:

Implied Transaction Value	$1,000.0	million
– Net Debt	(180.0)	million
= Implied Offer Value	**$820.0**	**million**

3. Calculating implied offer price per share:

Implied Offer Value	$820.0	million
/ Shares	23.000	million
= Implied Offer Price	**$35.65**	

4. Suppose that, in recent transactions, premiums paid have been in the 15-25% range. In light of this, based on premiums paid analysis, is the offer price above reasonable?

Premium to Current Stock Price   **19.5%** ($35.65 vs. $29.83)

Answer:
Yes, the implied premium over the current stock price is in the range of expected premiums paid.

....

SUMMARY
Chapter 4

TOPIC 1: OVERVIEW OF ACQUISITION COMPARABLES ANALYSIS

Along with Public Comparables Analysis, Acquisition Comparables Analysis is one of two major comparison-based methods used to determine the value of a company. While the Public Comparables method compares similar companies, Acquisition Comparables Analysis compares similar transactions. A key difference is that Acquisition Comparables Analysis typically leads to a higher price for the company being acquired. This reflects expected **synergies**, along with the benefit the acquiring company expects to obtain in being able to take control of the target's daily operations.

TOPIC 2: DETERMINING THE PRECEDENT TRANSACTIONS

The first step in performing acquisition comparables analysis is determining the list of similar precedent transactions. Your goal is to find transactions where the target deal and the deals you have selected all have similar business and financial characteristics. Knowing why a deal happened is sometimes critical in helping you to justify a certain premium or discount multiple.

Choosing comparable acquisitions, like choosing a peer group, is a subjective process with analytical limitations and governed by a wide range of factors, some intangible. It is often difficult to find "pure deal comps" for a given company.

TOPIC 3: MECHANICS OF SPREADING AN ACQUISITION COMPARABLE

After you have determined the peer group and gathered the relevant information, the next step is to calculate the offer value for each company in the deal list. Offer Value is similar to Equity Value (or Market Value) but it includes the control premium.

> **Offer Value =**
> **(Offer Price per Share x TOTAL Potential Shares Outstanding)**
> **– Option Proceeds**

Remember that **total shares** outstanding reflect the basic shares outstanding plus the potential shares from in-the-money" options and convertible securities.

When calculating Offer Value, for the sake of speed and simplicity many finance professionals just deduct option proceeds from the Offer Value for the in-the-money options, instead of assuming that the option proceeds are used to buy back the shares (as happens under the Treasury Stock Method).

After calculating offer value, the next step is to derive transaction value by adding Net Debt (assuming no preferred stock or noncontrolling interest) of the target.

Once the valuations have been derived, practitioners commonly calculate the multiples based on the latest twelve months (LTM) results.

A Few Complications to Watch For

Acquisitions where less than 100% of the target company is bought are quite common. And yet when the multiples are being analyzed for such a transaction, practitioners commonly make the mistake of not "grossing up" the offer value.

Acquirers frequently use stock as a form of consideration when making a takeover offer. The offer price is calculated as:

> **Offer Price per Share = Acquirer Stock Price x Exchange Ratio**

> **Exchange Ratio = (Offer Price / Acquirer Stock Price)**
> **x % Stock Consideration**

Premiums Paid Analysis

The percentage premium paid can be calculated as:

> **Premium (%) = (Offer Price / Target's Price) – 1**

A typical premiums paid analysis calculates the premiums in relation to the target's stock price **1 day**, **1 week** and **1 month** before the announcement of the deal to try to control for the effect of information leaks on the price. It may be appropriate to calculate premiums using an unaffected share price, that is, what the price was before the company announced it is considering being taken over, or market rumors.

Analyzing Acquisition Multiples

A practitioner needs to know the story for each transaction in order to understand why the deal has a high or low multiple compared to similar deals.

Besides the three main considerations that typically influence multiples—company size, risk and growth—it is important to also understand the impact of potential synergies on the price paid and the corresponding multiple.

Imputing Valuation Ranges

Valuation is really an umbrella term, and practitioners can mean different things when they talk about valuation. A company's value can be analyzed as a price per share, as an Equity Value or Enterprise Value, as a multiple of an operating or financial metric, or even as a premium.

It is an important skill to be able to imply or impute valuation. This means implying one type of valuation when all you have is information about another kind of valuation. For example, if an analyst were to give you an expected EBITDA multiple, you should be able to calculate the implied Equity Value per share.

MASTERY QUIZ
Chapter 4

QUESTION #1

True or False:

When determining whether an option is in the money for an acquisition, you should use the share price one day prior to the announcement of a takeover.

QUESTION #2

True or False:

When converting from Transaction Value to Offer Value, <u>add</u> debt and <u>subtract</u> cash (assuming no preferred stock or noncontrolling interest).

QUESTION #3

Assume Company A is currently trading at $44.67 and Company B offers a 25% premium to Company A's current stock price. What is the implied offer price per share by Company B?

A. $55.84
B. $33.50
C. $51.37
D. $60.30

QUESTION #4

ABC Corporation buys 18.6% of XYZ's Corporation's equity for $55.8 million. What is the appropriate Offer Value for multiples analysis?

A. $55.8 million
B. $300.0 million
C. $168.2 million
D. Not enough information available

QUESTION #5

The primary difference between an acquisition comparable multiple and a public comparable multiple is that the acquisition comparable multiple typically _____.

A. Factors in a control premium.
B. Provides a measure of relative value.
C. Cannot be calculated with public information.
D. Is lower.

QUESTION #6

Given the following facts, what is the implied Offer Value?

Facts

Share Price One Day Prior to Announcement	$20.00
Offer Price	$24.00
Basic Shares Outstanding	10.000 million
Options Outstanding	0.500 million
Average Option Exercise Price	$8.00
Net Debt	$17.5 million

A. $240 million
B. $206 million
C. $265.5 million
D. $248 million

QUESTION #7

Based on an acquisition comparables analysis, assume that the appropriate LTM EBITDA multiple for a takeover of XYZ Company is 8.0x. Also, assume that XYZ Company has 40 million shares outstanding, no options, $100 million of Net Debt, $125 million LTM EBITDA and a current share price of $18.00. What is the implied premium assuming an 8x EBITDA transaction multiple?

A. 38.9%
B. 25.0%
C. 20.0%
D. None of the above

ANSWER KEY
Chapter 4

ANSWER #1

False

In an acquisition, the <u>offer</u> price is typically used to determine whether an option is in the money.

ANSWER #2

False

When converting from Transaction Value to Offer Value, <u>subtract</u> debt and <u>add</u> cash.

ANSWER #3

A — $55.84

Company B will offer a 25% premium to Company A's current stock price. To calculate the offer price, you would multiply the current stock price * (1 + 25%) =

Current Stock Price	$44.67
x Premium to current price	125.0%
Offer Price	**$55.84**

ANSWER #4

B — $300 million

When analyzing a transaction, 100% acquisition is typically assumed for multiples analysis. Therefore, gross up the Offer Value to assume a 100% acquisition. If $55.8 million represents 18.6% of the Offer Value, $300.0 million represents 100% of the equity.

Equity Purchase Price	$55.8 million
/ Percentage	18.6%
100% Gross up Offer Value	**$300.0 million**

ANSWER #5

A — Factors in a control premium

While both provide measures of relative value and can be calculated with public information, acquisition comparables multiples are typically <u>higher</u> than public comparables multiples as they factor in a control premium.

ANSWER #6

D — $248 million

In-the-Money Options Outstanding	0.500	million
x Average Option Exercise Price	$8.00	
= Option Proceeds	**$4.0**	**million**
Basic Shares	10.000	million
+ In-the-Money Options	0.500	
= Total Potential Shares	10.500	million
x Offer Price	$24.00	
	$252.0	million
– Option Proceeds	(4.0)	
= Offer Value	**$248.0**	**million**

ANSWER #7

B — 25.0%

Assumed LTM EBITDA Multiple	8.0x	
Shares Outstanding	40.000	
LTM EBITDA	$125.0	million
Net Debt	$100	million
Assumed LTM EBITDA Multiple	8.0x	
x LTM EBITDA	$125.0	million
= Implied Transaction Value	**$1,000.0**	**million**
Implied Transaction Value	$1,000.0	million
- Net Debt	(100.0)	
= Implied Offer Value	**$900.0**	**million**
Implied Offer Value	$900.0	million
/ Diluted Shares	40.000	million
= Implied Offer Price	**$22.50**	
Implied Offer Price	$22.50	
vs. Current Share Price	$18.00	
= Implied Premium	**25.0%**	

CHAPTER 5
Discounted Cash Flow Analysis

QUICK SUMMARY

Discounted Cash Flow Analysis—or DCF for short—is a valuation approach employed by finance professionals to estimate a company's value using its projected future cash flows, and discounting on the basis of the risk of those cash flows.

Once you have gone through this chapter, you should be able to

* *Perform the mechanics of Discounted Cash Flow analysis;*

* *More specifically, derive a discount rate, calculate projected cash flows, and calculate a terminal value;*

* *Value a company on the basis of DCF analysis.*

TOPIC 1: OVERVIEW OF DISCOUNTED CASH FLOW ANALYSIS

As we learned in Chapters 3 and 4, financial professionals often use relative valuation techniques to determine a company's value by comparing it to similar companies, often its direct competitors. DCF valuation takes a different approach. The question it seeks to answer is this: Leaving aside how a company compares with other firms, how much cash flow will this company generate from this date onward? After all, if a for-profit company does not generate cash, it is typically worth little.

In DCF valuation, you estimate a company's future cash flows over some reasonable number of years called a **forecast period** (since you cannot estimate cash flow for an indefinite period). You then obtain the present value of those cash flows by discounting them, using a risk factor that is represented in a discount rate called the ◀**weighted average cost of capital (WACC)**▶. The stream of future cash flows needs to be discounted because $1,000 generated in ten years' time is worth considerably less than $1,000 today. Virtually every investor would rather have $1,000 today than $1,000 in ten years.

Finally, you sum the discounted cash flows from your forecast period, and add to this the **terminal value** of the company to capture the cash flows that will occur after the forecast period. After all, these cash flows have value as well. The present values of the projected cash flows from your forecast period, together with the present value of the terminal value, give you the company's total estimated **Enterprise Value**. What remains now is to check your inputs and assumptions in a number of ways that will be described later in the chapter. That, in a nutshell, is Discounted Cash Flow Analysis.

From our overview, we can see that a DCF valuation has three basic components:

- **Cash flows**, or more precisely, unlevered free cash flows (UFCF);
- **A terminal value** for the company (TV);
- **A discount rate**, called the weighted average cost of capital (WACC), which we will use to discount the future cash flows and the terminal value to their present values.

Later in the chapter, we will take a closer look at each of these elements. But first, let's briefly examine the strengths and drawbacks of DCF analysis in comparison to other well-known valuation approaches.

DCF Analysis: A Real-Life Case
Back in October 2014, Apple was trading around $100 per share. Was it undervalued? Some people certainly thought so. Activist Carl Icahn thought at the time that Apple's share could be worth as much as $203 (given certain assumptions and projections).

Various practitioners had performed a discounted cash flow of Apple at that time using assumptions such as a 9% discount rate and 10-12% free cash flow growth to arrive at a various valuation prices.

How did these investors and practitioners come up with their valuation? Specifically, how can you use a discounted cash flow analysis to value a company like Apple?

TOPIC 2: STRENGTHS AND POTENTIAL LIMITATIONS OF DCF VALUATION

Strengths

DCF analysis has some real advantages compared to other valuation methods. In fact, many professionals may place more weight on DCF-based estimates than on estimates derived from relative valuation. Here are some benefits of using the DCF method:

Advantage 1

DCF analysis is an intrinsic valuation method that attempts to measure the theoretical value of the company independent of current market conditions. By contrast, relative valuation techniques are accurate only to the degree that the market is correct in valuing the companies and transactions you are comparing to your target. Markets can overvalue or undervalue assets because conditions and perceptions change in response to many different events. Intrinsic valuation, however, is less sensitive to these market-driven considerations.

Let's say Company A's share price is trading at a lower multiple compared to that of its peer, Company B. Does this mean Company A is undervalued? Not necessarily. Even though Company A's stock may be trading low by comparison, its intrinsic, DCF-based value could tell a different story—that its stock should command a higher price. Relative valuation yields useful results, but you will get a fuller picture if you also value the company on its own terms—its ability to generate robust cash flows over a period.

> **UNLEVERED FREE CASH FLOWS**
>
> DCF analysis uses a particular type of cash flow called **unlevered free cash flows**, which are referred to as UFCF for short. UFCF are a firm's cash flows independent of its capital structure. They are the cash flows that are available after a firm has covered operating expenses, such as capital expenditures and working capital requirements, but before any principal and interest payments are made to debt holders, or dividends are paid to equity holders. Put differently, UFCF are cash flows available to all capital holders.

ASK THE FINANCE GURU

Have relative valuation techniques ever led to higher stock prices?

Yes. A good example was during the technology boom of the late 1990s. Most tech stocks then were trading at high multiples, but the relative valuation approach could support higher prices because the entire sector was overvalued.

Advantage 2

The DCF method offers a highly flexible model. It allows you, for example, to make forward-looking adjustments, such as increasing the company's expected sales growth rate, or factoring in improvements in operating margins, in order to see how these improvements impact projected cash flows. In turn, you can analyze how that would affect the company's estimated value. Because DCF analysis is forward-looking, you can also adjust for non-operating items such as excess assets, or make incremental strategic changes in synergies or in the company's expansion plans and view their effect on your valuation range.

Advantage 3

A DCF analysis is always obtainable. By contrast, it is not always possible to find a good peer group in public comparables analysis, or a good deal list in acquisition comparables analysis. With DCF analysis, all you need is a projection of cash flows and a discount rate. In addition, you can perform a DCF valuation for a private company. It does not limit you to publicly traded companies.

ASK THE FINANCE GURU

What's the idea behind looking for intrinsic value?

In the investment world, the key to maintaining a competitive advantage is in discovering valuable information your competitors lack. Value investors constantly pore over industry numbers, ratios, and trends looking for indications that the true value of some company exceeds what the market currently values it at, because the market somehow has gotten it wrong and undervalued it. They use different methods to try to get at this real value. One such method is Discounted Cash Flow Analysis. The eureka moment in DCF analysis is when you arrive at a valuation that differs from what the market says it is, and you have a reasonable and defensible reason for why the DCF analysis differs from the current valuation. If this does happen, it may be an indication that the market has incorrectly priced the stock, which may provide investors with an arbitrage opportunity.

Limitations

Compared to other valuation methods, DCF analysis does have some potential limitations.

Limitation 1

DCF valuation is based on predicted cash flows. In some ways, it is really a sophisticated and educated form of crystal ball gazing, and it is never perfect. Speculating on the future is hard. Also, the projections you use typically come from research analysts, from your own internal model or estimates, or from the company itself, if it is a client of yours or if you are privy to private information. Depending on the source, certain biases are possible. For example, projections can be optimistic because it is natural for a company to want to put its best foot forward, touting the likelihood of tremendous synergies, future growth, and other upside potential. Optimistic biases can result in DCF calculations that overstate company value. You also risk overstating company value if the weighted average cost of capital that you are using in discounting the cash flows to their present value is derived from less risky peers, and hence lower than it should be.

On the other hand, projections can also be more pessimistic than they need be. They can reflect doubts about the company or concerns about the market for its products and services. If you plan to use analyst research as the basis of free cash flow projections, it is a good idea to use several different reliable analysts in order to obtain as broad and as balanced a perspective as possible. You may also want to consider running various scenarios for the DCF projections and stress-testing your numbers.

Limitation 2

Even though DCF analysis, in its mechanics, is an objective calculation based on the use of present value, in many ways it is quite a subjective process. DCF valuation requires using your discretion to make numerous inputs and assumptions, and different people can make them differently. This means there can be a wide variation in results.

Limitation 3

Besides their subjectivity, DCF equations also happen to be set up in a way that make the analysis itself highly sensitive to changes in your key inputs and assumptions, especially the following:

- Free cash flow projections, such as changes to growth rates or margins;
- The estimated terminal value (discussed later in the chapter);
- The assumed discount rate (discussed later in the chapter).

Ultimately, the quality of your valuation can only be as good as the inputs and assumptions you make. In fact, DCF analysis is so sensitive to initial assumptions that professionals typically present the results as a range of estimated values rather than as a single value.

> **TIPS OF THE TRADE**
>
> There are situations in which comparable valuation analysis is difficult, and DCF analysis becomes almost a forced alternative. For instance, it may be hard to find comparable companies for a small, niche manufacturer of a unique product. A company might be a first of its kind, providing a unique product or service. An example would be Synaptics Incorporated: a developer and supplier of custom-designed human interface solutions that enable people to interact more easily and intuitively with a wide variety of mobile computing, communications, entertainment, and other electronic devices (at the time of this writing). Finding a peer group for it could be difficult because they have specialized products (e.g., clear screens that have touch capabilities). You still should try to find the closest group of comparables in order to undertake a comparables valuation, but consider placing more weight on your DCF analysis.

Summary: Steps of a DCF Valuation

1. Calculate the company's weighted average cost of capital (WACC) by:
   * finding out the company's cost of debt, and
   * calculating its cost of equity using an estimation model such as CAPM.

2. Select an appropriate forecast period by considering when the firm will reach a steady state condition.

3. Project the firm's unlevered free cash flow for each year in the forecast period by calculating the firm's EBIT from EBITDA, tax-effecting the EBIT, and making various cash flow adjustments.

4. Discount each unlevered free cash flow by the WACC to determine their present value, and add them up.

5. Calculate the firm's terminal value to capture the value of its cash flows beyond the forecast period, using the Exit Multiple Method, the Perpetuity Growth Rate Method, or both.

6. Derive the firm's total Enterprise Value by:
   * calculating the present value of its terminal value, and
   * adding this to the net present value of the free cash flows you calculated earlier.

7. Derive Equity Value from Enterprise Value by subtracting debt, preferred stock, and noncontrolling interest and adding cash and cash equivalents; then calculate Equity Value per share using diluted shares via TSM.

8. Create a reasonable and defensible range of estimated DCF values by running sensitivities with your assumptions and inputs.

9. Examine the entire valuation picture by:
   * comparing your estimated range of DCF-based equity values per share with the valuation ranges derived from the comparable analyses, and
   * asking if the differences among the ranges are reasonable and defensible.

As we have already seen, to undertake DCF analysis you need three things:

- Unlevered free cash flows (UFCF)
- A terminal value for the company (TV)
- A weighted average cost of capital (WACC) used to discount future values to the present

Each of these needs to be calculated. Let's start with WACC.

TOPIC 3: CALCULATING THE WEIGHTED AVERAGE COST OF CAPITAL

In DCF analysis you determine a company's value by estimating its future free cash flows over a number of years, then discounting those cash flows by a risk factor called the **weighted average cost of capital** (WACC). WACC captures the risk of those future cash flows. WACC is a blended discount rate. It blends two things: the cost of the company's equity capital (cost of equity), and the cost of its debt capital (cost of debt). Applying WACC to the future cash flows discounts them to their present value. You can also think of WACC as the blended rate of return that the company's equity and debt investors require to cover the risk of investing in the company. Put another way, it represents the company's cost of capital considering the risk of its operations and assets over the next several years.

The formula for weighted average cost of capital (WACC) is:

$$\text{WACC} = K_e \times \frac{E}{D+E} + K_d \times (1\text{-}T) \times \frac{D}{D+E}$$

where

- K_e is the cost of equity
- K_d is the cost of debt (pre-tax)
- E is the market value of equity
- D is the market value of debt, and
- T is the marginal tax rate

The weighted average cost of capital is the cost of equity times the percentage of equity in the capital structure, plus the cost of debt times the percentage of debt in the capital structure—and with a small adjustment (1 - t) applied to the cost of debt to capture the fact that it is after-tax, not pre-tax debt. Multiplying the cost of debt by the percentage of debt in the company's capital structure, and likewise the cost of equity by the percentage of equity, is what gives you a "weighted" or blended average.

> **DO YOU KNOW**
> … why after-tax debt is used rather than pretax? Because interest expense is tax-deductible. This means that, assuming a company generated enough operating profit to make use of the IRS's interest tax shield, its after-tax cost of debt will be lower than its nominal or pretax cost of debt. After-tax interest expense is therefore the true cost of borrowing.

Let's examine each component of WACC, starting with the market value of debt (D) and the market value of equity (E). Together, these make up the company's capital structure.

Calculating D

 Practitioners typically use the ◀**Book Value**▶ of a company's debt as a practical proxy for the Market Value of its debt. But be careful. If there are recent substantial changes in the risk-free rate or in the company's credit profile, the Market Value could be substantially different from the Book Value.

Calculating E

 This is calculated similarly to the method used in public comparables analysis: Share price times number of ◀**diluted shares**▶ outstanding (Chapter 3).

Calculating K_d

Cost of debt is what it costs the company to borrow/issue new long-term debt in the market. You can think of it as consisting of two components: the risk-free rate of long-term borrowing, plus a small "spread" (to account for the possibility of the company defaulting) that is based on the company's credit rating or credit profile. A good proxy for the first of these components, the risk-free rate of borrowing, is the 10- or 30-year US Treasury bond because it is virtually default-proof.

If the company's debt is publicly traded, you can directly observe its cost of debt in the market. If the debt is not publicly traded, you will need to estimate it using one of the following methods:

1. If you work in a financial institution, obtain a quote from debt capital markets professionals. The quote, usually a "spread" over a risk-free benchmark, will be based on the company's risk/credit profile.

 2. Examine the company's debt footnote (in its ◀**10-K**▶ or ◀**Annual Report**▶). The weighted average cost of debt based on coupon rates may yield a rough estimate. But be careful here. Check to see if interest rates may have changed since the issuance, and whether the company's credit profile has changed.

3. If the company had a recent debt issuance, you can find out what the interest rate was.

4. Finally, you can look to see if a comparable company has publicly traded debt or has had a recent debt issuance. As with any relative analysis, draw your conclusions

with care. Ask yourself, how similar is the risk/credit profile of the company you are comparing to that of the one you are valuing?

1 – T:

Recall that because interest expenses are generally tax-deductible, the true cost of borrowing is the after-tax cost of debt—not the higher, nominal pre-tax figure. To turn the pretax cost into after-tax cost, K_d is multiplied by $(1 - T)$, where T is generally the marginal tax rate.

Calculating Ke

Unlike Kd, you cannot directly observe Ke in the market. You will need to use an estimation model to determine it. The most widely used model is the Capital Asset Pricing Model (CAPM):

$$K_e = r_f + [\beta \times (r_m - r_f)]$$

where

* r_f is the risk-free rate of return
* ß (◄**beta**►) is a measure of risk
* r_m is the rate of return in the market, and
* $r_m - r_f$ is the market risk premium

Let's unpack the CAPM formula for cost of equity Ke.

Risk-free rate (r_f)

The risk-free rate r_f is the rate of return on an ultra-safe, "zero risk" investment. In the US, the benchmark for this is a Treasury security with a long maturity.

ASK THE FINANCE GURU

Is there a common reference for the risk-free rate of borrowing?

Yes. The risk-free benchmark used to be the 30-year U.S. Treasury bond, but the federal government stopped issuing it in October 2001. The 10-year Treasury bond is now the benchmark. It is currently the most widely traded long bond. In February 2006, however, the government began reissuing the 30-year bond and it may yet again replace the 10-year note as the risk-free benchmark. Note that T-bonds and T-notes have longer maturities than Treasury bills. All three are classified as Treasury securities.

Market risk premium ($r_m - r_f$)

The market risk premium ($r_m - r_f$), also called the equity risk premium, is the difference between the expected return on investment in the equity markets (r_m) and the return on a risk-free investment (r_f). It is the additional return an investor expects in order to be compensated for the added risk associated with investing in equity rather than holding a guaranteed, riskless, sure-bet asset such as a government Treasury bond. You can think of it as the investor's "reward" for bearing equity risk.

Let's walk through a simple illustration: if investors expect an overall market return of 12% and the current risk-free rate in the country is 5%, what would the market risk premium be?

Return of the market	12%
– Risk-free rate	5%
Market risk premium	7%

While estimates vary, during 2014 most practitioners were using a US market risk premium in the range of 5.0% to 7.0%. Duff & Phelps (formerly known as Ibbotson Associates) is a commonly quoted source of future US market risk premiums. They use a method based on historical data in which the long-term average income return on US Treasury securities is subtracted from the long-term average stock market return over the same time period.

ASK THE FINANCE GURU

Does the market risk premium vary by country?
Yes, it does. The basic principle of including a "reward" premium for bearing equity risk is the same everywhere in the world. But because equity market returns (r_m) and risk-free rates (r_f) vary by country, market risk premium estimates ($r_m – r_f$) also naturally differ from country to country. When you are undertaking a DCF valuation, use the market risk premium appropriate for the country in which the company you are valuing is based.

Beta(ß)
The return rates (r_m) and (r_f) are market/country statistics. Beta is a company-specific measure. Beta measures the volatility of a company's stock price compared to the overall market. If a company's beta is 1.0, that means it is as risky as the overall market; the company's stock price should mirror the movements of the general market. If the market rises 10%, for example, it can be expected that the company's stock price will also rise 10%. A beta of 1.0, in other words, means that returns on the stock can be expected to equal overall market returns. If the firm's beta is greater than 1.0, the stock is riskier than the overall market. To compensate for this, investors will expect and demand higher returns, and the company's cost of equity will therefore be higher. If beta is less than 1.0, the stock is less risky than the overall market,

investors will require lower returns, and cost of equity will be lower.

In short, in the CAPM formula the market risk premium $(r_m - r_f)$ is multiplied by the coefficient beta to reflect the higher equity cost that a riskier stock commands. Information services such as Bloomberg provide estimates of beta.

Flow Chart for WACC

Capturing Risk in the Cost of Equity Formula

Just as cost of debt is the risk-free rate of borrowing plus a "default" spread, cost of equity is the risk-free rate plus a second element that is added to account for a company's risk relative to the overall market. Why does equity entail a risk? The cost of equity is the return rate the equity investors expect based on the company's risk. The greater the level of perceived risk, the higher the expected return.

In other words, the riskier the investors believe the venture is, the higher the returns they will demand. Equity investors carry greater risk—and thus require higher returns—because they are subordinate to a company's debt holders and preferred stockholders in the pecking order of who gets paid first when earnings come in and in a bankruptcy situation. Equity investors, in other words, have only a residual claim on assets. They claim whatever residual value remains after the debt holders and preferred stockholders have been paid. The premium over a risk-free investment $(r_m - r_f)$ in the CAPM formula for cost of equity captures this greater risk that equity investors take.

Calculating WACC

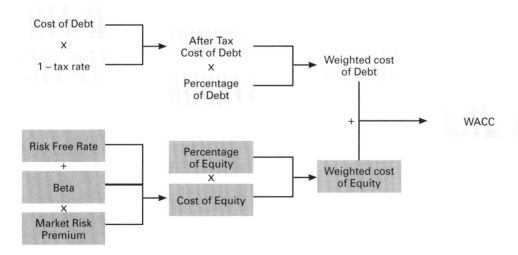

Assuming you know a company's optimal or likely capital structure, and now that you know how to determine, source or estimate the market value of equity (E), market value of debt (D), marginal tax rate (T), the cost of debt (K_d), cost of equity (K_e), the market risk premium ($r_m - r_f$), and the risk coefficient ß (beta), you are ready to calculate WACC.

Exercise

In the example below, let's calculate WACC for Talimara Corp. Suppose your research has turned up the following information. The first thing to do is to calculate Talimara's cost of equity under CAPM.

Assumptions

Risk-Free Rate	4.0%	
Market Risk Premium	7.0%	
Levered Beta	1.3	
		% of total
Market Value of Debt	$350.0	35.0%
+ Market Value of Equity	650.0	65.0%
=Total Capitalization	$1,000.0	
Marginal Tax Rate	35.0%	
Cost of Debt	6.6%	

Risk Free Rate	
+ Beta x Market Risk Premium	
= Cost of Equity	

Answer:

Risk Free Rate	4.0%
+ Beta x Market Risk Premium	9.1%
= Cost of Equity	**13.1%**

Using the cost of equity figure you just worked out, determine Talimara's WACC. Remember to use the company's after-tax cost of debt, not its pretax cost.

Exercise

	Cost		Weighting		Weighted Avg. Cost
Equity		x		=	
Debt		x		=	
				WACC	

Answer:

	Cost		Weighting			Weighted Avg. Cost
Equity	13.1%	x	65.0%	=		8.5%
Debt	4.3%	x	35.0%	=		1.5%
				WACC		**10.0%**

TOPIC 4: CALCULATING UNLEVERED FREE CASH FLOWS

Having calculated Talimara's WACC, the next step is to project its future unlevered free cash flows. To determine their present value, we will then discount the cash flows by the discount rate (WACC) that you just calculated. Unlevered free cash flows, you will recall, are cash flows that are independent of the company's capital structure. That is, they are independent of how the company's assets were financed. They are the company's cash flows before you subtract interest expense from them.

The idea behind this is that the true Enterprise Value of a company is independent of the particular way in which its assets happen to have been paid for. After all, they could have been financed using any number of combinations of debt and equity, and at many different borrowing rates. Each of those combinations would have yielded a slightly different interest expense, and yet the company's core business operations would remain the same regardless. Thus, factoring a company's financing costs into an estimate of its cash flows would yield somewhat arbitrary results.

The following is a widely used method for calculating unlevered free cash flows for one time period:

Step One
Find the company's EBITDA. EBITDA is a reasonable proxy for operating cash flow (see Chapter 2). Because EBITDA is before interest expense and therefore before the effects of the capital structure, it allows you to separate the company's operating activities from its financing activities.

Step Two
Remove depreciation and amortization from EBITDA, if they are tax-deductible. This will give you EBIT.

Step Three
"Tax-effect" the EBIT figure because taxes are a cash outflow. This means you need to use the after-tax EBIT.

FINANCIAL FACTOID

What does unlevered mean in the phrase "unlevered free cash flows"? In finance, leverage means debt. Debt, if you think about it, serves as a lever that allows you—gives you the leverage—to undertake transactions you otherwise could not. "Unlevered" roughly means "unhinged" or "free of the lever of debt."

Unlevered (debt-free) free cash flow is cash that is available to all capital holders—in particular, before debt holders are paid. It is free cash flow that can be paid to both debt and equity holders in the form of interest payments, repayment of debt principal, dividends, or a share buyback.

"Free" means the excess cash beyond what is needed to fund a company's operations and therefore available to capital holders.

TIPS OF THE TRADE

Besides D&A, there may be other non-cash items you need to consider. For example, changes in deferred taxes can be significant to a company's cash flow generation, and when they are, they are usually analyzed. Rule of thumb: consider any change in any asset or liability that impacts cash flow.

Step Four

Make cash flow adjustments. (Recall that EBITDA and EBIT are not actual cash flow.) Add back the ◀**non-cash**▶ expenses such as depreciation and amortization. Subtract ◀**capital expenditures**▶ because they are a cash outflow; they represent purchases such as new equipment, buildings and machines. Finally, add or subtract working capital needs such as cash spent to increase inventories, depending on whether the net change in working capital is positive (an increase) or negative (a decrease).

Here is a summary of the four steps in table form:

Unlevered Free Cash Flow	Explanation of Components
EBITDA	EBITDA: Common proxy for operating cash flow
Less: Depreciation & amortization	Captures tax shield on D&A
= EBIT	
Less: Taxes	Typically at the marginal tax rate
= Tax-affected EBIT	Yields after-tax operating income
+ Depreciation & amortization	Add or subtract the appropriate cash flow impacts.
- Capital expenditures	Remember that D&A are non-cash expenses!
+/- Changes in net working capital	
+/- Changes in other non-cash items	
= **Unlevered Free Cash Flow**	

ASK THE FINANCE GURU

Is there another way to calculate unlevered free cash flows?

Yes, an alternative is to start with net income. Unlevered Free Cash Flow = Net income + depreciation & amortization – capital expenditures – changes in working capital + interest expense times (1 – the marginal tax rate). As long as you use the same tax rate, this approach should yield the exact same answer as the EBITDA-based approach.

Selecting a Forecast Period: Steady State

Now that you know how to calculate unlevered free cash flow for one time period, your next step is to forecast the cash flows you expect the company to generate in the future. But there is an immediate question. The company could be around for 100 years or longer; how far into the future should you try to project the company's free cash flows in order to arrive at a DCF value? Clearly, you have to stop somewhere. In practice, finance professionals typically select a forecast period (also called "projection period" or "forecast horizon") of 5 to 20 years. How long the period is depends on the characteristics of the company and its industry.

In selecting an appropriate forecast period, an important criterion is to consider when the company will reach a **"steady state"** condition characterized by a normal business environment. (A flight analogy for "steady state" would be after a jet plane takes off, climbs through the cloud layer, and then reaches cruising altitude where you can now take off your seatbelt.) There are certain markers you should look for when you are trying to forecast when a company will reach steady state. One steady state marker is when a company is sustaining its capital investment—that is, all new capital spending by the company is simply to replace what they are using in a given year through depreciation. Another telling sign a company is at steady state is when its working capital needs have stabilized.

As with any projection into the future, however, predicting when a company will reach steady state can be a challenge. Industry factors can come into play: for example, a company in a **growth** sector may take longer to reach steady state than one in a **mature** industry. Second, the company itself may be at an earlier **stage** of its **life cycle** compared to other companies in the same industry. For instance, Apple and Microsoft compete in broadly the same industry, but Microsoft is at a more mature stage of its life cycle and closer to steady-state growth than Apple.

Third, you need to ask whether it is feasible and reasonable to project out a longer-term forecast period. And finally, if the industry or company you are analyzing is cyclical, you need to make sure that your forecast period does not end in the valley or at the peak of the business cycle, and that it includes one or more full business cycles. If your forecast period ends in the trough or at the apex of a business cycle, it will throw off the calculation of the final year of your forecast period. In turn, this will distort the calculation of the company's terminal value (which we will discuss shortly).

Discounting the Free Cash Flows: Time Value of Money

Let's recall our big picture: in DCF analysis, you are trying to determine the value of a company by forecasting its future cash flows for a certain forecast period, discounting them on the basis of the risk associated with each of those cash flows, and then adding them up. The future cash flows need to be

RULE OF THUMB
In a DCF analysis, the end of the forecast period you select can occur at, or after, the time at which the firm is expected to reach steady state, but it should not occur before it reaches steady state, because things are still changing.

A WORD ON TERMINOLOGY
Other names for tax-affected EBIT are:
• NOPAT, which means net operating profit after-tax
• Unlevered Net Income
• EBIAT, which means earnings before interest and after-taxes

discounted because of a basic premise called the time value of money.

Simply put, a dollar today is worth more than a dollar tomorrow. Why? Because the dollar today can be invested. The central concept is the opportunity cost of future money. Future money is worth less than money today because waiting for future money compels you to forego investment returns. The formula for the time value of money is:

$$FV = PV \times (1 + g)^n$$

where
- FV is future value
- PV is present value
- g is the growth rate or rate of return, and
- n is the number of periods (commonly expressed in years)

Let's use this formula in an easy example. Assuming a 10% rate of return for one year, $1 today would be worth $1.10 one year from now:

$1.10 = \$1.00 \times (1 + 10\%)^1$

Assuming another 10% growth in year 2, $1 would grow to $1.21 by the end of year 2:

$1.21 = \$1.10 \times (1 + 10\%)^1$
or
$1.21 = \$1.00 \times (1 + 10\%)^2$ where the 10% growth is compounded over two years

> **FINANCIAL FACTOID**
> In the Present Value formula, the discount rate r is typically substituted for the growth rate g. Is that cheating? No. Recall that like a growth rate, a discount rate can be expressed as a required rate of return. So "r" and "g" are really just mirror images of each other.

What we have just done is calculate the future value of a dollar from its present value. DCF discounting is just the reverse of this. It is calculating present value (PV) from future value (FV). Let's start with the same time-value-of-money formula, but then solve for PV by simply rearranging the terms:

Since $FV = PV \times (1 + g)^n$
$PV = FV / (1+r)^n$
where r is the discount rate or required rate of return.

Thus, at a 10% discount rate or WACC, $1.21 two years from now is worth $1.00 today:

$1.21 / (1 +10\%)^2 = \$1.00$

In DCF valuation, when you are discounting a stream of future cash flows for a number of years, you simply add up the individual pieces:

Present value of future cash flows =
$CF_1 / (1+r)^1 + CF_2 / (1+r)^2 + \ldots + CF_n / (1+r)^n$

Exercise

Let's walk through an exercise to discount projected unlevered free cash flows (UFCF):

	Projected Fiscal Year Ending December 31				
	20x1	*20x2*	*20x3*	*20x4*	*20x5*
EBITDA	$78.7	$81.9	$85.2	$88.6	$92.1
Less: Depreciation & Amortization	(30.0)	(32.0)	(33.0)	(33.3)	(34.5)
EBIT	48.7	49.9	52.2	55.3	57.6
Less: Taxes @ 35.0%	(17.1)	(17.5)	(18.3)	(19.3)	(20.2)
Tax-effected EBIT	31.7	32.4	33.9	35.9	37.5
Plus: Depreciation & Amortization	30.0	32.0	33.0	33.3	34.5
Less: Capital Expenditures	(32.5)	(32.5)	(33.0)	(34.0)	(34.5)
Less: Changes in Working Capital	(1.5)	(2.0)	(2.5)	(3.0)	(3.5)
Unlevered Free Cash Flow	**$27.6**	**$29.9**	**$31.4**	**$32.2**	**$33.9**

Assuming a discount rate of 9.5%, what is the present value (as of January 1, 20X1) of the UFCF?

$PV = FV / (1 + r)^n$

The formula for discounting assuming end-period cash flows:

$NPV = \$27.6 / (1 + 9.5\%)^1 + \$29.9 / (1 + 9.5\%)^2 + \$31.4 / (1 + 9.5\%)^3 + \$32.2 / (1 + 9.5\%)^4 + \$33.9 / (1 + 9.5\%)^5$
= **$118.0**

Answer:
$118 million

TOPIC 5: CALCULATING TERMINAL VALUE

By now, it has probably occurred to you that the total value of the company we are analyzing is greater than the sum of the present (discounted) value of the free cash flows that will be generated during the forecast period. What do we do with the cash flows that will occur after the forecast period? They have value too, and cannot be forgotten/ignored.

Finance professionals use a **terminal value** to capture the value of the company's cash flows beyond the forecast period. (In fact, for a company which posted losses for its first several years as a start-up, the terminal value calculation can be especially important.) Two methods are widely used to project the terminal value:

A. The Exit Multiple Method: Assumes that, at the end of the forecast period, the company is worth (or can be "sold for") a multiple of an operating metric, e.g., a multiple of EBITDA.

B. The Perpetuity Growth Rate Method: Assumes that the company's free cash flows will grow at a moderate, constant rate indefinitely.

It is important to become familiar with both methods for two reasons: both are routinely used in DCF valuation. Second, they are often used in conjunction with each other, because doing so allows you to check the results of one method against the other.

A. Exit Multiple Method

The Exit Multiple Method, also called the Terminal Multiple Method, estimates the terminal value of a company by applying a valuation multiple (for example, EV/EBITDA) to a relevant operating metric (for example, EBITDA).

| **Terminal value$_n$ = Multiple x Financial Metric$_n$** |
| where $_n$ equals the final year of the forecast period. |

Estimating the company's terminal value using a financial metric as of the last year of the forecast period results in a value at the end of year N. You will therefore need to discount this terminal value back to the beginning of the valuation date (Year Zero) so you can add it to the present values of the cash flows from the forecast period. The discount rate you would typically use for this is WACC.

There are many important considerations that need to be taken into account when determining the exit multiple. The most

> **RULE OF THUMB**
> If you used an equity value multiple rather than an Enterprise Value multiple as the terminal multiple, you would need to add Net Debt back for the final year of the forecast period in order to gross up Equity Value to Enterprise Value. It is not necessary to do this in the Perpetuity Growth Rate Method, because it already yields an Enterprise Value.

common type of multiple used is an Enterprise Value multiple to EBITDA. This, however, will vary from industry to industry.

Most practitioners begin with the current trading multiple and then examine whether that multiple is sustainable and reasonable. If it is not, they make adjustments to reflect the estimated multiple in a steady-state environment. A public comparables multiple estimates what the company is worth in the public market on a stand-alone basis. If you expect the company under analysis to be acquired after the forecast period, you might use a multiple determined by looking at a comparable transaction analysis. Note that a comparable transaction multiple reflects a ◄**control premium**▶ (a premium the acquirer pays for the benefit of taking control of the company's operations) as well as potential ◄**synergies**▶ from a merger. It therefore estimates what the company might be sold for.

Exercise

Let's calculate the terminal value for Talimara Corp. Assume it has the following projected unlevered free cash flows:

	Projected Fiscal Year Ending December 31				
	20x1	*20x2*	*20x3*	*20x4*	*20x5*
EBITDA	$78.7	$81.9	$85.2	$88.6	$92.1
Less: Depreciation & Amortization	(30.0)	(32.0)	(33.0)	(33.3)	(34.5)
EBIT	48.7	49.9	52.2	55.3	57.6
Less: Taxes @ 35.0%	(17.1)	(17.5)	(18.3)	(19.3)	(20.2)
Tax-effected EBIT	31.7	32.4	33.9	35.9	37.5
Plus: Depreciation & Amortization	30.0	32.0	33.0	33.3	34.5
Less: Capital Expenditures	(32.5)	(32.5)	(33.0)	(34.0)	(34.5)
Less: Changes in Working Capital	(1.5)	(2.0)	(2.5)	(3.0)	(3.5)
Unlevered Free Cash Flow	**$27.6**	**$29.9**	**$31.4**	**$32.2**	**$33.9**

The terminal year EBITDA is circled. Using an exit multiple of 7.0 times 20*x*5 EBITDA and a 9.5% WACC, what is the present value of Talimara's terminal value?

To determine the company's total estimated Enterprise Value, you would then add this discounted terminal value ($409.6 million) to the present value of the unlevered free cash flows you are expecting Talimara to generate during the forecast period.

B. Perpetuity Growth Rate Method
The Perpetuity Growth Rate Method calculates a company's terminal value on the basis of the assumption that the company

will continue to grow at a moderate, steady rate forever (hence the term "perpetuity"). It is calculated off of a normalized cash flow, which is the company's unlevered free cash flow at steady state (meaning the last year of the forecast period).

$$\text{Terminal Value} = \frac{FCF_n \times (1 + g)}{(r - g)}$$

where
- FCF is the normalized free cash flow in period N
- g is the nominal perpetual growth rate, and
- r is the discount rate or WACC

The nominal perpetual growth rate (g) is the company's sustainable long-run growth rate. This rate can be higher than inflation but should not exceed the growth rate of the overall economy. Rates vary by situation and company, but the typical range is 2% to 5%. The discount rate (r) is usually the weighted average cost of capital.

Like the Exit Multiple Method, the Perpetuity Growth Rate Method yields the value of the company as of the end of the forecast period. You will therefore need to discount this terminal value back to Year Zero, your valuation date, in order to arrive at its present value, and then add this to the present value of the free cash flows from the forecast period.

Exercise

Let's calculate the terminal value for Talimara using the perpetuity growth rate approach. Again, assume that Talimara has the following projected unlevered free cash flows:

The unlevered free cash flow for the terminal year is circled.

	Projected Fiscal Year Ending December 31				
	20x1	**20x2**	**20x3**	**20x4**	**20x5**
EBITDA	$78.7	$81.9	$85.2	$88.6	$92.1
Less: Depreciation & Amortization	(30.0)	(32.0)	(33.0)	(33.3)	(34.5)
EBIT	48.7	49.9	52.2	55.3	57.6
Less: Taxes @ 35.0%	(17.1)	(17.5)	(18.3)	(19.3)	(20.2)
Tax-effected EBIT	31.7	32.4	33.9	35.9	37.5
Plus: Depreciation & Amortization	30.0	32.0	33.0	33.3	34.5
Less: Capital Expenditures	(32.5)	(32.5)	(33.0)	(34.0)	(34.5)
Less: Changes in Working Capital	(1.5)	(2.0)	(2.5)	(3.0)	(3.5)
Unlevered Free Cash Flow	**$27.6**	**$29.9**	**$31.4**	**$32.2**	**$33.9**

Assuming a WACC of 9.5% and a perpetuity growth rate of 4.0%, what is the present value of Talimara's terminal value under this method?

Year 5 unlevered free cash flow	
Perpetuity growth rate	
Unlevered free cash flow in perpetuity	Year 5 unlevered free cash flow (1 + Perpetuity Growth Rate)

Unlevered free cash flow in perpetuity	
/ (WACC - Perpetuity growth rate)	
= **Year 5 Terminal Value**	

/ **5 years discount factor**	$1.574 = (1 + 9.5\%)^5$
= **Present Value of Terminal Value**	million

Answer:

Year 5 unlevered free cash flow	$33.9
Perpetuity growth rate	4.0%
Unlevered free cash flow in perpetuity	$35.3 Year 5 unlevered free cash flow (1 + Perpetuity Growth Rate)

Unlevered free cash flow in perpetuity	$35.3
/ (WACC - Perpetuity growth rate)	5.5%
= **Year 5 Terminal Value**	$641.3

/ **5 years discount factor**	$1.574 = (1 + 9.5\%)^5$
= **Present Value of Terminal Value**	**$407.3** million

The final step is to estimate the firm's total Enterprise Value by adding the present value of the terminal value to the present value of the ◀**unlevered free cash flows**▶ (UFCF) you are expecting Talimara to generate during the forecast period. Note that the figure of $407.3 million differs slightly from the value you arrived at using the Exit Multiple approach. That is why it is a good idea to use the methods in conjunction and cross-check the results.

TOPIC 6: DERIVING A DISCOUNTED CASH FLOW VALUATION

Now that we have gone over the individual components of DCF analysis, we are in a position to put the entire puzzle together and derive a company valuation.

Recall that unlevered free cash flows are independent of capital structure decisions. This means that the present value of a company's UFCF yields an Enterprise Value, not an Equity Value. Similarly, a terminal value calculation also yields an Enterprise Value—whether you estimate it using the Perpetuity Growth approach (that is, using UFCF); using an exit multiple of an Enterprise Value metric such as EBITDA; or, for that matter, using an Equity Value multiple (such as P/E) and adding back Net Debt for the final year to gross up Equity Value to Enterprise Value.

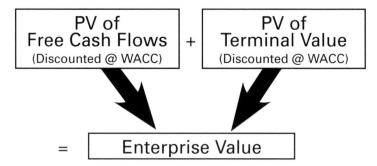

$$\begin{array}{ccc} \boxed{\begin{array}{c} \text{PV of} \\ \text{Free Cash Flows} \\ \text{(Discounted @ WACC)} \end{array}} & + & \boxed{\begin{array}{c} \text{PV of} \\ \text{Terminal Value} \\ \text{(Discounted @ WACC)} \end{array}} \end{array}$$

$$= \quad \boxed{\text{Enterprise Value}}$$

To derive Equity Value from Enterprise Value, subtract debt, ◀**preferred stock**▶ and ◀**noncontrolling interest**▶, and add cash and cash equivalents. Ideally, the timing for these balance sheet items should be consistent with the present value date. In practice, however, the most recent date is commonly used as a pragmatic estimate. For a public company, most professionals will calculate down to Equity Value per share, so they can compare the calculated intrinsic value to the current share price.

> **Equity Value =**
> **Enterprise Value – Debt, Preferred Stock & Minority Interests**
> **+ Cash & Cash Equivalents**

To calculate Equity Value per share, take the Equity Value calculated above and divide it by the number of diluted shares outstanding.

> $$\frac{\text{Equity Value}}{\text{Diluted Shares}} = \text{Equity Value Per Share}$$

Ideally, in terms of timing, the share information should be consistent with balance sheet items and the present value date. In practice, professionals commonly use the most recent share and option information.

Exercise

In the exercise we performed a few pages earlier for Talimara Corp., (under "Discounting The Free Cash Flows") the present value of Talimara's unlevered free cash flows was $118.0 million. The present value of its terminal value (using the EBITDA-based exit multiple method) was $409.6 million. Given that Talimara has $75.0 million of Net Debt and 15.000 million diluted shares outstanding, calculate its Enterprise Value, Equity Value and Equity Value per share.

Present Value of the Free Cash Flows	$118.0	million
+ Present Value of the Terminal Value	409.6	million
= Enterprise Value	**$527.6**	**million**

Enterprise Value		million
Less: Net Debt		million
= Equity Value		**million**

Equity Value		million
/ Diluted Shares Outstanding		million
= Equity Value per Share		

Answer:

Enterprise Value	$527.6	million
Less: Net Debt	(75.0)	million
= Equity Value	**$452.6**	**million**

Equity Value	$452.6	million
/ Diluted Shares Outstanding	15.000	million
= Equity Value per Share	**$30.17**	

TOPIC 7: CREATING AND COMPARING VALUATION RANGES

After performing public comparables analysis (Chapter 3), acquisition comparables analysis (Chapter 4), and DCF analysis, the grand goal is to figure out what the company is actually worth and, if it is a possible M&A target, what it could be sold for.

Suppose you have done these three analyses for Talimara Corp. Assume that an equity research analyst thinks that, for a public comparables valuation, a range of 7.0x to 9.0x LTM EBITDA is appropriate for Talimara and that, for an acquisition comparables valuation, a range of 9.0x to 11.0x LTM EBITDA is appropriate.

Let's say Talimara has an LTM EBITDA of $100.0 million, Net Debt of $200.0 million, and 20.000 million diluted shares outstanding. Recall the technique of imputing valuation ranges from Chapter 4. What is the range of Equity Values per share for the given multiples, under public comparables and acquisition comparables analysis?

Public Comparables Analysis

Multiple	7.0x	–	9.0x
x LTM EBITDA	$100.0		$100.0
= Implied Enterprise Value	$700.0 m		$900.0 m
- Net Debt	($200.0 m)		($200.0 m)
= Implied Equity Value	$500.0 m		$700.0 m
/ Diluted Shares	20.000 m		20.000 m
Implied Equity Value per share	**$25.00**	**–**	**$35.00**

Acquisition Comparables Analysis

Multiple	9.0x	–	11.0x
x LTM EBITDA	$100.0		$100.0
= Implied Transaction Value	$900.0 m		$1,100.0 m
- Net Debt	($200.0 m)		($200.0 m)
= Implied Offer Value	$700.0 m		$900.0 m
/ Diluted Shares	20.000 m		20.000 m
Implied Offer Value per share	**$35.00**	**–**	**$45.00**

In the last section, we derived a DCF Equity Value per share of approximately $30.00. Because of the subjective nature of the assumptions used in DCF, the estimated DCF value is typically expressed as a range of values rather than a single number. The most important thing is to create a reasonable and defensible range by sensitizing the discount rates, the exit multiples or perpetuity growth rate assumptions in your terminal value calculation, and possibly the key drivers in your UFCF projections. Assume that after running these sensitivities, your DCF value per share is $27.00 to $33.00, which centers the range around $30.00.

We can map out the valuation on a basis of Equity Value per share. Illustrating the data on a graph offers a particularly effective visual method for drawing comparisons:

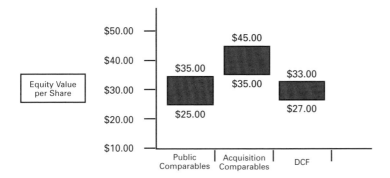

Let's compare the resulting valuation ranges. Notice that the valuation ranges from our public comparables analysis and from DCF analysis loosely overlap. Because both of these methods value a business on a stand-alone basis, it is fairly common to get this result when the comparable companies are reasonably valued in comparison to the target company's expected cash flow generation. Another way to look at this is that the DCF valuation is using reasonable assumptions compared to the public market comparables.

But there are situations where the DCF valuation and the public comparables values may differ a bit. What if the market is overvaluing or undervaluing the stock relative to the DCF valuation? What if there is another factor that is not captured in your DCF model? Are your DCF valuation assumptions reasonable? It is because of such questions that most practitioners cross-check the results from their DCF analysis and public comparables analyses to validate their work.

Now let's look at acquisition comparables analysis. The acquisition comparables method values the company from an M&A perspective. This means that a control premium and potential synergies are factored in, so it makes sense for the range to typically be higher than the public comparables and stand-alone DCF valuations.

Summarizing the ranges graphically allows you to examine the entire valuation picture. Are the differences between each valuation range reasonable? Is the premium implied by the higher valuation range from the acquisition comparables analysis justifiable? How much confidence do you have in the valuation from your public comparables analysis and in the assumptions you made in your DCF valuation? All of these are questions that practitioners face routinely, and being able to justify and defend these answers is as much of an art as it is a science.

SUMMARY
Chapter 5

TOPIC 1 & 2: OVERVIEW

DCF analysis estimates a company's value using its own projected future cash flows, discounted on the basis of the risk of those cash flows. To perform DCF valuation, you need the following components:

- Unlevered free cash flows (UFCF);
- A terminal value for the company (TV);
- A weighted average cost of capital (WACC), used to discount the future values of the UFCF and the TV to their present values.

Unlevered free cash flows are the cash flows available after a company has covered its main operating expenses, but before principal and interest payments and dividends—meaning, cash flows that are available to all capital holders and independent of capital structure.

DCF Strengths:

Compared to relative valuation, DCF comes closer to measuring a company's intrinsic worth because it is less influenced by external factors. Its flexibility allows you to quantify the changes in value from different operating assumptions. Finally, a DCF valuation is always obtainable, whereas public comparables and acquisition comparables analyses depend on finding a good peer group and a good deal list, respectively.

DCF Limitations:

DCF is based on projected cash flows, and it is hard to read the future. Projections from the company or from analysts can be optimistic, potentially resulting in overstated values. Projections can also be pessimistic. In addition, DCF requires using your discretion to make numerous inputs and assumptions, and the outcome is highly sensitive to the changes you make. Therefore, practitioners typically present a range of estimated values.

TOPIC 3: CALCULATING THE WEIGHTED AVERAGE COST OF CAPITAL

The Weighted Average Cost of Capital is the discount rate used to calculate the present value of future cash flows and the present value of the company's terminal value. It can be thought of as the required rate of return for both equity and debt investors (assuming there are no other capital holders such as preferred stock).

$$\text{WACC} = K_e \times \frac{E}{D+E} + K_d \times (1\text{-}T) \times \frac{D}{D+E}$$

where

- K_e is the cost of equity (post-tax)
- K_d is the cost of debt (pre-tax)
- E is the market value of equity
- D is the market value of debt, and
- T is the marginal tax rate

Because cost of equity Ke is not readily observable in the market, professionals commonly use the Capital Asset Pricing Model (CAPM) to estimate it.

$$K_e = r_f + [\text{ß} \times (r_m - r_f)]$$

where
- r_f is the risk-free rate of return
- ß (beta) is a measure of risk
- r_m is the rate of return in the market, and
- $r_m - r_f$ is the market risk premium

TOPIC 4 & 5. CALCULATING UNLEVERED FREE CASH FLOWS AND TERMINAL VALUE

After calculating WACC, the next step is to select an appropriate forecast period by considering when the firm will reach steady state; you then project its unlevered free cash flows (UFCF) over that period. The UFCF are then discounted by the discount rate (WACC) and added up.

Steady state is when the company reaches a stable growth environment while sustaining its capital investment needs. Forecast periods usually range from 5 to 20 years, depending on the industry, the company, and where it is in its life cycle.

A common approach to calculating UFCF is:

EBITDA
  Less: Depreciation & amortization

= EBIT
  Less: Taxes (@ Marginal Tax Rate)

= Tax-affected EBIT
  + Depreciation & amortization
  - Capital expenditures
  +/- Changes in net working capital
  +/- Changes in other non-cash items

= Unlevered Free Cash Flow

The resulting cash flow is unlevered because it is cash that can be returned to both debt and equity capital holders in the form of interest payments, repayments of debt, dividends, or a share buyback.

To capture the value of the company's cash flows beyond the forecast period, its terminal value (TV) is then calculated using the Exit Multiple Method, the Perpetuity Growth Rate Method, or both.

- Exit Multiple Method: Assumes that at the end of the forecast period, the company is worth (or can be sold for) a multiple of an operating metric, e.g., EV/EBITDA. Terminal value equals the selected multiple times financial metric

$$\text{Terminal Value} \quad = \quad \text{EBITDA}_n \times \text{Multiple}$$

- Perpetuity Growth Rate Method: Assumes that the company's free cash flows will grow at a moderate, constant rate indefinitely.

$$\text{Terminal Value} \quad = \quad \frac{\text{FCF}_n \times (1 + g)}{(r\text{-}g)}$$

where
  ◆ FCF is the normalized free cash flow in period N
  ◆ g is the nominal perpetual growth rate, and
  ◆ r is the discount rate or WACC

TOPIC 6 & 7: DERIVING A DISCOUNTED CASH FLOW VALUATION

You can now put the entire puzzle together. First, derive Enterprise Value by calculating the present value of the terminal value and adding this to the present values of the free cash flows you calculated earlier.

Then derive **Equity Value** from this Enterprise Value by subtracting debt, preferred stock and noncontrolling interest, and adding cash and cash equivalents. Finally, calculate **Equity Value per share** by taking the Equity Value and dividing it by the number of diluted shares outstanding. Finally, create a reasonable and defensible range of DCF values by running sensitivities around your assumptions and inputs.

Creating and Comparing Valuation Ranges

After undertaking public comparables and acquisition comparables analyses, calculate a range of Equity Values per share using the multiples from these analyses. Then examine the entire valuation picture by comparing your estimated range of DCF-based Equity Values per share with the valuation ranges you derived from the comparable analyses. Illustrating the data on a graph offers a particularly effective visual method for drawing comparisons. Finally, ask yourself if the differences among the ranges obtained through the three methodologies are reasonable and defensible.

....

MASTERY QUIZ
Chapter 5

QUESTION #1

True or False:

Selecting a higher levered beta will increase the value of my DCF analysis (everything else held constant).

QUESTION #2

True or False:

When performing a DCF analysis and deriving an Equity Value per share, one should calculate a precise, single value.

QUESTION #3

When calculating unlevered free cash flow for the purposes of a DCF valuation, which one of the following four items is not deducted from EBITDA?

A. Taxes
B. Change in working capital
C. Capital expenditures
D. Interest expense

QUESTION #4

With the perpetuity growth rate method, which one of the following components below is NOT necessarily needed to calculate the terminal value?

A. EBITDA exit multiple
B. Long-term growth rate of unlevered free cash flows
C. Unlevered free cash flow in the terminal year
D. Discount rate

QUESTION #5

Assume that the present value of the unlevered free cash flows for a company is $500 million. The present value of the terminal value is $3,000 million. Net Debt is $200 million. The cost of equity is 11% and the Weighted Average Cost of Capital is 9%. There are 100.0 million diluted shares outstanding. What is the Equity Value per share?

A. $15.00
B. $47.00
C. $32.00
D. $33.00

QUESTION #6

In calculating a terminal value using the perpetuity growth rate method, you initially assume that the required rate of return (r) is 10.0% and the perpetuity growth rate (g) assumption is 4.0%. After further research, you decide to lower the assumed long-term growth rate to 3.5% and the discount rate to 9.5%. What will happen to your DCF terminal value?

A. Increase
B. Decrease
C. Stay the same

QUESTION #7

Assume that Company A has a WACC of 10% and Company B has a WACC of 8%. Both companies have a projected year 5 terminal year EBITDA of $100.0 million, but Company A's exit multiple is 10.0x and Company B's exit multiple is 8.0x. Who has the HIGHER present value of the terminal value?

A. Company A
B. Company B
C. They are the same
D. There is not enough information provided

QUESTION #8

Using the WACC framework, suppose that a company's current cost of equity (Ke) is 10% and that the company's cost of debt is 6%. The tax rate is 38%. All else being equal, if the company's cost of debt suddenly increased by two percentage points (i.e. increased from 6% to 8%), what is the most reasonable statement about what would happen to the company's weighted average cost of capital?

A. Decrease
B. It must increase by 2%
C. Not change
D. You need to know the capital structure to get a better idea

QUESTION #9

Suppose a company's cost of equity is 10%, the company's cost of debt is 7%, and the company's debt/total capitalization is 30%. What is the company's weighted average cost of capital (WACC)?

A. 9.1%
B. 8.5%
C. 8.4%
D. Cannot be determined

ANSWER KEY
Chapter 5

ANSWER #1

False

In the context of the CAPM, selecting a higher beta will increase a firm's cost of equity and therefore the WACC. Given that the unlevered free cash flows will remain the same, using a higher WACC will result in a lower value of future cash flows discounted back to the present.

ANSWER #2

False

Valuation is both art and science, and DCF valuations are not any different. Even though the DCF methodology offers a very objective calculation in the form of present value, the inputs necessary to calculate a DCF valuation are still subjective. Practitioners should be careful in drawing too many concrete conclusions from a DCF analysis. Generally a valuation range is an appropriate answer, while a specific value is not.

ANSWER #3

D — Interest expense

Unlevered free cash flow is an operating measure independent of the capital structure of the company. Interest expense results from debt, a form of capital that should be ignored for the purposes of calculating unlevered free cash flow.

ANSWER #4

A — EBITDA exit multiple

EBITDA exit multiple is not needed in the perpetuity growth method because the exit multiple is utilized for the **EBITDA exit multiple method** of calculating terminal value. The **perpetuity growth method** needs the unlevered free cash flow in the terminal year, a long-term growth rate and a discount rate.

ANSWER #5

D — $33.00

The Enterprise Value of the firm is equal to the present value of the unlevered free cash flows plus the present value of the terminal value. Enterprise Value = $500 + $3,000 = $3,500. To get to Equity Value, subtract Net Debt. Equity Value = $3,500 – $200 = $3,300. To calculate Equity Value per share, take Equity Value divided by diluted shares outstanding. $3,300 / 100.0 million shares = $33.00.

ANSWER #6

B — Decrease

The denominator in the perpetuity growth rate formula equals: r – g. In the initial assumption, the denominator would be: 10.0% – 4.0% = **6.0%**. By changing the discount rate to 9.5% and the perpetuity growth rate to 3.5%, the denominator remains the same (9.5% – 3.5% = **6.0%**) in aggregate. But in the numerator (Free Cash Flow * (1 + growth rate), the lower growth rate will impact the projected free cash flow for next year. Therefore the terminal value will be lower.

ANSWER #7

A — Company A

Company A's present value of the terminal value is found by discounting 10.0 * $100.0 million or $1,000.0 million by 5 years at 10%. This would give you a value of $620.9 million. Company B's present value of the terminal value is found by discounting 8.0 * $100.0 million or $800.0 million by 5 years at 8%. This would give you a value of $544.5 million. Company A has the higher present value of the terminal value.

ANSWER #8

D — You need to know the capital structure to get a better idea

If the cost of debt increases and <u>all else stays</u> equal, then the WACC is most likely going to increase. But, just because the cost of debt increases, that doesn't mean that it will increase by 2% or by the after-tax amount of 2%. A key part of the question is not provided: what is the capital structure of the firm? That will determine the weighting of the cost of debt in the WACC formula.

ANSWER #9

D — Cannot be determined

The company's WACC cannot be determined because a tax rate was not given. You need to adjust a company's cost of debt for the tax shield [Kd * (1 – tax rate)] to calculate the after-tax cost of debt.

CHAPTER 6
Merger Consequences Analysis

QUICK SUMMARY

Merger Consequences Analysis is used to determine what an acquirer *could* afford to pay for a potential target, which may be different from what it will, in fact, eventually pay. For that reason, merger consequences analysis is often called **affordability analysis**. Another name for merger consequences analysis is ◄**pro forma**► analysis because, in determining the affordability for the acquirer, it seeks to answer the question of what the financial impact of the transaction will be. How much value will be added or taken away from the acquirer, if it is allowed to go through with the transaction at a given price?

Merger consequences analysis is often also referred to as ◄**accretion/dilution**► analysis because, in analyzing the acquirer's affordability, it tries to predict whether the intended transaction will increase *(accrete)* or decrease *(dilute)* the acquirer's earnings per share. Sometimes another metric, such as the acquirer's cash flow per share, is used.

Another affordability question that merger consequences analysis seeks to answer—this time, using credit analysis— is how much new debt the acquirer can take on without adversely affecting its credit rating.

In this chapter, you will learn how to perform the mechanics of merger consequences analysis. This includes using accretion/dilution analysis to determine how the proposed transaction will affect the acquirer's earnings per share (or EPS), and using credit analysis to determine the impact of the transaction on the acquirer's credit rating. We will also discuss the fundamentals of purchase accounting, especially the concept and creation of goodwill, and learn about other common complexities and considerations that arise during merger consequences analysis.

Fox Worried About Credit Implications from Raised Bid
To win over Time Warner's board, 21st Century Fox had to raise its stock-and-cash offer from its initial $85 a share, and had to increase the cash component as well. But to do so may require Fox to take on so much debt that its investment-grade credit rating would have been downgraded, analysts said. Generally speaking, a lower credit rating increases a company's borrowing costs. Fox wanted to preserve its investment-grade credit rating and thus was prepared only to consider a bid between $90 and $95 a share. But it was unlikely to raise the percentage of cash in the deal much beyond the 40% in the original offer. That offer was not high enough for Time Warner, which had wanted the offer raised to above $100 a share.

Merger Consequences Analysis: A Real-Life Case

How did 21st Century Fox's finance team analyze how much it could afford to pay in this M&A transaction? In this chapter, you will learn how to assess the financial impacts of a transaction such as this one, and how to draw affordability conclusions from such impacts.

TOPIC 1: THE BASICS OF MERGER CONSEQUENCES ANALYSIS

Many factors drive complexity in the M&A universe. Central among those factors are the financial impacts of a transaction. In this chapter, we will show how the key financial impacts of a corporate acquisition are determined. There are three considerations to examine when analyzing the financial impacts of an acquisition:

Business	Financing	Tax Considerations
• Allocation of the purchase price	• Offer of cash versus stock	• Is the transaction tax-free or taxable for the seller?
• Impact of potential synergies	• Impact on the buyer's earnings per share	• Are there potential tax benefits to the buyer?
	• Impact on the buyer's credit statistics	
	• What is the post-transaction ownership structure?	

A WORD ON TERMINOLOGY
Other common names for, or types of, merger consequences analysis:
- Financial impact analysis
- Accretion/dilution analysis
- Merger plans analysis
- Synergy analysis
- Pro forma analysis
- M&A analysis

We will mainly discuss the first two topics, business combination adjustments and financing considerations. The most important tax considerations are briefly discussed toward the end of this chapter, under "Other Analyses and Considerations."

Merger consequences analysis is helpful in several ways. First, it helps us to determine the price an acquirer can afford to pay, sometimes colorfully referred to as "the size of the acquirer's wallet." Second, it sheds light on the question, "What is the optimal form of consideration that should be given to the target's shareholders?" To put it more simply, "What cash-versus-stock mix would be best?" To a certain extent, this aspect of merger consequences analysis makes it a deal-structuring tool.

A simple analogy is the purchase of a car. Imagine that, after narrowing your choices to several cars, you ultimately select one model. Questions you are likely to ask yourself are: First, how much does this model generally sell for at other car dealerships (i.e., what are its comparables)? Second, can I afford to pay this price and stay within my budget? Third, if I plan to use a loan to buy the car, is there a constraint on my borrowing capacity? And finally, what are the measurable benefits of having this car?

In a similar way, an acquirer evaluates a potential target company and employs the valuation tools we have discussed in the book thus far to determine how much they *should* pay. The acquirer then uses the M&A analysis to establish the maximum price they can *afford* to pay. Merger consequences analysis—with its considerations of leverage, EPS and other important factors—is the tool that enables finance professionals to determine the price an acquirer can *afford* to pay, which is why it is sometimes referred to as an *affordability analysis*.

After determining the purchase price of your car, the next step is financing the purchase. Some of the financing options you may consider include leasing and using cash from either your savings or a loan. In the context of an acquisition, an acquirer can similarly use cash to finance the purchase of a target company. This cash can come from existing cash balances or from newly issued debt, stock or other securities. The acquirer will try to determine an optimal mix of cash and stock for the acquisition.

Two popular analyses used to determine a deal's affordability are, first, estimating the transaction's impact on the acquirer's **income statement**, and, secondly, considering the impact on its **balance sheet**. Let's start with the impact on the income statement.

A. Income Statement Impact

Income statement affordability is determined by EPS accretion/dilution analysis. A transaction is said to be accretive to EPS if the merged company's pro forma (meaning post-transaction) EPS exceeds the acquirer's pre-transaction EPS. The transaction is dilutive to EPS if the pro forma EPS is less than the acquirer's stand-alone EPS before the transaction. In a break-even transaction, there is no change between the "before" and "after" EPS figures. We can summarize these relationships as follows:

| Accretion | : | Pro Forma EPS > Acquirer's stand-alone EPS |

| Dilution | : | Pro Forma EPS < Acquirer's stand-alone EPS |

| Break Even | : | Pro Forma EPS = Acquirer's stand-alone EPS |

ASK THE FINANCE GURU

Question: Is accretion/dilution always measured as a change in EPS?

EPS impact is the most widely used measure of accretion/dilution and the default standard, since publicly traded companies are commonly valued on the basis of P/E multiples. However, if the company or sector does not trade particularly based on EPS, practitioners will analyze a transaction's impact on another metric, such as cash flow per share or dividends. But this is less common.

When calculating pro forma EPS to determine if the deal is accretive or dilutive, most finance professionals will base their calculations on consensus EPS estimates. Consensus EPS estimates reflect an aggregate of equity research analysts' projections and are provided by several information service providers. These providers aggregate equity research analysts' EPS projections of a company and provide their consensus estimates.

Pro Forma 2017E Accretion/Dilution %
50% Cash, 50% Stock

		Offer Price Per Share				
		$21.00	$21.50	$22.00	$22.50	$23.00
	$0.0	(3.1%)	(3.8%)	(4.6%)	(5.3%)	(6.1%)
Expected	$2.5	(1.3%)	(2.0%)	(2.8%)	(3.5%)	(4.5%)
Annual Pre-tax	$5.0	0.5%	(0.2%)	(1.0%)	(1.8%)	(2.5%)
Synergies	$7.5	2.4%	1.6%	0.8%	0.0%	(0.7%)
(in millions)	$10.0	4.2%	3.4%	2.6%	1.8%	1.0%
	$12.5	6.0%	5.2%	4.4%	3.6%	2.8%
	$15.0	7.8%	7.0%	6.2%	5.4%	4.6%

The chart above depicts changes in a sample acquirer's EPS for a transaction expected to occur during 2017. This analysis assumes that the acquirer is financing the transaction with 50% cash and 50% stock. It shows how the percentage of accretion or dilution (that is, the percentage by which the buyer's EPS is expected to increase or decrease compared to its standalone EPS) changes as the offer price per share (x-axis) and the expected annual pre-tax synergies (y-axis) vary. Accretive scenarios are shown with a gray background; dilutive scenarios have a white background. Observe that, as expected annual ◀**synergies**▶ increase (i.e., as you scan down any vertical column of the table), the deal becomes more accretive. That is, the buyer's post-transaction EPS rises by a greater percentage. Similarly, observe that, as the offer price per share increases (i.e., as you scan across any horizontal row), the deal becomes more dilutive to the buyer.

Later in the chapter, we will walk you through the analytics, rationale and intuition behind these movements in the table.

B. Balance Sheet Impact

A transaction's impact on the balance sheet is measured by examining the acquirer's pro forma (post-transaction) credit statistics. The aim of analyzing the balance sheet is to determine the acquirer's credit rating and thus its ability to finance the deal by issuing debt. You need to ask this question: What are the post-transaction ◀**leverage ratios**▶ and ◀**coverage ratios**▶? A commonly used financial ratio which measures leverage is Debt/EBITDA. This ratio examines how long it would take the company to pay off its debt load (numerator) using its current level of operating cash flow (denominator). Generally speaking, the lower the Debt/EBITDA multiple, the more conservative the company's leverage level and, thus, the lower its risk. It is also fairly common to analyze Interest Coverage, or EBITDA/Interest Expense. This ratio tells us how many times this operating cash flow (numerator) can "cover" the interest payments (denominator). Generally, the higher the Interest Coverage, the safer the company from a leverage risk perspective.

Here is a typical summary page demonstrating a transaction's impact on pro-forma credit statistics:

Pro Forma Balance Sheet Impact
50% Cash, 50% Stock

		Debt/EBITDA	EBITDA/Interest
	$21.00	3.1x	7.0x
Offer Price	$21.50	3.1x	7.0x
Per Share	$22.00	3.2x	6.9x
	$22.50	3.2x	6.8x
	$23.00	3.2x	6.7x

The chart illustrates how certain leverage/credit statistics change as the offer price per share changes (in a deal where the consideration paid is 50% stock / 50% cash). Observe that, as the offer price rises, the leverage/credit statistics deteriorate, since more debt is needed to fund the transaction.

TOPIC 2: PURCHASE ACCOUNTING

Net Identifiable Assets

Grasping the accounting aspects of an M&A transaction is an important part of understanding its financial impact. Purchase accounting is the set of accounting rules that governs how an acquirer recognizes and records an M&A transaction on its balance sheet. Whether the acquirer is a ◀financial▶ or ◀strategic▶ buyer, the purchase method is the appropriate accounting treatment for M&A transactions. Both US GAAP and IFRS (International Financial Reporting Standards) require the use of this system.

Purchase accounting begins with an examination of the target company's **Net Identifiable Assets**.

The calculation of net identifiable assets employs this sequence of formulas:

Net Assets = Assets – Liabilities

Identifiable Assets = Assets – Target's Existing Goodwill

Net Identifiable Assets = Identifiable Assets – Liabilities

*Note: technically you should also subtract noncontrolling interest. We are keeping the definition simplified for training purposes.

> **DO YOU KNOW**
> … what the difference between intangible and tangible assets is? Generally speaking, tangible assets are assets that clearly have physical existence, such as inventory, land or machinery. Intangible assets are assets that are valuable to the company but do not have an actual physical form, such as patents, copyrights, brand names, and other intellectual property

ASK THE FINANCE GURU

Question: How exactly does Tangible Book Value differ from Net Identifiable Assets?

Actually, they don't. The two mean the same thing.

- *Book Value = Assets – Liabilities*
- *Tangible Book Value = Book Value - Target's Existing Goodwill*
  *= **(Assets – Liabilities) – Target's Existing Goodwill***

- *Identifiable Assets = Assets – Target's Existing Goodwill*
- *Net Identifiable Assets = Identifiable Assets – Liabilities*
  *= **(Assets – Target's Existing Goodwill) – Liabilities***

As you can see, Tangible Book Value and Net Identifiable Assets are equivalent.

On the date of the acquisition, the target company's assets and liabilities are recorded at Fair Market Value, which is typically estimated by a professional appraiser using cash flow analysis, comparables analysis, and other techniques. Any increase in Net Identifiable Assets is called a "◀write-up▶". Professionals express this by saying the Net Identifiable Assets have been "written up" to Fair Market Value. Although write-ups are more common, net assets can also be written down. For example, scrapping a target company's inventory after acquiring it would be recorded as a write-down.

Goodwill

Goodwill is the difference between the purchase price and Fair Market Value of the target's Net Identifiable Assets. Goodwill is an intangible asset representing the portion of the purchase price that cannot otherwise be allocated to, or explained by, the Fair Market Value of the target's Net Identifiable Assets.

Purchase Price

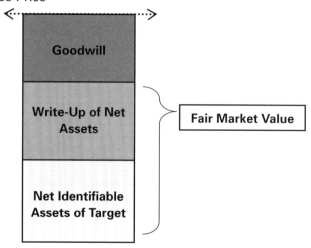

Let's go through a simple example to see how this works. Assume the following:

Purchase Price =	$500
Net Identifiable Assets =	$200
Fair Market Value =	$450

To calculate the write-up, we need to take the difference between the Fair Market Value and the value of the Net Identifiable Assets. Therefore, the write-up equals $250 ($450 - $200 = $250). This write-up represents the amount by which the Book Values of the target's Net Identifiable Assets must increase to make them equal to their Fair Market Values.

Items commonly written up are those on a target company's balance sheet which have a historic cost below the current Fair Market Value. Although it depends on the industry, the most substantial items that are commonly written up are PP&E, land, and certain ◀**identifiable intangible assets**▶ such as brand names and patents.

To calculate goodwill, you must take the difference between the purchase price and the Fair Market Value of the assets and liabilities. In the previous example, the goodwill recorded would be $50 ($500 - $450), or the excess of the purchase price over the Fair Market Value of the Net Identifiable Assets acquired.

ASK THE FINANCE GURU

What is the difference between goodwill and identifiable intangibles? Isn't goodwill an intangible asset?

Goodwill is a type of intangible asset. You cannot touch an intangible asset as you can a machine, but it is still an asset with value. Goodwill, however, is not an identifiable intangible asset. In this section, we learned that identifiable intangible assets are written up to Fair Market Value, whereas goodwill is allocated as a remainder from the purchase price. Under US GAAP, identifiable intangibles are recognized separately from goodwill if they

A. arise from a legal or contractual right or obligation, or

B. are capable of being separated from the acquired entity, meaning that the identifiable intangible can be sold, licensed, rented, or exchanged.

Patents and brand names are examples of identifiable intangibles that are separate from goodwill.

Note: IFRS has some other qualifying rules not specifically mentioned by US GAAP. Also, note that although IFRS rules vary slightly from the definitions above, they are similar in spirit. You are urged to seek outside accounting assistance for more detailed guidance.

To summarize, goodwill is calculated by first allocating the purchase price of a target company to its various components. Since all of the aforementioned components build up to the purchase price, or Offer Value of equity, you can add or subtract the components to or from the Offer Value of equity. The unallocated or residual amount is the goodwill created.

> **Offer Value of Equity**
> **Less: Net Identifiable Assets of Target**
> **Less: Write-up of Net Identifiable Assets**
> _____
> **= Goodwill Created**

Using the figures from the previous example:

Offer Value of Equity	$500
Net Identifiable Assets of Target	(200)
Write-up of Net Identifiable Assets	(250)
Goodwill Created	$50

This is just a simplified example, and the advice of qualified accountants will be important to ensure that the impact of the complexities arising from items—such as possible restructuring charges and deferred taxes—is properly captured in the allocation of the purchase price. Training The Street's live instruction training programs address many of the complex issues surrounding the purchase method of accounting.

It may also be important to understand and analyze any incremental depreciation or amortization expense that might arise from any write-ups. For example, increasing PP&E will probably result in additional depreciation expense as the increased value of the PP&E (the write-up portion) is depreciated over the estimated useful life determined at the time of the transaction. This can become very complicated and varies with the facts and circumstances surrounding each transaction. This topic is covered briefly at the end of this chapter.

Goodwill Created in Microsoft's Acquisition of Nokia Devices and Services business (NDS)

To offer a real-life illustration, here is an illustrative account of the goodwill created in Microsoft's Acquisition of NDS. The following financial information is taken from Microsoft's 10-K, dated February June 30, 2014 and summarized for training purposes:

In this case, the historical book value of Nokia's assets and liabilities is included in the fair value of the assets and liabilities below.

Consideration for NDS's Equity	$9,465 million
– NDS's Fair Market Value of Assets	(9,500)
+ NDS's Fair Market Value of Liabilities	5,493
= Residual Goodwill	$5,458 million

So the question one must ask is why an acquirer would pay more than the Fair Market Value of the Net Identifiable Assets. Is there additional value that is not currently reflected in the target's valuation? Many professionals view the following factors as potential sources of additional value:

- Premium to gain control of the target (often called "◀**Control Premium**▶").

    - Why would existing shareholders agree to cede control of the company without receiving a premium over the current market price?

    - Beyond this, the acquirer may very well have been involved in a bidding war with a third party and forced to pay more to win the bid.

- Synergies – incremental cost savings or additional net revenue realized from the combination of the companies' operations.

    - Additionally, there might be some intangible qualities of the target that represent value to the acquirer, such as a compelling strategic rationale.

- Other intangible benefits, such as brand equity, expertise, and so on.

Convergence of Global Accounting Standards

Great strides have been taken toward achieving the global convergence of accounting standards. Broadly speaking, US GAAP and International Financial Reporting Standards (IFRS) have similar accounting standards governing purchase accounting for transactions. Under both sets of standards:

- All M&A transactions must be accounted for under the purchase accounting method.

- For financial reporting purposes, there can be no amortization of goodwill or any indefinite life intangibles. The useful life of an indefinite life intangible, by definition is beyond the foreseeable future and therefore cannot be quantified. Goodwill is one type of indefinite life intangible. Companies are required to test goodwill and indefinite life intangibles annually for possible impairment, writing down the asset if it becomes impaired.

- By contrast, finite life intangibles such as patents, do have a quantifiable useful life and can therefore be amortized over their estimated useful lives.

Under purchase accounting, M&A-related transaction costs and restructuring charges are expensed. For illustrative and training purposes below, we will NOT be performing adjustments with regards to this rule. Please seek outside guidance for interpretation of the rule and analysis of its financial impact.

TOPIC 3: TRANSACTION ADJUSTMENTS

Let's analyze a couple of scenarios in a hypothetical M&A transaction to determine the financial impact of the deal. We will first analyze the purchase of a target in which the acquirer uses 100% stock as consideration. We will then examine a 100% cash purchase. Assume the following information for the acquiring and target companies and the proposed transaction.

Acquirer Information*	
Current share price	$18.00
Total existing debt	$200.0
Tax rate	40.0%
Interest on new debt	6.0%
Net Income	$53.4
Diluted shares outstanding	53.400
EPS	$1.00

Target Information*	
Current share price	$22.00
Total assets	$370.0
Total liabilities	220.0
Existing goodwill	25.0
Net Income	$13.9
Diluted shares outstanding	10.000
EPS	$1.39
Offer price (per share)	$27.50

Dollars and shares in millions, except per share data

A. 100% Stock Purchase

Imagine a 100% stock purchase funded entirely with the acquirer's shares, at an offer price of **$27.50**. If the target has no options outstanding, what is the implied Offer Value? This will determine the total price paid for the target's equity. (Refer to Chapter 4 if you need to review the calculation of Offer Value.)

Offer Value = Offer Price per Share x Target's Diluted Shares Outstanding

= $27.50 x 10.000 million
= $275.0 million

What is the goodwill created, assuming no write-ups?

Offer Value	$275.0	million
Less: Net Identifiable Assets	(125.0)*	
= Goodwill	$150.0	million

*Net Identifiable Assets = assets less existing goodwill less liabilities: $370 - $220 - $25 = $125

Next, what is the implied ◄**exchange ratio**►? The exchange ratio tells you how many shares the acquirer will need to issue for every share of the target. In a 100% stock-financed deal, it is a crucial statistic to analyze.

| **Exchange Ratio = Offer Price / Acquirer Price x % Stock** |

= $27.50 / $18.00 * 100% Stock
= 1.5278

In this transaction, the acquirer must issue 1.5278 of its shares for each share of the target that it wants to buy. The target's shareholders usually receive cash to cover the value of any fractional shares they should receive in the transaction.
In aggregate, how many shares must be issued to the target's shareholders?

| **Shares Issued by Acquirer = Exchange Ratio x Target's Shares Outstanding** |

= 1.5278 x 10.000 million
= 15.278 million

ASK THE FINANCE GURU

Question: What is the exchange ratio in transactions where the stock issued is not the only form of consideration?

When all, or even a portion, of the Offer Value delivered to the target is cash, there are two common ways to present an exchange ratio:

   A. Factor the percentage stock in the transaction into the exchange ratio, which is then referred to as the "actual ratio"; or

   B. Show the exchange ratio assuming 100% stock, which is referred to as the "theoretical ratio."

Both presentations are common. Just make sure the number of shares issued is correct.

As previously discussed, many professionals focus on the transaction's impact on EPS. Let's calculate the pro forma EPS under the transaction assumptions.

Pro forma EPS is calculated by dividing Pro Forma Net Income by pro forma shares outstanding. Here is the formula for pro forma EPS:

Pro Forma EPS = $\dfrac{\text{Acquirer's Net Income + Target's Net Income } \pm \text{ Adjustments}}{\text{Acquirer's Shares Outstanding + New Shares Issued}}$

The most important "adjustments" to Net Income are typically the after-tax impact of
* *Synergies*
* *Interest expense on new acquisition debt, and*
* *Incremental depreciation or amortization from certain write-ups.*

Assuming no synergies and write-ups, what is the Pro Forma Net Income?

What are the pro forma shares outstanding?

> **Pro Forma Net Income = Acquirer's Net Income + Target's Net Income**

Pro Forma Net Income = $53.4 million + $13.9 million
= $67.3 million

> **Pro Forma Shares Outstanding**
> **= Acquirer's Shares + New Shares Issued**

Pro Forma Shares Outstanding = 53.400 + 15.278
= 68.678 million

Finally, calculate the pro forma EPS:

Pro Forma EPS = $67.3 million/68.678 = **$0.98**

Is this proposed transaction accretive or dilutive?

Recall that the acquirer's stand-alone EPS is $1.00. Therefore, this transaction is *dilutive*. The acquirer would have generated EPS of $1.00 without the deal, and with the deal, it will make only $0.98—a dilution of $0.02 per share in absolute terms.

Accretion and dilution levels can be expressed either as an amount per share or as a percentage.

> **TIPS OF THE TRADE**
> Although M&A practitioners calculate accretion/dilution both as an amount per share and as a percentage, the percentage impact is often the more meaningful figure, because it shows the relative impact of the transaction on EPS.

As a Dollar Amount

> **$ Accretion/(Dilution) per Share**
> **= Pro Forma EPS - Acquirer EPS**

= $0.98 - $1.00
= ($0.02) Dilution per share

As a Percentage

> **% Accretion/(Dilution)**
> **= $ Accretion or Dilution / Acquirer EPS**

= ($0.02)/$1.00
= (2.0%) Dilution

Synergies

In an affordability analysis, we've learned that an important component is the calculation of the $/% accretion or dilution. Although the transaction may be dilutive, we have not yet factored in the impact of any potential synergies. If the transaction is dilutive, the next question an M&A practitioner will ask is this: What synergy amount would the acquirer need to make the deal "EPS break-even" or, in other words, accretion/dilution-neutral?

Let's try to determine **pre-tax synergies to break-even** by starting with the calculation of the **after-tax synergies needed**:

> **After-tax Synergies Needed = Dilution per Share**
> **x Pro forma Shares Outstanding**

= $0.02 x 68.678 million
= $1.4 million

A $1.4 million increase in Net Income would make pro forma EPS equal to $1.00 [($67.3 + $1.4) / 68.678]. This would bring the acquirer's EPS back to its pre-transaction EPS level. But the focus is usually on the pre-tax synergy amount primarily resulting from cost savings. To calculate pre-tax synergies to break-even, simply gross up the after-tax amount using the tax rate:

> **Pre-tax Synergies to Breakeven**
> **= After-tax Synergies Needed /(1 – tax rate)**

= $1.4 million/(1 – 40%)
= $2.3 million

The acquirer needs to achieve approximately $2.3 million in pre-tax synergies for the deal to be EPS-neutral. This number helps to place the dilution impact in a more measurable context. Is it reasonable to expect that these synergies can be achieved? As a guideline for assessing attainability, many M&A practitioners compare the pre-tax synergies needed to break even to the expected synergies announced in precedent transactions. Another method for getting estimates for the synergies needed is to receive guidance from the acquiring company's management team.

Question: What is the appropriate tax rate to use—the acquirer's, the target's, or a blend of the two?

The best tax rate to use is probably the estimated post-transaction effective tax rate. However, this can be hard to obtain until the companies and their tax advisors have determined it. Sometimes the acquirer's tax rate is used as a simplifying assumption, especially if the acquirer is significantly larger than the target. If the target is quite large in comparison to the acquirer, the blended average of the two companies may be appropriate.

Acquirer Information*		Target Information*	
Current share price	$18.00	Current share price	$22.00
Total existing debt	$200.0	Total assets	$370.0
Tax rate	40.0%	Total liabilities	220.0
Interest on new debt	6.0%	Existing goodwill	25.0
Net Income	$53.4	Net Income	$13.9
Diluted shares outstanding	53.400	Diluted shares outstanding	10.000
EPS	$1.00	EPS	$1.39
Transaction Expenses	$3.0	Offer price (per share)	$27.50

Dollars and shares in millions, except per share data.

B. 100% Cash Purchase

Now, let's use the same assumptions (shown above) to analyze a **100% cash purchase** (funded entirely using new debt issued by the acquirer) at an offer price of **$27.50**.

Question: Instead of raising debt, could an acquirer fund the deal with existing cash on hand?

Although companies can issue debt (or a mix of debt and equity) to fund significant acquisitions, companies with very large balances of excess cash can often finance a deal with cash on hand. Analytically, the opportunity cost of the income that could have been earned by using that cash for an alternative investment should be factored into the pro forma EPS calculation as a decrease of interest income.

The **Offer Value** remains the same as in the example with 100% stock consideration. Keep in mind that the offer price for the target company has not changed. The only thing that has changed in this second scenario is that the buyer is now paying for the target with cash. But it is still offering $27.50 per share.

= $27.50 x 10.000 million
= $275.0 million

Goodwill also remains the same: the equity purchase price is still $275 million to acquire a company with Net Identifiable Assets of $125 million (assuming no write-ups and no transaction expenses).

Offer Value	$275.0	million
Less: Net Identifiable Assets	(125.0)*	
= Goodwill	$150.0	million

* Net identifiable assets = assets less existing goodwill less liabilities: $370 - $220 - $25 = $125

However, because it is a 100% cash transaction, there are no shares issued to the target. So the **new debt issued** in the transaction is equal to the Offer Value.

Assuming a 6.0% interest rate on new debt, what is the interest expense from this new debt?

> **Incremental Interest Expense =**
> **New Debt Issued x Interest Rate**

= $275.0 million x 6.0%
= $16.5 million

Remember that this incremental interest expense is tax-deductible, so the impact on net earnings is the after-tax amount. Assuming a 40% tax rate, what is the after-tax interest expense needed to capture the ◀**tax shield**▶?

> **After-tax Interest Expense = Pre-tax Interest Expense**
> **x (1 – tax rate)**

= $16.5 million x (1 – 40%)
= $9.9 million

Factoring in the after-tax interest expense, what is the pro forma EPS?

> **Pro Forma Net Income = Acquirer's Net Income**
> **+ Target's Net Income – After-tax Interest Expense**

Pro Forma Net Income = $53.4 million + $13.9 million - $9.9 million
= $57.4 million

Because there are no new shares issued, the pro forma shares outstanding would simply equal the acquirer's stand-alone shares outstanding.

Pro Forma shares outstanding = 53.400 million
Pro Forma EPS = $57.4 million / 53.400 million = $1.075

As before, let's calculate the dollar amount and percentage of accretion/dilution:

As a Dollar Amount

> **$ Accretion/(Dilution) per Share =**
> **Pro forma EPS – Acquirer EPS**

= $1.075 – $1.00
= $0.075 accretion per share

As a Percentage

> **% Accretion/(Dilution) =**
> **$ Accretion or Dilution per Share / Acquirer EPS**

= $0.075 / $1.00
= 7.5% accretion per share

Credit Statistics

Recall that affordability is partially determined by the transaction's balance sheet impact. Balance sheet analysis is especially important when the transaction involves issuing debt. Using our 100% cash example, let's examine the impact that issuing debt has on:

A. Pro forma Debt
B. Pro forma Interest Expense
C. Pro forma EBITDA

Once you have calculated the pro forma credit statistics, you can then analyze and compare various credit metrics to get a sense of balance sheet affordability.

A. Let's start with debt. How able is the acquirer to raise debt and still maintain a particular credit rating? We've learned two of the most widely examined metrics for this:

- Debt/EBITDA: this gives you a sense of how much *leverage* there is, compared to cash flow (**◀leverage ratio▶**).

- EBITDA/interest expense: this gives you a sense of how many times operating cash flow can *cover* interest payments (**◀coverage ratio▶**).

ASK THE FINANCE GURU

Question: Is the target's debt always assumed? Can't it be refinanced?

Often, the target's existing debt does get refinanced. But make sure you properly capture the impact of a refinancing. The old target debt and interest expense will be eliminated, but the new acquisition debt and interest expense should reflect the refinanced amount.

From our 100% cash example above, assume that the acquirer has $200.0 million of existing debt, $12.0 million of existing interest expense, and $135.0 million of EBITDA. Assume also that the target has $50.0 million of existing debt, $4.0 million of existing interest expense and $52.2 million of EBITDA. What is the pro forma debt?

Answer:

If the acquirer intends to assume the target's debt, then the pro forma debt is the summation of: 1) acquirer's debt, 2) target's debt, and 3) new debt issued. Recall from the 100% cash exercise that the new debt issued was $275.0 million. Therefore, pro forma debt is equal to:

Pro Forma Debt = Acquirer's Debt + Target's Debt + New Debt

$525.0 million = $200.0 million + $50.0 million + $275.0 million

The acquiring company would more than double the dollar amount of its leverage!

B. Our next step is to calculate the pro forma interest expense. Again, the pro forma interest expense is the summation of:

   1) acquirer's interest expense,
   2) target's interest expense, and
   3) interest expense based on the new debt issued.
      The new debt issued was $275.0 million.

Based on a 6.0% interest rate on new debt, the interest expense is $275.0 x 6.0% = $16.5 million. What is the pro forma interest expense?

Pro forma Interest Expense = Acquirer's Interest Expense + Target's Interest Expense + New Interest Expense

$32.5 million = $12.0 million + $4.0 million + $16.5 million

Since EBITDA is before interest expense, there is no interest expense adjustment to it. Pro forma EBITDA (assuming no synergies) is just acquirer's EBITDA plus target's EBITDA.

Pro Forma EBITDA = Acquirer's EBITDA + Target EBITDA

$187.2 million = $135.0 million + $52.2 million

Given pro forma debt of **$525.0 million**, pro forma interest expense of **$32.5 million**, and pro forma EBITDA of **$187.2 million**, calculate the Pro forma Debt / EBITDA and Pro forma EBITDA / Interest Expense.

Answer:
Pro Forma Debt / EBITDA = $525.0 million / $187.2 million = 2.8x

EBITDA / Interest Expense = $187.2 million / $32.5 million = 5.8x (rounded)

So how much debt is the right amount? The level of debt an acquirer is willing to take on depends on their risk tolerance, desired credit rating, and how the capital markets view the company and the transaction. Questions professionals will ask include: Do they have enough cash flow to pay off the debt in the future? Will their debt capacity be so constrained in the future as to prevent them from making another acquisition or funding another project? For more information, please seek professional credit analysis and ratings resources.

If 2.5x Debt/EBITDA is the desired leverage ratio for the acquirer, this transaction would probably not be exclusively financed using debt. The acquirer would have to consider the tradeoffs between increasing its debt capacity and diluting its ownership. What would be the effect of the increased debt on the acquirer's credit rating? Will it decrease? Will it remain unchanged? Additionally, what is the desired currency (cash or stock) of the target, and how will paying with stock affect the acquirer's ownership profile?

TOPIC 4: RELATIVE P/E ANALYSIS

In a 100% stock transaction (before the impact of synergies or other transaction adjustments such as depreciation or amortization from write-ups), there is a quick way to calculate whether or not a deal will be accretive or dilutive. It is called relative P/E analysis.

Relative P/E analysis involves comparing the acquirer's P/E multiple with the offer P/E multiple.

To calculate the offer P/E multiple, divide the offer price per share by the target's stand-alone EPS.

TIPS OF THE TRADE
Although relative P/E analysis is not used to calculate the precise accretion/ dilution impact of a deal, you can use it to get a quick, "back-of-the-envelope" indication of direction.

By benchmarking to an amount of earnings, the relative P/E analysis gives us a sense of how much is paid (offer P/E) versus the value of the acquisition currency (acquirer's P/E).

Let's say that company A has a stock price of $50.00 per share, and company B a stock price of $14.00. Which company has the higher valuation? Actually, there is no way to tell from share prices alone. The reason is that these share prices are absolute figures. They are not benchmarked to a financial metric such as earnings per share.

Similarly, in an all-stock M&A transaction, when comparing the price paid or offered by an acquirer and the value of the acquirer's stock, you need to benchmark the offer to a level of earnings (target's Net Income). If the acquirer's P/E is greater than the offer P/E, then you know that the acquirer is using a stronger currency, relative to its earnings, than what it is paying or offering the target for its earnings. So, if the acquirer's stock price is more valuable or worth more, then they probably have to issue fewer shares, resulting in a less dilutive transaction. **If the acquirer P/E is *greater* than the offer P/E, the deal will be *accretive*.**

On the flip side, if the acquirer's P/E is less than the offer P/E, the value of the acquirer's currency is lower. If an acquirer's shares are worth less, it will probably have to issue more shares, causing a more dilutive result. **If the acquirer P/E is *lower* than the offer P/E, the deal will be *dilutive*.**

Question: How popular is this relative P/E analysis?
The relative P/E analysis is widely used to determine the relative strength of issuing stock for a transaction. Although it is only one consideration, generally speaking, companies trading at higher P/E multiples often want to issue shares for a transaction (as opposed to cash) because of the accretive impact on pro forma EPS.

Recall the following assumptions from our earlier example:

Acquirer's Price	$18.00
Acquirer's EPS	$1.00
Offer Price	$27.50
Target's EPS	$1.39

Will a 100% stock transaction be accretive or dilutive (assuming no synergies or write-ups)?

To calculate the acquirer's P/E multiple and the offer P/E multiple:

Acquirer's Stock Price	$18.00
/ Acquirer's EPS	$1.00
Acquirer P/E Multiple	**18.0x**

Offer Price	$27.50
/ Target's EPS	$1.39
Offer P/E Multiple	**19.8x**

This deal would be **dilutive** because the acquirer's P/E is *lower* than the offer P/E. Let's go through the rest of the process and actually calculate accretion/dilution.

Remember that relative P/Es assume no synergies or other purchase accounting adjustments.

What is the pro forma Net Income?

Acquirer Net Income	$53.4	million
+ Target Net Income	13.9	million
= Pro Forma Net Income	$67.3	million

What would be the number of shares issued?

Exchange Ratio =
Offer Price / Acquirer's Share Price x 100% stock

$27.50 / $18.00 x 100%
Exchange Ratio = 1.5278

New Shares Issued =
Exchange Ratio x Target's Shares Outstanding

= 1.5278 x 10.000 million
= 15.278 million

To calculate pro forma shares outstanding:

Acquirer Shares Outstanding	53.400	million
+ New Shares Issued To Target	15.278	million
= Pro Forma Shares Outstanding	68.678	million

How about pro forma EPS?

Pro Forma EPS = Pro Forma Net Income / Pro Forma Shares
= $67.3 million / 68.678 million
= $0.98

Compared to the original acquirer's EPS of $1.00, this deal would be *dilutive*.

But what if the acquirer's stock price were **$22.00** with the offer price remaining at $27.50?

To calculate the acquirer's new P/E multiple and the offer P/E multiple:

Acquirer's Stock Price	$22.00
/ Acquirer's EPS	$1.00
Acquirer P/E Multiple	**22.0x**
Offer Price	$27.50
/ Target's EPS	$1.39
Offer P/E Multiple	**19.8x**

Is this deal accretive or dilutive? The offer P/E remains the same. But now the acquirer's P/E is higher. This means there is relatively higher value in the acquirer's stock as a form of currency for the transaction, and thus fewer shares would need to be issued. This deal is *accretive*.

Here is the proof:

Exchange Ratio = Offer Price / Acquirer's Share Price
x 100% Stock

1.250 = $27.50 / $22.00 x 100%

Exchange Ratio	1.250	
x Target's Shares Outstanding	10.000	million
= New Shares Issued	12.500	million
Acquirer's Net Income	$53.4	million
+ Target's Net Income	13.9	
= Pro Forma Net Income	$67.3	million
Acquirer's Shares Outstanding	53.400	million
+ New Shares Issued	12.500	
= Pro Forma Shares Outstanding	65.900	million
Pro Forma Net Income	$67.3	million
/ Pro Forma Shares Outstanding	65.900	million
= Pro Forma EPS	$1.02	
Percentage Accretion	2% *(vs. $1.00)*	

Notice that the only real difference between the $18.00 acquirer stock price scenario and the $22.00 acquirer stock price scenario was the number of new acquirer shares issued to the target's shareholders. When the acquirer's share price is lower, the acquirer must issue more shares than when its share price is higher (assuming the same purchase price).

To summarize, although relative P/E analysis is not used to calculate the precise accretion/dilution impact of a deal, it can be used to obtain a quick, "back-of-the-envelope" indication of direction.

TOPIC 5: OTHER ANALYSES AND CONSIDERATIONS

In addition to evaluating accretion/dilution and credit rating impacts, merger consequences analysis entails many other analyses and considerations. We will now briefly look at several of them:

A. Combinations of Cash and Stock Consideration

A mixed financing structure is an option frequently chosen in M&A transactions. The target's shareholders often receive a combination of cash and stock from the acquirer. Mixed or not, the math is exactly the same as before. You just need to factor in the percentage stock for the new shares issued (remember that actual exchange ratio = theoretical exchange ratio x % stock) and the percentage cash for the new debt issued (% cash x Offer Value).

Recall our real-life example, in which AbbVie agreed to acquire Pharmacyclics. Here are the terms shared at announcement:

In the tender offer, AbbVie will acquire all of the outstanding shares of Pharmacyclics' common stock for $261.25 per share, consisting of cash and AbbVie common stock. Pharmacyclics' stockholders will be permitted to elect cash, AbbVie common stock or a combination, subject to proration. The aggregate consideration (based on information at time of announcement of the deal) will consist of approximately 58.3% cash and 41.7% of AbbVie common stock.

B. Impact of Synergies on Pro Forma Earnings

Recall from Chapter 4 (Acquisition Comparables Analysis) that synergies are an increase in cash flows that result from a merger of the operations of two companies. These combined cash flows create an enhanced effect that is greater than the sum of the cash flows of the individual stand-alone companies. There are revenue synergies and cost synergies, but the largest synergies are usually cost savings realized through the reduction of overlapping and redundant expenses. Realized synergies raise pro forma earnings, thus benefiting the resulting pro forma EPS.

Assume $5 million of pre-tax synergies are expected from cost savings. Using a 40% tax rate, this increase in profit would result in an additional $2 million in taxes: $5 million x 40%. Pro forma Net Income therefore would rise by $3 million [$5 million x (1 – 40%) or $5 million - $2 million].

This incremental benefit would then be factored into the previous pro forma EPS calculations.

C. Incremental Depreciation or Amortization from Write-Ups
Earlier, we discussed writing up assets to their Fair Market Value. Incremental depreciation or amortization expenses also impact pro forma earnings. Suppose a write-up of $150 million of PP&E has an estimated 10-year useful life. This will result in an additional $15 million of annual depreciation expense ($150 million/10 years), thereby lowering pro forma earnings.

ASK THE FINANCE GURU

Question: In an actual transaction, how are the potential synergies determined?

In M&A transactions, the synergies are commonly estimated by the management teams. They study the operations of the two companies for insights into the synergies that can be expected. Often, the acquiring company hires consultants who specialize in M&A deals to undertake the analysis. At the more preliminary stages of the transaction, examining synergies from precedent transactions—as a percentage of the target's sales, of SG&A, or of some other appropriate measure—may yield figures that can serve as a rough estimate of expected benefits until the actual analysis of the merger synergies is performed.

D. Exchange Ratio Analysis
Recall that the exchange ratio is the stock price per share offered to the target (offer price) divided by the acquirer's stock price. The exchange ratio tells you the number of shares the acquirer issued for each share of the target. The focus is on *relative* value: that is, the value paid to the target, compared to the acquirer's price.

The target's stock price divided by the acquirer's stock price yields an implied exchange ratio. Although this does not factor in a control premium (offer price is usually greater than target's stock price), the relationship still offers us a sense of relative value. Examining the historical stock prices and the implied "natural" exchange ratio over different time periods—a month, six months, last year, and so on—can help to determine the premium paid to target shareholders in a stock transaction.

E. Contribution Analysis

A contribution analysis looks at what each of the two parties is contributing in sales, EBITDA, EBIT, Net Income, and so on to the newly combined entity. It can be expressed on a percentage basis, with the acquirer's and target's contributions totaling 100%. The statistics are typically calculated before the impact of any merger adjustments such as synergies, incremental D&A from write-ups, or interest expense from new acquisition debt.

Let's walk through an exercise to see how this works. If an acquirer has sales of $150.0 million and the target has sales of $50.0 million, what would be the sales contribution of each side?

Answer:

The calculation would be:

Acquirer's Sales Contribution = $150.0 million / $200.0 million = 75.0%

Target's Sales Contribution = $50.0 million / $200.0 million = 25.0% [or 100% less 75%]

F. Pro Forma Ownership

When stock is issued to finance a transaction, the resulting pro forma ownership is often analyzed. Using our 100% stock example from earlier in this chapter, what is the percentage ownership of the target's shareholders?

Recall:

- Acquirer's shares   53.400 million
- New shares issued to target 15.278 million

Target Pro Forma Ownership =
New Shares Issued / Pro Forma Shares

= 15.278 million / (53.400 million + 15.278 million)

= 22.2%

The acquirer's post-deal ownership stake is now 77.8% and the target's is now 22.2%.

Implied ownership often brings up issues of control, especially when it is close to 50%-50%. If the target is going to own a significant portion of the new entity, board seats and management positions may need to reflect the nature of the post-transaction ownership split.

In a 100% stock deal, it is particularly meaningful to compare the pro forma *ownership* to the *contribution analysis*. In the example above, the acquirer is contributing 75% of the sales and will have a 77.8% post-deal ownership stake. Both the acquirer and the target need to make sure that their share of ownership in the post-deal entity reflects how much they have contributed to it.

G. Tax Considerations (US Corporate Tax Law)

Taxes are yet another consideration in the analysis of M&A transactions. Taxation is an advanced topic which deserves separate and substantial attention. As a quick introduction, however, let's briefly discuss two major acquisition structures: acquiring the target's *assets* (asset purchase), and acquiring the target's *stock* (stock sale).

For the following topics, please consult outside professional guidance. Also, seek non-US guidance for tax rules pertaining to non-US companies.

Asset purchase

Under current US tax law, an asset purchase has pros and cons for both the acquirer and the target. The following are in the acquirer's favor:

- The acquirer is allowed to pick and choose which assets of the target they want to buy.
- The assets acquired may be free of liabilities (negotiated as part of the transaction).
- The acquirer can step up the tax basis of the target's assets to their purchase price (instead of leaving them at their historical Book Values), creating tax-deductible amortization for the step-up of goodwill and tax-deductible depreciation for the step-up of PP&E.

However, since one of the parties must recognize a taxable event, an asset purchase is a taxable sale for the seller, with the taxable gain equal to the step-up in the tax basis.

Stock purchase

In a *stock purchase*, the acquirer assumes ownership of the entire target. There is no step-up in tax basis of the assets and therefore no tax deductibility of amortization or depreciation for the acquirer. The transaction can usually be structured to avoid, or at least defer, a taxable gain for the seller, depending on the cash and stock consideration mix.

Stock deals can also be structured with a *Section 338 election*. For tax purposes, this gives the acquirer the same step-up in tax basis as in an asset deal. In other words, with a Section 338 election, the transaction is still legally treated as a stock sale, but from a tax perspective it is treated as an asset sale. (A more common tax election is called a Section 338(h)(10), which applies to the purchase of a subsidiary.)

Since the impact of taxes on transactions is complicated and technical, it is always prudent to seek professional advice regarding M&A tax considerations.

ASK THE FINANCE GURU

Question: What exactly is cash EPS?

Since depreciation and amortization are non-cash expenses, some practitioners may calculate earnings and EPS before the non-cash D&A from purchase accounting adjustments (the write-ups). For example, an acquirer in the pharmaceutical sector may report cash earnings before the impact of the amortization expense resulting from the write-up of patents. Note that there is no standardized definition of cash EPS. Practitioners will vary in their treatment of non-cash items. If you see cash EPS, make sure that you are comfortable with how it is defined and how it impacts your analysis.

H. Qualitative Issues

Beyond the quantitative analyses, there are often qualitative issues that should be considered. Here are some examples:

- ◆ Integration:
  - • How will the products, services, administrative systems, and procedures of the two companies be integrated?
  - • Who will be the new senior officers? What will be the composition of the new board of directors?
- ◆ Will investors like the strategic rationale of the new company? What is the vision of the new company?
- ◆ Will there be a clash of organizational cultures between the two firms?

- ◆ Other transactional intangibles:
  - The name of the new pro forma company and the location of its headquarters
  - Regulatory issues
  - Employee relations
  - Public perception

While it may be difficult to attach specific dollar amounts to these qualitative issues, their impact is nonetheless real, and they will need to be discussed and addressed.

SUMMARY
Chapter 6

TOPIC 1: MERGER CONSEQUENCES ANALYSIS

Many factors drive the complexity of the M&A universe, including business combination adjustments, tax considerations and financing considerations. Merger consequences analysis helps to determine the price an acquirer can afford to pay. It also sheds light on the optimal form of consideration that should be given to the target's shareholders (the cash-versus-stock mix).

Two widely used methods for determining affordability are: (A) estimating a transaction's impact on the acquirer's income statement; and (B) estimating its impact on the acquirer's balance sheet.

- Income statement – what is the resulting accretion/dilution?

- Balance sheet – what is the transaction's effect on the acquirer's pro forma credit statistics and credit rating (which affects the acquirer's ability to finance the deal by issuing debt)?

TOPIC 2: PURCHASE ACCOUNTING

Purchase accounting is the set of accounting standards that govern how the acquirer will recognize the transaction on its balance sheet and on other core statements.

First, the target's Net Identifiable Assets are calculated as:

Net Identifiable Assets = Tangible Assets – Liabilities

Next, purchase accounting states that, on the date of the acquisition, the target's assets and liabilities must be recorded on the acquirer's balance sheet at Fair Market Value. Any increase in Net Identifiable Assets is called a write-up.

The difference between the purchase price and Fair Market Value of the target's Net Identifiable Assets acquired is goodwill. Sometimes, an acquirer pays more than Fair Market Value because of a control premium, revenue and cost synergies, and/or other intangible qualities of the target that have value to the acquirer.

TOPIC 3: TRANSACTION ADJUSTMENTS

In reviewing an M&A transaction, it is important to calculate various metrics to analyze affordability.

The Offer Value tells you how much the acquirer is offering for the target's equity. The exchange ratio tells you how many shares the acquirer will need to issue for every share of the target. The exchange ratio is calculated as:

> **Exchange Ratio = Offer Price / Acquirer Price x % Stock**

Pro forma EPS is the EPS of the new company post-transaction. It is calculated as:

$$\text{Pro Forma EPS} = \frac{\text{Acquirer's Net Income + Target's Net Income} \pm \text{Adjustments}}{\text{Acquirer's Shares Outstanding + New Shares Issued}}$$

Some common after-tax adjustments include interest expense on new acquisition debt, the impact of synergies, and incremental depreciation or amortization from any write-ups.

Accretion/dilution in EPS can be expressed as a per share amount or as a percentage:

> **$ Accretion/(Dilution) per Share =**
> **Pro forma EPS – Acquirer EPS**

> **% Accretion/(Dilution) =**
> **$ Accretion or Dilution per Share / Acquirer EPS**

If a deal is dilutive, practitioners may calculate the **pre-tax synergies to break-even**, or the dollar amount of synergies needed to break-even on an accretion/dilution basis. This is calculated by first determining the after-tax synergies needed, then grossing them up by dividing by 1 – tax rate.

> **After-tax Synergies Needed = Dilution per Share**
> **x Pro forma Shares Outstanding**

> **Pre-tax Synergies to Breakeven**
> **= After-tax Synergies Needed /(1 – tax rate)**

Another key consideration is a transaction's impact on the balance sheet. This is especially important when a transaction involves the issuance of new debt. It is important to analyze:

- ◆ Pro forma Debt
- ◆ Pro forma Interest Expense
- ◆ Pro forma EBITDA

Once you have calculated the pro forma credit statistics, you can then analyze these various metrics to get a sense of balance sheet affordability. What is the acquirer's ability to raise debt and still maintain a certain credit rating?

Two popular metrics examined are:

- Leverage ratio: Pro Forma Debt / Pro Forma EBITDA
- Coverage ratio: Pro Forma EBITDA / Pro Forma Interest Expense

TOPIC 4: RELATIVE P/E ANALYSIS

In a 100% stock transaction (before the impact of synergies or other transaction adjustments such as depreciation or amortization from write-ups), relative P/E analysis is a quick way to calculate whether or not a deal will be accretive or dilutive. Relative P/E analysis involves comparing the acquirer's P/E multiple with the offer P/E. The offer P/E is calculated by dividing the offer price per share by the target's stand-alone EPS. By benchmarking the share prices to a dollar of earnings, relative P/E analysis gives a sense of how much is paid (offer P/E) versus the value of the acquisition currency (acquirer's P/E).

If the acquirer P/E is greater than the offer P/E, the acquirer is using a stronger currency relative to its earnings than what it is paying or offering the target for its earnings (fewer shares need to be issued). **If the acquirer P/E is greater than the offer P/E, the deal will be accretive.**

On the other hand, if the acquirer's P/E is less than the offer P/E, the value of the acquirer's currency is lower (more shares need to be issued). **If the acquirer's P/E is lower than the offer P/E, the deal will be dilutive.**

TOPIC 5: OTHER ANALYSES AND CONSIDERATIONS

In addition to evaluating accretion/dilution and credit rating impacts, merger consequences analysis entails many other analyses and considerations:

- Combination of Cash and Stock Consideration
  - Factor the percentage stock into the calculation of the new shares issued and the percentage cash for the new debt issued.

- Impact of Synergies on Pro Forma Earnings
  - Realized synergies raise pro forma earnings, thus benefiting the resulting pro forma EPS.

- Incremental Depreciation or Amortization from Write-Ups
- Exchange Ratio Analysis
  - Examining the acquirer's and target's historical stock prices and the implied natural exchange ratio over different time periods can offer insights that will help determine the premium paid to target shareholders in a stock transaction.
- Contribution Analysis
  - What do both parties contribute in sales, EBITDA, EBIT, Net Income and so on?
- Pro Forma Ownership
- Tax Considerations (US Corporate Tax Law)
  - Deal structure: stock purchase or asset purchase
  - An asset purchase or Section 338 election can result in tax deductible depreciation and/or amortization for the step-up in the tax basis.
- Qualitative Issues
  - Integration of the two companies
  - Strategic rationale
  - Market reaction
  - Differing corporate cultures
  - Other transaction intangibles such as a new corporate name, regulatory issues and employee relations

MASTERY QUIZ
Chapter 6

QUESTION #1

True or False:

In an accretive deal, the pro-forma EPS is always greater than the acquirer's stand-alone EPS.

QUESTION #2

True or False:

If the acquirer P/E is lower than the offer P/E, the deal will be dilutive because the acquirer will issue fewer shares due to the relative strength of the acquirer's stock versus what is paid.

QUESTION #3

Net identifiable assets of the target company are calculated as follows:

A. Assets – Liabilities
B. Assets – Target's Existing Goodwill
C. Assets – Target's Existing Goodwill – Liabilities
D. Assets – Total Debt

QUESTION #4

When calculating goodwill under purchase accounting, which one of the following adjustments should NOT be made to the offer value of equity?

A. Subtract interest expense from the target's EBIT.
B. Subtract the tangible Book Value of the target.
C. Subtract the write-up of assets.

QUESTION #5

Assume that you are comparing two different M&A deals each with 100% stock considerations. In transaction A, the acquirer's stock price is $50.00, the target's price is $75.00, and the offered premium on the target's price is 25%. In transaction B, the acquirer's stock price is $5.00, the target's price is $10.00 and the offered premium on the target's price is 10%. Which of the following statements is true about the two exchange ratios?

A. Transaction A has a higher exchange ratio.
B. Transaction B has a higher exchange ratio.
C. The exchange ratios are the same in both transactions.
D. There is not enough information given to calculate
  the exchange ratio.

QUESTION #6

For ABC Corporation, assume the following:

- ◆ Pre-tax cost of debt = 6.0%
- ◆ EPS = $1.00
- ◆ Net Income = $100.0 million
- ◆ Tax rate = 40%

For XYZ Corporation, assume the following:

- ◆ EPS = $1.00
- ◆ Net Income = $10.0 million
- ◆ Shares Outstanding = 10.000 million

If ABC buys XYZ using 100% cash (financed by new debt) for $16.67 per share, what is the dollar amount of accretion for this transaction?

A. $0.00
B. $0.04
C. $0.05
D. $0.06

QUESTION #7

The CEO of a company is contemplating acquiring another company. The CEO will only consider an accretive transaction. You run the merger analysis and find the deal is currently dilutive by $0.05 before the impact of synergies. Here are some other assumptions:

- ◆ Pro forma shares = 300.000 million
- ◆ Tax rate = 40.0%

The CEO also says he thinks he can reasonably achieve $20.0 million of pre-tax cost synergies. What should the CEO do?

A. Do the deal.
B. Don't do the deal.
C. There is not enough information provided.

QUESTION #8

Assume an acquiring company is thinking about funding an acquisition with a mix of cash and stock. They would like to keep their Debt / EBITDA ratio below 3.0x. The acquiring company has a P/E multiple of 20.0x. It is going to offer $30.00 per share for the target, which has an EPS of $2.00. The target has 100.000 million diluted shares outstanding. The pro forma EBITDA is estimated to be $1,500.0 million. Which of the following statements is the most correct?

A. The deal is accretive based on the relative P/E methodology.

B. The deal would ensure that the company remains investment grade.

C. You do not have enough information to know the exact affordability to the acquirer.

QUESTION #9

Which of the following statements is the least correct about relative P/E analysis?

A. Gives a sense of how much is paid versus the value of the acquirer's acquisition currency.

B. Can be done for 100% stock transactions.

C. Utilizes an offer P/E metric, which is defined as the target's stock price / target's standalone EPS.

D. Would be accretive if the acquirer's P/E is greater than the offer P/E.

ANSWER KEY
Chapter 6

ANSWER #1

True

Accretion is defined as occurring when a deal's pro forma EPS is greater than the acquirer's stand-alone EPS.

ANSWER #2

False

It is correct that the deal will be dilutive given that the acquirer's P/E is lower than the offer P/E, but the rationale behind the dilutive deal is that the acquirer is paying with a **lower-valued currency**. Therefore, the acquirer will issue **more** shares due to the **lack of relative strength** of its stock versus what is paid.

ANSWER #3

C — Assets – Target's Existing Goodwill – Liabilities

The amount that a potential acquirer is willing to pay for a target company under purchase accounting begins with a base value of Net Identifiable Assets. That base value is calculated as the Target's Assets – Target's Existing Goodwill – Liabilities = Net Identifiable Assets.

ANSWER #4

A — Subtract interest expense from the target's EBIT.

The target's interest expense and EBIT are both income statement items. Goodwill created is based upon the Net Identifiable Assets of the target, i.e., balance sheet items. Tangible Book Value and write-ups are adjustments that will be made to the Offer Value of equity to derive the goodwill created.

ANSWER #5

B — Transaction B has a higher exchange ratio.

The offer price in transaction A is calculated by $75.00 x (1 + 25%) = $93.75. Therefore the exchange ratio for transaction A is found by taking $93.75 / $50.00 = 1.875. The offer price in transaction B is calculated by

$10.00 x (1 + 10%) = $11.00. Therefore the exchange ratio for transaction A is found by taking $11.00 / $5.00 = 2.200. Transaction B has the higher exchange ratio.

ANSWER #6

B — $0.04

The first step is to get to pro forma EPS. This is found by taking Pro Forma Net Income divided by pro forma shares outstanding. Pro Forma Net Income would be found by taking the acquirer's Net Income plus the target's Net Income plus any adjustments. In an all-cash deal, this would include the effect of the after-tax interest expense. After-tax interest expense would be $6 million: [$16.67 offer price x 10.000 million shares x 6% interest rate x (1-40%)]. Therefore, the Pro Forma Net Income would be $100.0 + $10.0 - $6.0 = $104.0 million.

Pro forma shares would just be the shares of ABC; since this is an all-cash deal, there would be no new shares issued. **Although the shares of ABC are not provided, they can be implied by taking the Net Income divided by the EPS ($100.0 million / $1.00 = 100.000 million shares).** Therefore, the pro forma EPS = $104.0 / 100.000 = $1.04. If you subtract ABC's stand-alone EPS of $1.00, the accretion is $0.04.

ANSWER #7

B — Don't do the deal.

This is an exercise in calculating the pre-tax synergies needed to break even. Once the pre-tax synergies have been calculated, we can see if there are enough synergies past break-even to make the deal accretive.

Net Income dilution is equal to:

EPS dilution x Pro forma shares = $0.05 x 300.000 million = $15.0 million

Grossed up for taxes:

Net Income dilution / (1 – tax rate) = $15.0 million / (1 – 40%) = $25.0 million

The pre-tax synergies to break-even are $25.0 million. If the CEO thinks the company can only extract $20.0 million in synergies, then the deal would remain dilutive. Greater than $25.0 million in synergies would be required.

ANSWER #8

C — You do not have enough information to know the exact affordability to the acquirer.

The relative P/E methodology does not work in this situation because it is a mix of cash and stock. We don't know the cost of debt of the acquirer and therefore do not know the dilutive effect of interest expense on the pro forma Net Income. The total Offer Value of the equity is $30.00 x 1,000.0 million shares = $3,000.0 million. But we are not provided any information about the percentage of debt versus equity. Affordability analysis can be thought of as the income statement affordability (accretion/dilution) and the balance sheet affordability (maintaining desired credit statistics). There is not enough information to make an exact analysis.

ANSWER #9

C — Utilizes an offer P/E metric, which is defined as the target's stock price / target's standalone EPS.

Relative P/E analysis does give a sense of how much is paid versus the value of the acquirer's acquisition currency. It is also utilized for 100% stock transactions. The relative P/E analysis states that if the acquirer P/E is greater than the offer P/E, then the deal is accretive. Relative P/E analysis does utilize an offer P/E metric. **But the offer P/E is calculated as the offer price / target's standalone EPS.**

CHAPTER 7
Leveraged Buyout Analysis

LBO ANALYSIS: AN OVERVIEW

A ◀**leveraged buyout**▶—LBO for short—is the acquisition
of a company using very high amounts of debt financing,
along with a relatively modest amount of equity capital from
the financial sponsor itself, typically a private equity firm. In
truth, LBO transactions are simply acquisition transactions in
which the debt capital frequently makes up a large portion of
the total purchase price.

From the acquirer's viewpoint, **Leveraged Buyout Analysis** is
a set of tools the acquirer's valuation team uses to determine
what price it can pay for a target in order to earn a particular
return on its equity investment. Ultimately, however, whether
a particular LBO transaction will succeed or not depends
on a mutual meeting of the minds among all three major
stakeholder groups: the financial buyers, the lenders, and
the selling shareholders.

In this chapter, we will look at the key features of an LBO
transaction, walk through the mechanics of LBO Analysis,
discuss how LBOs are financed, and learn when and
why it sometimes makes sense to add substantial debt
to a company's balance sheet. We will identify the main
stakeholders involved in a typical LBO, determine the
implications of the transaction for each of them, and examine
how success is ultimately achieved and measured. We will
also discuss how these stakeholders' perspectives differ and
what makes an LBO attractive to each group.

LBOs: A Real-Life Case

The leveraged buyout of Heinz in 2013 was one of the largest
in history at the time of its announcement.

3G Capital Management, LLC through its fund, 3G Special Situations Fund III LP and Berkshire Hathaway Inc. entered into a definitive merger agreement to acquire H. J. Heinz Company from BlackRock, Inc. and other shareholders for $23 billion in cash on February 13, 2013. The transaction will be financed through a combination of cash provided by Berkshire Hathaway and affiliates of 3G Capital; rollover of existing debt, as well as debt financing that has been committed by J.P. Morgan and Wells Fargo.

How did finance professionals decide that Heinz was a good candidate for an LBO? What financial criteria did the transaction have to meet in order for it to take place? As a choice of strategy, is it unusual for private equity firms to invest heavily in fresh, new, growth-oriented capital projects after taking a company private in an LBO?

These are questions you will be able to answer by the end of this chapter.

TOPIC 1: THREE SETS OF PLAYERS; THREE POINTS OF VIEW

Each of the three sets of players in an LBO transaction—buyers, lenders, and selling shareholders—must be satisfied with the terms of the deal, given the risks each believes it is taking. Let's walk through an overview of the goals of each group.

Group One: The Financial Buyers

In Chapter 6, we focused on strategic buyers in our discussion of Merger Consequences Analysis and Accretion/Dilution techniques in the context of M&A transactions. Our focus in this Chapter is on a different kind of equity holder, called a ◀**financial buyer**▶. Financial buyers are quite a different breed from ◀**strategic buyers**▶. To see how they differ, let's begin with an analogy from the real estate industry that helps capture what financial buyers really do in an LBO transaction: "home flipping." In real estate, a home flipper is someone who buys a run-down home and renovates it, with plans to sell it in a few years at a profit, but no real intention of living in it for any length of time. The table below summarizes the close parallels between home flippers and financial buyers in an LBO:

	Home Flipping	**LBO**
Target	Run-down home	Undervalued company
Buyer	Home flipper	Financial buyer, e.g. a private equity firm
Financing sources	Personal cash (equity) + bank mortgage	Financial buyer's cash (equity) + debt borrowed from various sources
After the acquisition	Renovate and improve home	Improve the acquired company's operations to achieve efficiency and/or growth
Debt repayment	Pay down with rental income and other cash flow sources, not personal cash	Pay down using acquired company's own free cash flow, not financial buyer's own cash
Exit strategy	Sell to another home buyer	Sell to a public or private buyer (either a strategic or financial buyer), or take the company public via an ◀IPO▶
Success defined as	Achieving profit (selling price minus initial purchase price and renovation costs)	Achieving a particular ◀**internal rate of return (IRR)**▶on the investment, often exceeding 20-25% annually

The table shows that just as the motivations of a home flipper differ from those of someone who purchases a home intending to live in it for the next 2-3 decades, so do the objectives and interests of a financial buyer in an LBO transaction diverge from those of a strategic buyer in a merger deal. A financial buyer's priorities diverge further still from the priorities of the other stakeholders in an LBO transaction.

Strategic buyers are in it for the long term. A memorable way to couch the difference is this: while strategic buyers are interested in a marriage with real synergies, the typical financial buyers look for a relatively temporary dating experience, with quick but high returns. Their time horizon is shorter. For that reason, financial buyers do not like to compete with strategic buyers for the same deal. The strategic buyers tend to be willing to pay more, since they see greater possibilities for long-term integration. They are willing to invest more of their own cash and stock in the transaction.

Financial buyers, by contrast, involve as little of their own cash as possible in the transaction. They raise capital from investors such as insurance companies, endowments, pension funds, institutional investors and wealthy families, and then actively search for an undervalued company to acquire and turn around, typically within a 3-to-5-year time frame. In place of ◄**synergies**► and ◄**accretion**► to earnings per share, financial sponsors typically measure their success in terms of the internal rate of return (IRR) that they can expect to achieve. *(IRR will be covered more fully later in the Chapter.)*

Strategic buyers tend to be other companies, often in the same industry as the target. They estimate a deal's affordability by analyzing the potential synergies between them and the target, and then determining whether the transaction will result in accretion to their earnings per share. *Financial buyers, on the other hand, buy a firm and try to create value by taking on additional debt (◄leverage►) while using the cash flows of the acquired company to pay down that debt.*

Group Two: The Lenders

Lenders provide the debt financing to support the leveraged buyout of the company. As you might guess, their priorities differ quite a bit from that of the financial buyers. While the financial buyers are concerned with maximizing the internal rate of return on their equity investment, lenders are concerned with whether their debt capital and interest will be repaid. They care little about equity returns. Lenders typically ask the following three questions:

- **Is the deal's risk level reasonable?** Can the target company reasonably support the amount of leverage? Excessive debt could create a huge future cash flow obligation for the company in the form of interest payments and repayment of ◄**principal**►.

- **How certain is it that the borrowers will fully repay the principal and make the interest payments?** Lenders want their interest payments to be paid on time and want the principal to be ◄**amortized**► according to the pre-determined schedule.

- **Overall, how much confidence is there in the financial buyer?** The financial buyer is essentially the captain of the ship and will, directly or indirectly, be hiring managers, running the company's operations (or at least advising on them), and handling valuation and financing issues. It is important to determine the financial buyer's track record in making these decisions. Also, what is their strategic plan for the company after the LBO transaction?

There are two main kinds of lenders in an LBO: ‹**senior debt**› and ‹**subordinated debt**› lenders. Their characteristics will be explored more fully under Topic 2, "Funding a Leveraged Buyout – TargetLBO, Inc." But briefly:

* **Senior debt** holders, as their name suggests, come first in the capital structure. They are first in line to get paid should the company be ‹**liquidated**› because of a ‹**default**›. Senior debt is often backed ("securitized") by the operating assets of the purchased business, further lowering its financial risk. Because senior debt is less risky, senior debt holders receive a lower interest rate. From a lender's perspective, the greater the risk an investment poses, the higher the interest rate they will charge on the borrowed funds.

* **Subordinated debt** ranks below senior debt in the capital structure. In the event of a default, subordinated debt holders get paid only after the senior debt holders have been compensated. Subordinated debt is thus more risky and carries a higher interest rate.

ASK THE FINANCE GURU

Question: How much debt can the buyer use in an LBO transaction?

Lenders and credit agencies use a variety of credit statistics to measure (i) the target company's overall debt burden compared to other forms of capital, and (ii) the cash flow it generates. Later in this chapter we will cover the parameters lenders typically use to assess the buyer's debt capacity and credit-worthiness.

Group Three: The Selling Shareholders

The final set of primary players in an LBO transaction is the target's shareholders. Their central motivation is to get the best price for the shares they hold. So long as the purchase price and premium paid are high enough, the selling shareholders are typically happy and likely to get on board with an LBO transaction, especially since they generally receive cash for their shares. Receiving cash means they have no ongoing ownership stake in the company after the LBO transaction, and therefore do not have to worry about what happens to the company. An exception is when the target is a family-owned business. In such cases, the selling shareholders may want to retain some ownership in the company along with the financial buyer.

A Meeting of the Minds

The challenging but necessary condition for making an LBO transaction work is that all three parties involved must be satisfied that it is a sufficiently attractive deal. Two out of three will not cut it. A potential deal may make great sense to two of the three players, but if the offer price is not high enough for the seller, or the rate of return is not high enough for the buyer, or the deal seems too risky for the lender, there will be no deal. In Topic 5, Understanding the Dynamics of an LBO, we will examine more fully how the motivations of the three parties differ.

The Target Company

Even with perfect harmony among the parties, there can be no deal if the target company itself is not a suitable LBO candidate. Let's discuss what makes for an attractive LBO candidate. The selection criteria vary by industry and sector —for example, a risk level or a rate of return that is acceptable in one industry may not be in another. But in general, there are four common, company-specific characteristics that a good LBO candidate must have. It must:

A. **Be an undervalued company**: Companies may be **undervalued** because they have struggling operations, or have had past difficulties, or have image problems. Or they could just be out of favor with the market. Undervalued companies are especially desirable to financial buyers. By their very definition, such companies often have potential for upside if their operations can be improved. Sometimes what a distressed company needs is a fresh injection of new capital and forward-looking management.

B. **Have current or expected stable cash flows**: Because of the very high leverage used in LBOs, financial buyers closely examine the target company's potential to generate **stable cash flows** during the investment period. Why? Because if, after paying its operating costs and making investments in the business, the company still has excess cash flows, the buyers can use this cash to pay down the debt borrowed to finance the purchase.

C. **Have manageable, predictable investment needs**: LBO candidates are usually **mature, stable** companies. They

> ### WORDS TO KNOW
> What is the key difference between **subordinated debt**, **high yield** bonds, and **junk** bonds? Essentially, there is none. In the event of a default, subordinated debt is less likely than senior debt to be repaid because it ranks lower in the pecking order. For that reason, subordinated debt is typically rated **non-investment grade**, or sub–investment grade. "High yield bonds" and "junk bonds" are simply other terms for non-investment grade bonds. During the 1980s, they were often called junk bonds. Today, the term "high yield" is more in vogue, but all three mean the same thing.

have predictable, foreseeable research and development costs and capital expenditure needs. R&D and capital expenditures are potentially large uses of cash, so being able to predict them is extremely important. This is cash that could otherwise be used to pay down debt—it is important to know how much of it will be available.

D. **Present a viable exit strategy:** In the end, financial buyers typically seek to exit from their investment by selling the company to a strategic buyer or another financial buyer, or by taking the company public in an initial public offering (◄**IPO**►). Therefore, it is important to find a target company that allows the financial buyer to develop a good exit strategy.

> **FINANCIAL FACTOID**
> Can an LBO have more than one financial buyer? Yes. Example: The March 2005 buyout of SunGard for $10.4 billion, the largest leveraged buyout in 15 years, involved seven private equity firms! The participation of multiple players makes it all the more critical to get a good grasp of the underlying motivations and agendas of each party.

ASK THE FINANCE GURU

Question: Can you undertake a leveraged buyout on private as well as publicly-traded companies?

Yes. An LBO firm can acquire either a publicly traded or privately owned company, or even a single division of a corporation. For example, in June 2014, in a deal valued at approximately $4 billion, Johnson & Johnson sold its blood testing subsidiary to the Carlyle Group. Public company buyouts, by comparison, tend to be larger and higher profile than buyouts of private firms.

TOPIC 2: FUNDING A LEVERAGED BUYOUT: TargetLBO, Inc.

Let's look at the mechanics of an LBO transaction—its structure, its economics, and the incentives that emerge at various stages of the deal itself—from the perspective of each of the three big players we discussed earlier.

Suppose that a financial buyer has expressed interest in purchasing and arranging financing for a hypothetical company which we will call **TargetLBO, Inc**. How do we analyze this? Some of the questions we need to ask include: What are the motivations of the sellers, the lenders, and the financial buyers in this transaction? What is the benefit of using large amounts of debt? And are there widely accepted parameters in determining the optimal amount of debt?

Let's first discuss the sellers, TargetLBO's shareholders. So long as the purchase price is right, the selling shareholders are generally not too concerned about the details of how the deal is financed or who does it. As in a real estate deal, the consideration paid to the sellers is 100% cash. This allows them to walk away with no further interest in the company.

ASK THE FINANCE GURU

Question: Are there cases where the sellers care about funding?

Yes. In certain LBOs, some sellers retain an equity stake in the new firm. This is known as ◀rollover equity▶. It can happen for different reasons. For example, the financial buyer might need to retain key management personnel to run operations, and giving them an ownership stake may serve as a performance incentive. If some of the sellers retain a stake in ownership, this essentially makes them equity owners, instantly altering their interests: as owners, they now become concerned about the levels of debt financing.

Another instance in which the sellers care about the financing is with a privately-owned family business, as the sellers are personally concerned about the legacy of the enterprise and its continuing success. Too risky a capital structure may cause the post-LBO company to fail, resulting in restructuring, lay-offs, or even a liquidation of the business.

That leaves us with the lenders and the financial buyers. How do they go about determining the deal's financing structure? Assuming that the acquisition of TargetLBO is a typical LBO, there will be three sources of capital:

A. Senior debt
B. Subordinated debt
C. Sponsor equity

Usually, financial sponsors want to use as much debt and put down as little of their own cash (equity) as possible. The less cash a financial buyer infuses into a transaction, the higher the returns on its investment and the more cash is available for it to invest in other projects. On the other hand, it is important that the financial buyer not over-lever the target company. From a capital structure standpoint, excessive leverage is risky. Too much debt can become unmanageable and hamper the target company's financial flexibility and could potentially lead to default.

If debt levels are manageable and can be paid down efficiently, however, this often creates a beneficial effect to the buyer called **leveraged returns**. The phrase essentially means that, in terms of value or return on investment, the debt holders (the lenders) are limited to receiving interest and principal payments and if the firm were sold at a higher price in the future, or if it were to generate larger cash flows and profits than expected, all of this upside would go to the financial sponsor. There will be more information on leveraged returns under Topic 4. The central point here is that financial sponsors have an incentive to use a lot of debt. That being said, sponsors typically first seek the cheapest form of debt, senior debt. It carries the lowest interest rate because its holders incur the least risk.

Senior Debt

A large part of the debt capital structure in a leveraged buyout usually comes in the form of loans from commercial and investment banks. Hedge funds are also a growing source of loan capital. Bank loans are typically called senior debt because they are usually ◀secured▶ by the assets of the target company itself. In the event that something goes wrong, the lending banks have seniority in laying claim to the company's assets.

A second feature of senior debt in the form of bank loans is that it tends to have a maturity of 5-8 years, which is shorter than other capital structure instruments. This means that, both *chronologically* and in terms of *priority*, senior debt holders are repaid before the subordinated bond holders and other capital providers. Because of these two features— seniority and earlier maturities—bank loans carry lower risk, and thus lower interest rates, than other forms of capital.

Nevertheless, debt itself is inherently risky. Senior debt lenders, therefore, do not lend unlimited amounts of debt to an LBO transaction—there is a point at which they will stop. In terms of our example, once senior debt is maxed out, the financial buyers of TargetLBO, Inc. will need to tap into the subordinated debt market if they need more financing.

Subordinated Debt

Subordinated debt typically comes from financial institutions, high yield funds, merchant banks, and hedge funds. It is usually unsecured, meaning that it is not backed by the target company's assets. This makes it riskier. Subordinated debt also tends to have a longer maturity (8-10 years), making it of longer duration than the other pieces of the capital structure. Finally, subordinated debt typically has a "bullet" structure.

As a result of subordination, longer maturities, and bullet structures, subordinated loans require a higher interest rate. They usually make up between 15% and 35% of an LBO's total capital structure.

Credit Ratios

The next obvious question is this: How much senior debt and subordinated debt can the financial buyer borrow? In our

> **WORDS TO KNOW**
>
> A ◀bullet payment structure▶ means that no repayment (amortization) takes place during the interim period at all. The entire principal is paid along with the very last interest payment at the end of the bond's term. During the interim period, only interest is paid.

example, the answer lies in TargetLBO's credit ratios. Credit ratios determine the viability of a company and, thus, how much a financial buyer can borrow to finance it. There are different kinds of credit ratios, as well as alternative metrics, but some of the most widely used are:

A. Leverage Ratios:

These are multiples that measure the debt burden on the company in relation to a proxy for operating cash flow, such as EBITDA.

- Senior Debt/EBITDA
- Total Debt/EBITDA

B. Coverage Ratios:

These multiples measure the company's ability to make its required interest payments. Coverage ratios also use a proxy for operating cash flow.

- EBITDA/Interest Expense
- (EBITDA – Capital Expenditures)/Interest Expense

C. Other Key Statistics:

- Equity Investment/Total Capital: This tells lenders how much the financial buyer will contribute to TargetLBO's total capital structure.
- Collateral for lenders, such as inventory, accounts receivable, and **property, plant and equipment (PP&E)**.

In a typical buyout such as TargetLBO's, both the lenders and the financial buyers will use ratios and statistics such as these to keep borrowing levels within reasonable limits— reasonable, at least, for a highly leveraged transaction. Remember that one of the main priorities of senior debt holders is to get their principal repaid in the near future. They therefore tend to request an amortization schedule that requires full payment in 5-8 years.

In terms of their actual numerical values, credit ratios change constantly, depending on the interest rate environment and current conditions in the lending market. This, in turn, affects the borrowing limits of financial buyers. For example, in a more flexible, low-interest-rate market, a private equity firm can secure higher levels of debt financing. In a tighter market with higher interest rates, in which it is more difficult to secure favorable terms on a loan, the financial buyer may settle for lower levels of debt and a higher equity contribution to the deal.

Here are some general benchmarks taken from recently completed LBO transactions:

Total Debt/EBITDA	4.5x to 5.5x or less
Senior Bank Debt/EBITDA	3.0x or less
EBITDA/Interest Expense	Greater than 2.0x
EBITDA – Capital Expenditures/Interest Expense	Greater than 1.6x
Bank Debt Repayment	5 to 7 years
Equity Contribution From Sponsor (%)	25% to 30+%

ASK THE FINANCE GURU

Question: What typically happens with the target company's existing debt?

The existing debt of the target company either stays with the business (is assumed by the acquirer) or is refinanced. Typically, since the post-LBO company will have substantially more leverage than the pre-LBO company, most lenders put ◀covenants▶ in place to force a refinancing in the event of an LBO.

Equity Contribution from Sponsor

Although leveraged buyouts do involve high levels of debt financing, they are rarely funded with 100% debt. The financial sponsor typically needs to provide some amount of equity capital to fill the gap between the purchase price of the company and the amount of debt they were able to raise. The reason is simple: lenders want the sponsors to have some vested interest in the project—some "skin in the game," as it is sometimes put.

Let's see how the math works for TargetLBO, our hypothetical company. Assume that the company currently has an EBITDA of $140.0 million per year and $70.0 million in Net Debt. Its financial buyers have approached lenders and, based on the company's profile, have determined that they can borrow up to 5.5x total debt/EBITDA. What is the maximum amount of debt the financial buyer can borrow?

Answer:

Total Debt Capacity = Leverage Multiple x EBITDA	

= 5.5 x $140.0 million
= $770.0 million

Sometimes, the ◀covenants▶ of the existing debt may be broken by the high leverage levels of the post-LBO transaction company. Therefore, part of the new debt raised may be used to pay off the existing debt.

Given that TargetLBO's existing debt is $70.0 million, how much of the total debt capacity will be new debt, assuming that the financial sponsor will have to refinance the company's existing debt?

Answer:

New Debt = Total Debt Capacity – Refinancing Existing Net Debt

= $770.0 million – $70.0 million
= $700.0 million

Suppose the financial buyer is willing to contribute 23% of the total purchase price (which includes the refinancing of the existing debt).

A. What is the maximum amount the financial buyer can pay for TargetLBO?

B. What is the dollar amount of the financial buyer's equity contribution?

Answer to A.

With 23% from the buyer, total debt of $770.0 million represents 77% of the purchase price.

Setting up a proportion may help:

$$\frac{77\%}{100\%} = \frac{\$770}{x}$$

Solving for the total purchase price (x), we get:

Total Purchase Price = Total Debt Capacity / % Debt Contribution

= $770.0 million / 77%
= $1,000.0 million

In a more general form, the maximum purchase price for a firm can be expressed as:

Total Purchase Price = Total Debt Capacity / (1 – % Equity Contribution)

Answer to B.
To calculate the dollar amount of equity:

| **Equity Contribution = Total Purchase Price - $ From Lenders** | |

= $1,000.0 million - $770.0 million
= $230.0 million

OR

= *Total Purchase Price x % Equity Contribution*
= $1,000.0 million x 23%
= $230.0 million

Assuming that the deal closes on the $1,000.0 million purchase price (including debt refinancing), what is the Enterprise Value/EBITDA multiple?

Answer:
Enterprise Value/EBITDA Multiple = $1,000.0 million / $140.0 million = 7.143x

Thus far, we have examined the goals and motivations of the three main groups of players in an LBO transaction: financial buyers, lenders, and selling shareholders. We also discussed how the priorities of financial buyers differ from those of strategic buyers. We next looked at the four primary criteria that make a target company an attractive LBO candidate: (1) An undervalued company that has (2) the potential to generate stable cash flows, along with (3) moderate, predictable R&D and capital expenditure needs, and which presents its financial buyers with (4) the possibility of a viable exit strategy.

Finally, we considered the mechanics of an LBO transaction, including what makes the use of debt attractive, what determines the right amount of debt in the capital structure, and how credit ratios are employed to determine the maximum (or optional) amount of senior debt and subordinated debt that a financial buyer can borrow—or the optimal amount it should borrow.

In a sense, however, the real task begins once the transaction is completed: how does the financial buyer turn around the acquired company to create value? Topic 3 will address this fundamental question.

TOPIC 3: DE-LEVERAGING AND MAXIMIZING VALUE

In Topic 2, we discussed and walked through the financing stages of the leveraged buyout of a hypothetical company called TargetLBO, Inc. Once the financial components of the transaction have been decided, the buyout has been structured, and the deal has closed, TargetLBO's financial sponsors will turn their attention to the next important phase of the process: creating value in order to maximize the return on their equity investment before they exit the company, typically in three to five years.

The following are several different ways that financial buyers create value for themselves:

- ◆ Repay as much of the debt as possible (also known as ◀**de-leveraging**▶ the investment)
- ◆ Make operating improvements to the business to increase TargetLBO's available cash flow

- ◆ Achieve ◀**multiple expansion**▶ upon sale of the business

A. De-leveraging

As mentioned in the opening section of Topic 2, a financial buyer's motivations closely parallel those of a home flipper. Smart home flippers try to pay off as much of their mortgage as possible, as quickly as possible. The same holds true for the financial buyer in an LBO. Just as paying down the mortgage increases the value of the owner's equity in the home, paying down debt raises the buyer's equity returns. This affects value creation in two ways:

1) The firm's capital structure becomes less risky because it has less debt and less interest expense to cover.

2) The residual Equity Value in the firm increases.

B. Operating Improvements

Operating improvements generate increased cash flow and can come in many forms. The following are two common ones:

- ◆ **Sales growth**

  Sales growth is often called "top line" growth and can be achieved in a number of different ways, including growth through market expansion (entering into new markets) and growth through market share gains (improving positions in current markets). Developing an entirely new product segment can also raise sales, but this often requires additional cash investment up front before it improves cash flow.

◆ **Margin improvements**
Free cash flow can also be boosted through margin improvements and improved efficiencies.

Bear in mind that achieving operating improvements is easy to do on paper, but much harder to do in reality. Sometimes the company's existing managers are already trying to increase sales growth and maximize profits. Whatever you are planning to do, they have likely thought of it already. Nevertheless, operating improvements is one of the major strategies financial buyers use to create value.

C. Multiple Expansion
Financial buyers evaluating the feasibility of an LBO transaction commonly use the conservative assumption that they will sell the business at the same Enterprise Value-to-EBITDA multiple at which they purchased it. However, the possibility exists that the buyer could sell the company for a higher multiple than what it was bought for. This could be a reflection of operating improvements, a change in the market environment, a low initial purchase price, or any combination of these.

Calculating Residual Equity Value Under Each Scenario
Let's consider the effect that each of these three value-enhancing investment strategies has on the residual Equity Value of our hypothetical firm TargetLBO:

A. Scenario 1: De-leveraging Only
The initial capital structure of the TargetLBO buyout looks like this:

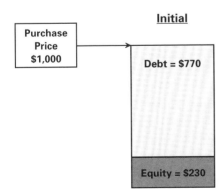

Assume that the financial buyer uses TargetLBO's free cash flows to pay off $470.0 million of its debt, so that in year 5 we have the following:

- Net Debt = $300.0 million
- EBITDA = $140.0 million
- Financial buyer can sell company for 7.143 x EBITDA (i.e., the selling multiple is 7.143 x EBITDA). Conservatively, assume the seller can sell the company for the same multiple of EBITDA for which they purchased the company.

What is the residual Equity Value for the financial buyer?

Answer:

The Sale Price in Year 5 (Enterprise Value) = Selling Multiple x Year 5 EBITDA

(Enterprise Value) = 7.143 x $140.0 million
= $1,000.0 million

Residual Equity Value = Enterprise Value – Net Debt

= $1,000.0 million – $300.0 million
= $700.0 million

The above scenario is actually a very conservative one. It assumes that there has been **no increase** of the exit sale price over the original purchase price, **no growth** in EBITDA, and **no multiple expansion**. Later in this section, we will discuss what happens if the seller can increase the selling multiple. For now, the main point should be clear even in this conservative scenario: even if TargetLBO were to sell at the exact same valuation, the financial buyer's Equity Value would still rise from $230.0 million to $700.0 million because of the diligent pay-down of debt. Even before the occurrence of any growth in the business, the financial sponsor has more than *tripled* its investment ($700/$230)—just from de-leveraging. Clearly, it is important for the financial buyer to use free cash flows to de-lever as quickly as possible.

It should be mentioned here that, well before the deal is structured and finalized, TargetLBO's buyers would also have looked at its capital expenditure needs. High capital expenditure requirements make a company less attractive as an LBO candidate. Why? Because they affect how quickly a financial sponsor can de-lever the TargetLBO. ◂**Capital expenditures**▸ are among a company's largest cash outflows, and every dollar forgone in capital spending is a dollar that could have been used to pay down debt. On the other hand, if a company is currently spending inefficiently on capital expenditures, this might make for an attractive target.

Certain capital expenditures, however, are not discretionary, and a business would suffer if those expenditures were reduced. Good managers and LBO firms therefore look for other ways to improve free cash flow without cutting what are called **maintenance capital expenditures**, the bare minimum required capital expenditure to maintain the business. One such way is to undertake operating improvements.

B. Scenario 2: De-leveraging + Operating Improvements

Now let's apply operating improvements to TargetLBO to see how they increase its value. Imagine that the buyers have succeeded in improving margins, growing the company's sales, and paying down even more of its debt than had originally been expected.

Let's assume that Year 5 EBITDA has now improved to $155.0 million from its previous level of $140.0 million and that, through de-leveraging, Net Debt in year 5 has been cut to $250.0 million from the post-LBO amount of $770.0 million. Assume there is no multiple expansion, and so the sale multiple remains 7.143 times EBITDA. What would the new residual Equity Value be?

Answer:

The Sale Price in Year 5 = Selling Multiple x Year 5 EBITDA

(Enterprise Value) = 7.143 x $155.0 million
= $1,107.2 million

Residual Equity Value = Enterprise Value – Net Debt

= $1,107.2 million - $250.0 million
= $857.2 million

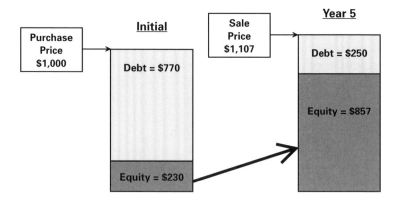

In this scenario, the initial $230.0 million equity investment grows 3.7 times ($857.2 million / $230.0 million). Notice that improving margins and increasing sales has a dual impact. First, it makes more free cash flow available for paying down debt, which increases the residual Equity Value. Second, even with no **multiple expansion**, it also allows TargetLBO's buyers to sell the company at a higher price because they are selling it using a higher EBITDA figure.

ASK THE FINANCE GURU

Question: Can the financial buyers run the business any better than the existing management? What can they do that hasn't been done already?

It can be a challenge to improve operations beyond what the company is already doing, but it can be done, and it often is. First, financial buyers look for undervalued companies that may be running inefficiently. Second, financial sponsors may bring industry expertise and/or a fresh operating strategy to the company. Third, taking a public company private often gives the management team greater leeway to develop a longer-term strategy over a couple of years instead of the pressure of the quarterly earnings mindset that drives a public company to focus rather narrowly on current earnings. Fourth, a financial buyer may have previously invested in a portfolio of similar companies and thus already experienced the learning curve necessary for improving this kind of company. And finally, the buyer may be able to unlock potential synergies by merging together two or more of its portfolio companies.

OTHER VALUE-ENHANCING STRATEGIES

Management incentive plans

Yet another way to spur improvements is to set up incentives for management in the form of stock options or stock grants. An ownership stake enables management to share in any upside the firm might generate. In fact, in our hypothetical case, the new CEO of TargetLBO will receive an attractive equity ownership package from the buyers to motivate her performance and encourage her management team to develop an operating plan to:

- initiate aggressive cost reduction plans,
- create clear, focused growth strategies,
- change and improve marketing strategies, and
- improve efficiency in decision-making.

The going private effect

LBO transactions offer a side benefit to the managers of a publicly traded target company—because the company is being taken private, the management is likely to receive less public scrutiny. In fact, to win over management, financial sponsors are increasingly selling the image of a leveraged buyout as a "going private transaction." Why? Because going private relieves the CEO and management team of the pressures of reporting periodic earnings, allowing for easier implementation of long-term strategic plans.

C. Scenario 3: De-leveraging + Operating Improvements + Multiple Expansion

So far, our analysis has assumed that the financial buyer sells TargetLBO at the same Enterprise Value-to-EBITDA multiple at which the company was purchased: 7.143 times. To be conservative, buyers often use this assumption when evaluating potential LBO transactions. In practice, however, they are often able to sell the business for a higher multiple, reflecting operating improvements, an improved M&A market, a low initial purchase price, or a combination of these. In this third scenario, we assume that an expanded multiple is achieved.

As we did in Scenario 2, let's assume that TargetLBO's financial sponsor has succeeded in improving margins and has been able to pay down more debt than originally expected. Year 5 EBITDA has now improved to $155.0 million and Net Debt in year 5 has been cut to $250.0 million. But this time around, let's imagine that because of a favorable M&A market for this kind of company, the buyer can sell the company on the open market at a higher multiple: 8.0 times. What would the new residual Equity Value be?

Answer:

The Sale Price in Year 5 = Selling Multiple x Year 5 EBITDA

(Enterprise Value) = 8.0 x $155.0 million
= $1,240.0 million

Residual Equity Value = Enterprise Value – Net Debt

= $1,240.0 million – $250.0 million
= $990.0 million

This $990.0 million is 4.3 times the initial investment of $230.0 million.

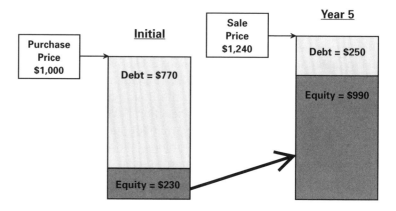

To summarize, depending on how effective their investment strategy is, TargetLBO's financial sponsors can improve their residual Equity Value in the company by the following amounts:

	De-leveraging Only	De-leveraging + Improving Margins	De-leveraging + Improving Margins + Multiple Expansion
Residual Equity Value	$700.0 million	$857.2 million	$990.0 million
Improvement Over Initial Investment of $230.0 million	3.0 times	3.7 times	4.3 times

In Topic 3, using the example of the hypothetical target firm TargetLBO Inc., we examined how financial buyers create value for themselves. They create value primarily in three ways: (A) by paying down their debt—referred to as de-leveraging their investment; (B) by making operating improvements through stronger sales, improved margins, and other value-driving strategies such as management incentive plans; and/or (C) by trying to sell the business at a higher Enterprise Value-to-EBITDA multiple than what they bought it for (i.e., by achieving multiple expansion).

Finally, we performed some calculations to examine the impact of the three main value-enhancing techniques (de-leveraging, operating improvements, and multiple expansion) on the acquired company's available free cash flow, its EBITDA, and ultimately its residual Equity Value, noting that a combination of the three typically yields the best results.

Topic 4 follows chronologically from Topic 3. In Topic 4, we will discuss the fundamental measure used by financial buyers to evaluate the success of an LBO deal: the internal rate of return.

ASK THE FINANCE GURU

Question: Merger Consequences Analysis is regarded as a form of affordability analysis. Is that also true of Leveraged Buyout Analysis?

Yes; like Merger Consequences (see Chapter 6), LBO Analysis can be considered another type of affordability analysis. Why? One of the overarching questions that guides LBO Analysis is this: "What price could a private equity investor pay for this public company and still receive the rate of return the buyer is reasonably demanding?" It is fairly straightforward to calculate this IRR after the deal is done. Hindsight, after all, is 20/20. LBO analysis, however, is actually done before the transaction, while the parties are still contemplating the deal. Like Discounted Cash Flow valuation (Chapter 5), LBO analysis is characteristically forward-looking. The private equity investor needs to estimate the company's future free cash flows and exit sale price. This "guesstimate" is more art than science—albeit highly educated art.

TOPIC 4: MEASURING SUCCESS FROM THE BUYER'S PERSPECTIVE

Understanding how private equity investors measure their investment performance is a key to understanding their motivations, and hence a key to analyzing an LBO transaction. In Topic 3, we discussed how financial buyers attempt to maximize value. In Topic 4, we will look at how financial buyers calculate the return on their investment using the internal rate of return (IRR) formula. We will also explore how leverage significantly increases the potential for higher returns.

Ultimately, financial buyers realize value from their investment when they exit it, usually in one of these three ways:

- **A sale:** Selling the company to a strategic buyer or another financial buyer (an M&A event).
- **An IPO:** Taking the company public through an initial public offering.
- **A special dividend:** Re-levering the company with new debt and paying out a special dividend to the owners.

ASK THE FINANCE GURU

Question: Of the three exit strategies, is one better than the others?

Each approach has its benefits and downsides. It depends on the financial buyer's goals. The advantage of strategy #1, selling the company outright, is that the financial buyer may be able to "unwind" the entire position (that is, realize the entire value of the investment) at a premium. In the second strategy—taking the company public—it is virtually impossible for the financial buyer to sell all of its stock at once on the open market, because this might cause the share price to plummet. Market dynamics also limit an all-at-once sale. So strategy #2 is usually not a full exit. Also, IPO pricing is typically done at a discount. In a hot IPO market, however, the business can and often does get a good valuation. Strategy #2 also gives the buyer the opportunity to benefit from future upside in the investment. Exit strategy #3, a dividend payment, does not represent a full exit from the company. But it does allow the sponsor to take some money out of the investment and continue to have a stake in it, however, the company now has an additional debt burden.

We will focus our discussion on just the first of these three exit strategies—the sale of the company to another buyer—because it is the only one that represents a complete exit and a fundamental change of ownership. But first, what exactly does the internal rate of return (IRR) measure, and what is the formula for calculating it?

The Internal Rate of Return: Measuring Investment Performance

To measure their returns from an LBO investment, financial buyers rely heavily on internal rate of return (IRR) analysis. Similarly to what we learned in DCF Analysis in Chapter 4, IRR calculations rely on the concept of the time value of money. Future money has less value than present money.

ASK THE FINANCE GURU

Question: How common are special dividends?

This depends on market conditions. From the late 1990s up until 2002, special dividends of post-LBO companies were uncommon. Since 2004, however, there has been a sharp increase in the frequency of special dividends financed through new debt (known as "leveraged recapitalizations"). Abundant debt capital at attractive rates had allowed for this boom. The credit crunch of 2008-2011, however, reversed this trend. Special dividends made a comeback in the early 2010s as credit markets opened back up and became more liquid.

The difference between DCF and LBO analyses is this: in DCF valuation, the target company's free cash flows are projected out over a number of years, then discounted back to the present using some pre-determined discount rate (the weighted average cost of capital, or WACC). Adding the present value of the company's cash flows to the present value of its terminal value gives you the company's Enterprise Value. In DCF analysis, valuation experts know what the discount rate is; what they do not know is the present value of the company's cash flows and terminal value (the firm's Enterprise Value). That is what they solve for.

In LBO analysis, valuation experts know—or at least can estimate—the initial equity investment they are making in the company, and the company's future value (called its "exit value" in LBO analysis). What they do not know and must solve for, using a calculator or spreadsheet, is the discount rate (the internal rate of return), which represents the annual return on their investment.

The IRR is defined as the discount rate that equates the present value (PV) of an investment's cash inflows to that of its cash outflows. This can be expressed as the condition where

> **PV (Inflows) = PV (Outflows)**

Viewed another way, the IRR is the discount rate (r) that causes the net present value (NPV) of the investment to equal zero:

$$CF_0 + \frac{CF_1}{(1 + r)^1} + \frac{CF_2}{(1 + r)^2} + \ldots + \frac{CF_n}{(1 + r)^n} = 0$$

To measure investment performance in an LBO transaction, we simply solve for the unknown discount rate (r).

> **TIPS OF THE TRADE**
>
> In DCF valuation, you know (1) the free cash flows, (2) the terminal value, and (3) the discount rate (WACC), and you solve for (4) the company's **present value**— that is, its Enterprise Value.
>
> In LBO analysis, by contrast, you know (1) the free cash flows, (2) the exit value, and (3) the initial investment, and solve for (4) **the discount rate**—that is, the internal rate of return to the equity investment of the financial buyer.

In the context of an LBO investment, the outflow is the initial equity investment (CF_0) that the financial buyer made in the company. The inflows are the proceeds realized upon exiting the investment. To simplify the analysis, let's assume that there are no cash flows (for example, dividends) received in the interim period. This simplifying assumption allows us to rewrite the equation as:

$$CF_0 + \frac{CF_n}{(1 + r)^n} = 0$$

Solving for r yields:

$$r = \left[\frac{CF_n}{CF_0} \right]^{1/n} - 1$$

This is commonly shown as:

$$IRR = \left[\frac{FV}{PV} \right]^{1/n} - 1$$

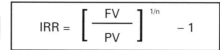

where:

- ◆ FV is the future value
- ◆ PV is the present value, and
- ◆ n is the number of periods

Calculating IRR

Using the formula for IRR that we just worked out, let's calculate the return on a financial buyer's investment in TargetLBO Inc. We will consider the same three scenarios introduced in Topic 3 when we examined the effect of different investment strategies on residual Equity Value.

Scenario 1 will assume that the only strategy the financial buyer employs is de-leveraging. Scenario 2 will assume that the buyer pursues two strategies: de-leveraging and margin improvements. Finally, Scenario 3 will assume that the buyer uses all three value-enhancing strategies: de-leveraging, improving margins, and multiple expansion.

Calculating and comparing the results of these three scenarios will give you a more intuitive feel for how, for a given initial investment, a change in the residual Equity Value of a business affects the rate of return the financial buyer receives; it will also give you a sense of how successful the LBO transaction is from the buyer's perspective.

ASK THE FINANCE GURU

Question: Are exits ever shorter than three to five years?

Rarely. Exiting an LBO investment in less than three to five years is the exception rather than the rule. For example, the private equity firm Kohlberg Kravis Roberts (KKR) has held onto their investments an average of seven years. But as a high-profile example of a quick flip, investors in Hertz, the rental car company, approximately doubled their investment in about one year, using a special, financially engineered dividend and an IPO.

Scenario 1: De-leveraging Only

Initial Investment = $230.0 million (the remaining $770.0 million was funded by the lenders to provide a buyout price of $1,000.0 million)

Future residual Equity Value = $700.0 million[1]

What is the IRR for this investment transaction?

Answer:
The IRR calculation is shown here:

$$-\$230 + \left[\frac{\$700}{(1 + r)^5}\right] = 0$$

$$r = \left[\frac{\$700}{\$230}\right]^{1/5} - 1$$

The IRR for this de-levered-only investment is 24.9%.

Scenario 2: De-leveraging + Improving Margins

Having discussed the effect of de-leveraging, let's look at a scenario in which the buyer pursues two strategies: paying down debt and improving the business's margins. Recall from our hypothetical TargetLBO case in Topic 3 that TargetLBO was able to (1) improve year 5 EBITDA to $155.0 million and (2) de-lever (that is, cut Net Debt) from $770.0 million to $250.0 million. In the process, it was able to capture residual Equity Value of $857.2 million.

Keeping the initial investment in the company at the same level ($230.0 million), and assuming a residual equity value of $857.2 million, what is the new IRR?

---

1 This scenario assumes that, in projected year 5:, Net Debt balance is down to $300.0 million; EBITDA is $140.0 million; the selling multiple is 7.143x; and there are no dividends paid to the sponsor.

Answer:

$$r = \left[\frac{\$857.2}{\$230.0} \right]^{1/5} -1 \ = 30.1\%$$

Having quantified the dual benefit of having both improving margins and de-leveraging, we can see that Scenario 2 generates a higher IRR than just de-leveraging alone.

Scenario 3: De-leveraging + Improving Margins + Multiple Expansion

Our third and final scenario demonstrates that an even higher IRR can be achieved if de-leveraging and improved operating performance are combined with multiple expansion.

Under Scenario 2, in which TargetLBO improved its year 5 EBITDA to $155.0 million, de-levered to $250.0 million, and sold at a higher multiple of 8.0x EBITDA, the financial buyer was able to capture $990.0 million of residual Equity Value. Keeping the initial investment the same at $230.0 million, what is the new IRR?

Answer:

$$r = \left[\frac{\$990.0}{\$230.0} \right]^{1/5} -1 \ = 33.9\%$$

In conclusion, from the perspective of the financial buyer preparing for an exit event, the success of the TargetLBO deal can be measured by the rate of return (IRR) the buyer receives. That IRR depends on the choice of investment techniques, and on what combination of them, if any, is used. To summarize:

	De-leveraging Only	De-leveraging + Improving Margins	De-leveraging + Improving Margins + Multiple Expansion
IRR to Financial Buyer	24.9%	30.1%	33.9%

ASK THE FINANCE GURU

Question: What internal rates of return do financial buyers consider acceptable?

That depends. Different financial buyers have different acceptable thresholds for their investments (this threshold is called a ◄hurdle rate►). Financial buyers tend to demand a higher IRR for a higher-risk investment, and accept a lower IRR for a lower-risk investment. But typically, private equity firms aim for returns of 18% to 25%, or higher.

De-leveraging: the Concept of Leveraged Returns

In Scenario 1 above, the IRR of 24.9% resulted from the value of the equity increasing over time. The Equity Value rose because a substantial portion of the debt used in financing the transaction was repaid during the five-year period, leaving a greater residual Equity Value when the buyer exited the investment.

The de-leveraging of the balance sheet, together with the resulting increase in investment returns, creates what is known as leveraged returns. The term captures the idea that using greater amounts of debt leverage, and thus smaller amounts of equity, raises equity returns (IRR).

Simply stated, one of the major advantages of leverage is that the financial buyer can put up less initial capital. In addition, if the company is sold at a higher price, or if it generates larger cash flows and profits than expected, all of that upside goes to the financial buyer. The banks and other lenders receive only their principal and interest because their rate of return is fixed.

Are there disadvantages to increased leverage? Yes; it places added stress on a company and its managers to perform, increases the company's financial risk, and raises the likelihood of default. Furthermore, high debt levels give the company less financial flexibility in the future should things go wrong with its business operations.

In Topic 4, we calculated the financial sponsor's return on investment, under three different investment strategies, using the internal rate of return (IRR) formula. Topic 5 expands our view of the LBO transaction. We will now look at it not only from the perspective of the buyers, but also from the viewpoint of the other main stakeholders—the sellers and lenders. The buyers remain the primary driving force of an LBO transaction. But as we will see, a successful deal, depends on reaching a meeting of the minds. This requires good negotiating skills that go beyond the ability to work out the math on paper.

TOPIC 5: UNDERSTANDING THE DYNAMICS OF AN LBO

Reaching a Meeting of the Minds: the Role of Negotiation

 In the TargetLBO deal that we analyzed in Topics 3 and 4, assuming that the ◀**hurdle rate**▶ or minimum required return of the financial buyer is around 20%–25%, the transaction would appear to be a good investment under each of the three scenarios we considered. But Topics 3 and 4 defined success solely in terms of the returns to the buyer as an equity investor. Our discussion was entirely from the financial buyer's perspective. For an LBO transaction to occur, all the stakeholders must walk away satisfied with the deal's economics.

Satisfying all the parties, however, is not easy. More often than not, a potential transaction fails because one or more of the parties was uncomfortable with the proposed terms. The graphic below summarizes each party's primary motivations and interests. The little triangular intersection of the three circles represents the possibility of a successful LBO transaction:

Lenders

Sellers: Are we receiving a fair price?

• Fair value relative to comparable companies and transactions

LBO Firm: What is the expected IRR?

• IRR exceeding 20-25% assuming an exit typically in 4-6 years
• Exit strategy (sale or IPO)
• Fit with other fund investments

Purchase Price

Level of Debt Financing

Investor IRR

Lender: What is the certainty of interest payments and debt repayments?

• Cash flow & coverage ratios
• Certainty of interest & debt payments (low default risk)
• Confidence in LBO sponsor

If the lenders are uncomfortable with the credit profile of the newly debt-burdened company, they will be reluctant to risk their capital. Lending money to a risky company at 7% is not a terribly attractive investment, unless there is reasonable certainty that it will be paid back.

ASK THE FINANCE GURU

Question: What are a bank's incentives for lending to a risky LBO transaction?

Debt investors are after a return on capital, so lending allows that money to be put to work. Second, the debt that banks issue is senior debt. It is not riskless, but it is the safest form of debt. Third, banks can sometimes look forward to receiving additional investment-banking business from the company and the private equity sponsors—in the form of underwriting fees on issuing debt, M&A advisory fees if the business is later sold, or an equity underwriting fee if the company goes public in an IPO.

Sellers

If the sellers are not happy with the price they receive, they will not sign off on the deal, either, regardless of how glowingly the lenders and financial buyers talk about the transaction.

The challenge of satisfying all three parties lies partly in the fact that they often have conflicting viewpoints. How divergent these perspectives are depends on the deal structure. Keeping all other things equal, let's imagine that we could increase the leverage used in the deal structure. The table below summarizes how this change would leave each of the three parties: satisfied, disappointed, or indifferent.

Effect of Increasing the Leverage		
Financial Buyer	**Lenders**	**Sellers**
• **Satisfied**	• **Disappointed**	• **Indifferent**, assuming the purchase price has not changed
• Get leveraged returns	• More Debt = more risk, less certainty of repayment	• They usually receive 100% cash

Now, let's imagine that we could raise the purchase price, keeping all other things equal:

	Effect of Increasing the Purchase Price	

Financial Buyer	**Lenders**	**Sellers**
• **Disappointed**	• **Disappointed**	• **Satisfied**
• Increases equity investment = loss of leveraged returns = lower IRR	• More Debt = more risk, less certainty of repayment	• Get higher price!

It is easy to see from this that the perspectives of the three parties change in different ways depending on the deal structure. The changes in each party's satisfaction level demonstrate the conflicting nature of their perspectives.

Let's revisit our TargetLBO case study one final time. Assume that the company has an LTM EBITDA of $140.0 million and $70.0 million in Net Debt. The financial sponsor, after approaching a new group of lenders, determines that it can now borrow up to 6.0x total debt to EBITDA. The sponsor is willing to contribute its own equity for up to 30% of the purchase price and is targeting an IRR of 25%.

Also, this time around, assume that the **sellers** want a price of $1,120.0 million for the whole firm (including refinancing of existing debt), instead of the $1,000 million previously used in the analysis.

Finally, in year 5 assume:

- ♦ An exit with no multiple expansion
- ♦ EBITDA = $145.0 million
- ♦ Net Debt = $350.0 million

Will this deal work under these assumptions?

Answer:

For the deal to work, we need to examine the viewpoints of all three parties.

Sellers: We can assume that the sellers are happy with the $1,120.0 million price, since that is what they are demanding.

Lenders: The lenders will lend up to 6.0x total debt / EBITDA. Therefore, the maximum leverage is:

$$= 6.0 \times \$140.0 \text{ million}$$
$$= \$840.0 \text{ million}$$

Financial buyer: The financial buyer is looking for an IRR of at least 25.0%, with no more than 30% equity contribution.

So, the initial equity investment by the financial sponsor is:

$1,120.0 million – $840.0 million = $280.0 million equity investment

The buyer's equity contribution is:

$280.0 million / $1,120.0 million = 25.0%

Since the sponsor was willing to contribute up to 30% of purchase price, we can assume that the sponsor is comfortable with the equity contribution of 25% in this scenario. However, we still need to see if the IRR is greater than 25%.

The buyout multiple is:

$1,120.0 million / $140.0 million = 8.0 x

From this, we can calculate the residual Equity Value for a year 5 exit:

Enterprise Value = 8.0 x $145.0 million = $1,160.0 million

Residual Equity Value = $1,160.0 million – $350.0 million = $810.0 million

$$\text{IRR} = \left[\frac{\$810}{\$280} \right]^{1/5} -1 = 23.7\%$$

ASK THE FINANCE GURU

Question: How would you know if the lenders are comfortable with the pay-down of debt? Do you need a financial model?

Typically, an LBO model forecasts the projected cash flows and debt schedule of the target company for the next several years. From this model, you would be able to keep track of the interest payments and debt balances over time. Specifically, you would double-check to make sure that all senior debt is paid down according to schedule. For simplicity, we have generated the numbers in this Chapter from an LBO model and provided only the necessary detail.

Observe that the rate of return (23.7%) is less than the buyer's targeted IRR of 25%. This poses a problem. Unless the deal's parameters change—for example, more leverage is used or a lower purchase price is offered—we should assume that the financial sponsor is unlikely to pursue this deal. At this point, given that it is facing a return lower than its targeted IRR, the financial sponsor has some hard choices to make. It has three main alternatives:

- **Relax its 25% hurdle rate.** After all, 23.7% is quite close to the 25% that it wanted.

- **Try to obtain a little more debt financing from the lenders.** LBO transactions are driven by relationships, and financial sponsors often have considerable clout with their lenders, especially in light of the myriad of fees they pay.

- **Try to negotiate a new purchase price just low enough to make the IRR slightly more attractive.** Bear in mind that the target shareholders would have to be willing to accept this lower purchase price.

Which of these three alternatives will work in practice is a *fact-driven, context-dependent,* and *relationship-governed* question, not a math-driven one. This is where intangibles come into play. The important point to grasp about the dynamics of LBO transactions is that they are as much about *negotiating* as they are about the fundamentals of deal mechanics or the soundness of the math. Good negotiating skills are essential to making a potential deal work because no matter how promising a deal seems, the deal won't happen unless the current shareholders are willing to sell and the lenders are willing to provide the right amount and type of leverage.

However, the entire process begins with picking the right candidate company, because no amount of savvy negotiating will turn the wrong kind of company into a suitable LBO candidate. Recall that LBO candidates are often troubled or out-of-favor companies. They usually have strong, stable cash flows. They can either be private companies (non-core divisions of a conglomerate) or public firms (publicly traded companies that are undervalued). Once a target has been selected, success lies in having the flexibility and insight to recognize that the different parties involved have very different motivations, and then moving the deal forward with this fundamental reality in mind. A successful deal occurs when there is a good balance in the trade-offs among debt leverage, equity contribution, and purchase price—the three assets that represent the lenders, the sponsoring private equity firm, and the selling shareholders, respectively.

SUMMARY
Chapter 7

In this chapter we covered the following topics:

- ◆ Three Sets of Players; Three Points of View
- ◆ Funding a Leveraged Buyout: TargetLBO, Inc.
- ◆ De-leveraging and Maximizing Value
- ◆ Measuring Success from the Buyer's Perspective
- ◆ Understanding the Dynamics of an LBO

A leveraged buyout, or LBO, is the acquisition of a company using very high levels of debt capital and a relatively small proportion of equity financing. This creates a highly leveraged transaction. The repayment of debt and the resulting strengthening of the company's balance sheet are referred to as de-leveraging.

TOPIC 1: THREE SETS OF PLAYERS; THREE POINTS OF VIEW

LBO transactions have three main stakeholders:

- ◆ Financial buyers
- ◆ Lenders
- ◆ Selling shareholders

Each has different priorities and approaches the deal from a different perspective.

A. The financial buyer is usually the key driving force behind an LBO transaction. One of its main goals is to achieve a suitable return on its equity (as measured by the Internal Rate of Return) upon exiting the investment by:

- ◆ selling the company to a strategic buyer, or to another financial buyer;
- ◆ selling it to the public in an IPO; or
- ◆ re-levering the company using new debt, along with a special dividend payout to the owners.

The financial buyer's time horizon, which is much shorter than that of a strategic buyer, is typically 3-5 years.

B. Lenders such as banks provide most of the capital in an LBO. They offer **senior** and **subordinated debt** to financial buyers to finance the transaction. Given the deal's inherent risks, the priority of lenders is to have a high degree of certainty that the debt principal and interest will be repaid.

C. The **selling shareholders** essentially just want a fair price for the company. They will usually go along with various capitalization structures and financing choices as long as they feel that shareholder value is being maximized.

Three phases of an LBO transaction: for an LBO transaction to take place, 1) the right company must first be found, 2) the three main parties must then agree to a price, and finally 3) the funds must be raised.

We just summarized Phase 2. Let's review Phase 1. A good LBO candidate normally has the following characteristics:

- It is undervalued, perhaps because it is distressed.
- It has, or possesses the potential to generate, stable, predictable cash flows.
- It has moderate, predictable capital expenditure and/ or R&D needs.
- It presents the financial sponsors with the possibility of a viable exit strategy.

Let's now turn to Phase 3, raising the funds.

TOPIC 2: FUNDING A LEVERAGED BUYOUT: TargetLBO, Inc.

There are typically three main sources of capital for LBO transactions:

1) Senior debt
2) Subordinated debt
3) Sponsor equity

The financial buyers want to use as much debt, and as little of their own cash (equity), as possible. Using low amounts of their own cash gives them greater flexibility to sponsor other deals. Increased debt also provides an effect called leveraged returns (discussed in Topic 4).

The financial sponsors first try to raise senior debt, which is secured and less risky. It is also the cheapest form of capital. Only after maxing out senior debt does the financial sponsor tap into the subordinated debt market. Subordinated debt is typically unsecured, riskier, and requires a higher coupon because, in the event of a default, senior debt is paid ahead of it. Subordinated debt is also bullet-structured, which means that the principal is repaid only at the very end of the period.

In determining how much debt it should borrow, the sponsor uses credit ratios, especially the following:

- Senior Debt/EBITDA
- Total Debt/EBITDA
- EBITDA/Interest Expense
- (EBITDA - Capital Expenditures)/Interest Expense
- Equity Investment/Total Capital
- Collateral for lenders such as inventory, accounts receivable and property, plant and equipment

In a more flexible, low-interest-rate market, a financial buyer can secure higher levels of debt financing. In a tighter market with higher interest rates, where it is more difficult to secure favorable terms on a loan, a financial buyer may settle for lower leverage levels.

Credit ratio parameters change constantly in response to interest rates and other market and economic conditions. If you are evaluating a company as an LBO candidate, you are urged to seek professional advice and more than one outside resource to help you to determine what is appropriate in light of the company's growth profile and cash flows.

TOPIC 3: DE-LEVERAGING AND MAXIMIZING VALUE

After the deal has been structured and the buyout completed, the financial buyer turns its focus to maximizing the value of its equity investment until it exits from the investment, which it will typically do after three to five years. During this period, the sponsor tries to enhance its return on investment by the following means:

- Paying off as much debt as possible, or de-leveraging the investment, in order to (A) reduce the risk of its capital structure and (B) boost its residual Equity Value.

- Launching operating improvements through sales growth, management incentive plans, margin improvements, and efficiency improvements in order to increase the cash flow generated by the company.

- Achieving multiple expansion (selling the company for a higher Enterprise Value-to-EBITDA multiple) upon exiting the business, based on operating improvements, an upward turn in the M&A market environment, a low initial purchase price, or a combination of these.

Timing

In an effort to time the sale of the business so that it coincides with a period in which the multiples are at or close to a high (perhaps owing to a favorable M&A market for this type of company), the sponsor keeps a close watch on the company's enterprise multiples—especially EV/EBITDA.

TOPIC 4: MEASURING SUCCESS FROM THE BUYER'S PERSPECTIVE

Ultimately, financial buyers realize value from their investment when they exit it (referred to as an **exit event**). Exiting usually occurs through:

A. A sale: They sell the company to a strategic buyer or another financial buyer (an M&A event).

B. An IPO: They take the company public in an IPO.

C. A special dividend: They re-lever the company with new debt and pay out a special dividend to the owners.

To measure their returns from an LBO investment, financial buyers rely heavily on internal rate of return (IRR) analysis. The IRR is defined as the discount rate that equates the present value (PV) of an investment's cash inflows to that of its outflows:

$$CF_0 + \frac{CF_1}{(1+r)^1} + \frac{CF_2}{(1+r)^2} + \ldots + \frac{CF_n}{(1+r)^n} = 0$$

A simplified version that assumes no dividends is:

$$CF_0 + \frac{CF_n}{(1+r)^n} = 0$$

Solving for r yields:

$$r = \left[\frac{CF_n}{CF_0}\right]^{1/n} - 1$$

Or:

$$IRR = \left[\frac{FV}{PV}\right]^{1/n} - 1$$

where

- FV is the future value
- PV is the present value, and
- n is the number of periods

Private equity firms and other financial buyers usually have a threshold or hurdle IRR that they consider acceptable for their investment, and below which they are reluctant to go. Different financial buyers have different hurdle rates. Knowing what hurdle rate a financial buyer is using will help the other parties in negotiating an LBO transaction.

Equity investors try to enhance their return on investment in different ways. One way is to use debt, which provides an effect called "leveraged returns" that is beneficial to the financial buyer. If the company is sold at a higher price, or if it generates larger-than-expected cash flows and profits, all of this upside goes to the financial buyer. The banks and other lenders are limited to receiving only their interest and principal payments; their rate of return is fixed.

In short, the primary factors that boost IRRs for private equity investors are:

- Repaying debt (referred to as de-leveraging)
- Making operating improvements while they own the business
- Achieving multiple expansion upon selling the business

These factors can work in tandem. In other words, combining them potentially boosts the financial buyer's IRR even more.

TOPIC 5: UNDERSTANDING THE DYNAMICS OF AN LBO TRANSACTION

Although the financial buyer tends to be the primary driving force of an LBO transaction, in order for a deal to occur, all the stakeholders (buyers, lenders, and sellers) must be satisfied with the deal's economics. Satisfying all parties is not always easy, and potential transactions can fall apart if one or more of the parties is uncomfortable because the terms of the deal do not meet their internal requirements or expectations.

The viewpoints of the three main players in an LBO transaction tend to diverge, and their positions can change depending on the deal structure. For example, adding more leverage, or raising the purchase price, affects the parties differently. It benefits some and is a disadvantage to others. The success of an LBO transaction therefore depends as much on skillfully negotiating among the parties as on getting the math of the deal mechanics right. Put differently, LBO transactions are as much relationship-driven and context-based as they are formula-driven. Over time, having excellent negotiating skills can be as much a creator of value as having excellent quantitative skills or picking the right LBO candidate in the first place.

MASTERY QUIZ
Chapter 7

QUESTION #1

True or False:

Financial sponsors' returns in an LBO transaction are assessed by calculating the net present value (NPV) of future cash flows.

QUESTION #2

Calculate the pro forma (post-deal) leverage, as measured by total debt to EBITDA, of the newly-indebted LBO target assuming EBITDA of $100.0 million, a transaction purchase price multiple of 8.0x, and an equity contribution of 30.0% of the purchase price.

A. 8.0x
B. 6.5x
C. 2.4x
D. None of the above

QUESTION #3

Your boss has asked you to put together a due diligence list to help determine whether or not the company she will be visiting is a good LBO candidate. Which of the following questions is probably most important when assessing whether or not a company is a good LBO candidate?

A. Is the company publicly-traded or private?
B. Does the company have higher-than-average operating margins compared to its peers?
C. Are the company's cash flows stable?
D. Is the company located in the US or internationally?

QUESTION #4

A company with $100.0 million of debt was purchased for $900.0 million by maximizing debt capacity at 6.3x EBITDA. The financial buyer funded the transaction using $270.0 million of equity. What was the company's EBITDA at the time of purchase?

A. $100.0 million
B. $124.4 million
C. None of the above.
D. There is not enough information to answer the question.

QUESTION #5

All of the following except one could be considered incentives that encourage management to operate a post-LBO company effectively. Which one is NOT an incentive?

A. Stock options
B. Greater cushion in operating performance given the equity sponsor's new equity contribution
C. Lack of public shareholder scrutiny
D. Fewer appearances on the news networks

QUESTION #6

Which statement is NOT typical in the context of an LBO transaction?

A. It is typical to assume an exit multiple identical to the transaction multiple at the time of the purchase.
B. Financial buyers, strategic buyers, and equity sponsors are more or less synonymous with one another.
C. The amount of leverage a company can take on is crucial to determining the price a financial sponsor can pay.
D. Financing parameters move around considerably given changing market conditions, so it is difficult to come up with hard and fast rules without knowing the current market conditions.

QUESTION #7

True or False:

High yield bonds typically have longer maturities than bank loans.

QUESTION #8

Bank loans are typically_____, while high yield bonds are typically_____. Select the choice of terms that best completes the sentence.

A. Amortized; bullet maturities
B. Amortized; amortized
C. bullet maturities; amortized
D. bullet maturities; bullet maturities

QUESTION #9

A candidate for an LBO transaction has current year EBITDA of $1,000.0 million. A financial buyer can use leverage up to 6.0x debt / current year EBITDA and wants to contribute 25.0% of the purchase price with sponsor equity. Assuming a projected year 5 sale of the company and no multiple expansion, what is the exit multiple at year 5?

QUESTION #10

Imagine that a financial buyer is deciding between two separate investments (investment A and investment B) that coincidentally have the same current year EBITDA of $100.0 million. In both cases, the maximum amount of leverage allowed is 5.5x debt / current year EBITDA and the equity contribution is 30%. Investment A has an exit potential in projected year 3 with a 7.9x EBITDA exit multiple, $125.0 million in EBITDA and Net Debt of $500.0 m. Investment B has an exit potential in projected year 5 with a 7.9x EBITDA exit multiple, $150.0 million in EBITDA and Net Debt of $450.0 million. Assuming that the financial buyer only wants to maximize IRR, which of the following statements is true?

A. The buyer should take investment A.
B. The buyer should take investment B.
C. The buyer is indifferent between the investments.
D. There is not enough information to make a decision.

QUESTION #11

A financial buyer has just invested $1,500.0 million in a company buyout and used $4,500.0 million of debt financing. The buyer is planning to sell the company in 3 years for an 8.0x exit multiple.

But the buyer has an operational decision in the meantime. The buyer can sell some assets of the company to pay down debt. If this is done, the year 3 Net Debt balance goes down to $3,000.0 million and EBITDA will be $770.0 million.

If these assets are not sold, there is more future EBITDA (since assets are expected to generate future cash flow), but the trade-off is that the buyer cannot use the proceeds of the asset sale to pay off more debt. It is estimated that the Year 3 EBITDA under this case would be $800.0 million and the Net Debt would be $3,500.0 million.

Assume that there is some burden of selling assets and that the financial buyer is only willing to sell assets if it boosts IRR more than 5.0 percentage points (5.0%) versus not selling the assets. Also assume that the exit multiple is 8.0x under both cases. What should the buyer do?

A. The buyer should not sell the assets.
B. The buyer should sell the assets.
C. The buyer is indifferent between the choices.
D. There is not enough information to make a decision.

ANSWER KEY
Chapter 7

ANSWER #1

False

Equity investors use internal rate of return (IRR) to assess returns of an LBO transaction. While both NPVs and IRRs factor in the time value of money and risk, NPV requires using a pre-determined discount rate. IRRs, in effect, back into discount rates and thereby eliminate the need for picking one.

ANSWER #2

D — None of the above. The answer is 5.6x.

The transaction value = 8.0 x $100.0 million = $800.0 million. 70.0% (or 1 – 30% equity contribution) of the $800.0 million purchase price is financed using debt for total debt of $560.0 million. Total debt of $560.0 million divided by EBITDA of $100.0 million results in a debt / EBITDA multiple of 5.6x.

ANSWER #3

C — Are the company's cash flows stable?

Public, private, US and international companies can all make potentially good LBO candidates. While higher-than-average margins may suggest higher cash flows and greater ability to service debt, higher margins are by no means necessary in an LBO candidate. In fact, high margin companies are likely to be valued higher than their peers, making them potentially less likely to be **undervalued** —another key characteristic of a good LBO candidate. Even a lower-margin business can be a good LBO candidate provided the company generates enough **stable, predictable** cash flow to service high debt loads.

ANSWER #4

A — $100 million

The purchase price multiple and the debt multiple both use a common EBITDA, so you could attack this problem in two ways.

The easier approach is to focus on the leverage multiple: first calculate the amount of debt $630.0 million = $900.0

million - $270.0 million. If the total debt to EBITDA is 6.3x, then the EBITDA is $100.0 million ($630.0 million / 6.3x).

An alternative and more complicated approach is to focus on the purchase price multiple. We're given the purchase price of $900.0 million but need to calculate the purchase price multiple to eventually determine the EBITDA of the company. Fortunately, the debt proportion is known [($900.0 million – $270.0 million) / $900.0 million = 70%], so we can determine the purchase price multiple by dividing the debt multiple by the debt proportion of 70% (6.3x / 70% = 9.0x). Finally, to calculate the company's EBITDA, we divide the $900.0 million purchase price by the calculated multiple of 9.0x to solve for the unknown EBITDA of $100.0 million ($900.0 million / 9.0x = $100.0 million).

ANSWER #5

B — Greater cushion with respect to operating performance given the equity sponsor's new equity contribution.

The high debt levels actually create less room for declines in operating performance. Instead, they serve as a powerful motivation to focus on cash flow generation that will be needed to make interest and principal payments on the company's debt.

ANSWER #6

B — Financial buyers, strategic buyers, and equity sponsors are more or less synonymous with one another.

Financial buyers and strategic buyers are very different. Strategic buyers are typically companies that operate the same, similar or complementary businesses as the target. Financial buyers are private equity investors that invest in businesses without necessarily owning other similar businesses. Equity sponsor is simply another name for a financial buyer.

ANSWER #7

True

Bank loans are typically repaid in 5 – 7 years. High yield bonds typically have maturities of 8 to 10 years.

ANSWER #8

A — Amortized, bullet maturities

Bank loans are typically amortized, meaning that required principal payments are made throughout the life of the loan. By the time the bank loan matures, a majority of the principal has already been repaid. In contrast, a high yield bond typically does not require principal payments, leaving the entire principal due to be repaid upon maturity ("bullet maturity").

ANSWER #9

8.0x

The maximum leverage allowed is $6,000.0 million (6.0 x $1,000.0 million). If this represents 75.0% of the contribution, the maximum transaction value is $8,000.0 million ($6,000.0 million / 75.0%). The buyout multiple is calculated as transaction value / EBITDA. The initial buyout multiple is 8.0x ($8,000.0 million / $1,000.0 million of EBITDA). Assuming no multiple expansion means that in year 5, the exit multiple for the investment is the same as the buyout multiple. Therefore, it is 8.0x as well.

ANSWER #10

A — The buyer should take investment A.

The maximum leverage allowed is $550.0 million (5.5 x $100.0 million). If this represents 70% of the contribution, the maximum transaction value is $785.7 million ($550.0 million / 70.0%). The equity contribution is $235.7 million ($785.7 x 30.0% or $785.7 million - $550.0 million).

With investment A, the exit year transaction value is $987.5 million (7.9 x $125.0 million) and the residual Equity Value is $487.5 million ($987.5 million - $500.0 million). Therefore the IRR of investment A is calculated as:

$$\text{IRR A} = \left[\frac{\$487.5}{\$235.7} \right]^{1/3} - 1 = 27.4\%$$

With investment B, the exit year transaction value is $1,185.0 million (7.9 x $150.0) and the residual Equity Value is $735.0 million ($1,185.0 million - $450.0 million). Therefore the IRR of investment B is calculated as:

$$\text{IRR B} = \left[\frac{\$735.0}{\$235.7} \right]^{1/5} - 1 = 25.5\%$$

ANSWER #11

A. The buyer should not sell the assets.

Without selling the assets, the exit year transaction value is $6,400.0 million (8.0 x $800.0 million) and the residual Equity Value is $2,900.0 million ($6,400.0 million - $3,500.0 million). Therefore the IRR under this scenario is calculated as:

$$IRR = \left[\frac{\$2,900.0}{\$1,500.0}\right]^{1/3} - 1 = 24.6\%$$

With selling the assets, the exit year transaction value is $6,160.0 million (8.0 x $770.0 million) and the residual Equity Value is $3,160.0 million ($6,160.0 million - $3,000.0 million). Therefore the IRR under this scenario is calculated as:

$$IRR = \left[\frac{\$3,160.0}{\$1,500.0}\right]^{1/3} - 1 = 28.2\%$$

$$
\begin{aligned}
\text{Difference in IRRs} \quad &= \quad 28.2\% - 24.6\,\% \\
&= \quad 3.6\%
\end{aligned}
$$

The percentage difference of 3.6% does not clear the hurdle rate of 5.0%.

HOTWORD GLOSSARY

8-K

Report of unscheduled material events that would be of importance to shareholders, such as acquisitions or the resignation of the CEO

10-K

Comprehensive annual filing with the SEC

10-Q

Quarterly filing with the SEC to update a company's financial position since its fiscal year end

14D-9

A target company's response to a tender offer, including the recommendation of the target's board of directors

20-F

Comprehensive annual filing for a non-US company traded in the US

·· **A** ··

Accretion

An increase in the equity position of a share of stock because of the reduction of shares outstanding or an increase in net income; often used in the context of a merger or acquisition

Annual Report

Comprehensive annual filing to shareholders; similar to the 10-K

Amortization of debt

Amortization, with regards to debt, means paydown of the debt balance or the repayment of the principal amount. Be careful because "amortization" can mean different things to different people! (To "amortize" intangibles means to spread the cost of the asset over a useful life, much like depreciation of fixed assets)

B

Beta

An equity beta measures the degree to which a company's equity returns vary with the return of the overall market

Book Value

The value of net assets (assets less liabilities) that belong to a company's shareholders, as stated on the balance sheet

C

Capital expenditures

Investments in property, plant and equipment or related assets

COGS

Stands for Cost of Goods Sold. Usually the first main expense line item on an income statement

Collar

In an acquisition, an upper and lower limit that will be paid for shares of the company to be acquired

Control premium (or takeover premium)

Percentage increase in value paid over the target's equity value prior to announcement to gain control over the target

Convertible securities

Any instrument that can be converted into common shares. This instrument is typically issued as debt, which can later be converted into common shares

Coverage Ratio (or leverage ratio)

A measure of a company's ability to meet interest payments, usually expressed in terms of a measure of profitability over interest expense such as EBITDA / Gross Interest Expense

Covenant

A rule set up by a lender that the borrower must adhere to such as a leverage limit or a working capital minimum

D

D&A

Stands for Depreciation and Amortization. Refers to expenses recorded to allocate certain assets' costs over their useful lives

Default

Failure to meet interest or principal payments when due

Deleverage (or delever)

To pay down debt principal. In a leveraged buyout, certain lenders will require the principal of their loan to be paid down according to a pre-determined schedule

Diluted shares

Basic shares plus any potential shares from options and convertible securities

Dilution

A decrease in the equity position of a share of stock because of the issuance of additional shares or a decrease in net income; often used in the context of a merger or acquisition

E

Enterprise Value

The value of both equity and debt capital plus noncontrolling interest & preferred stock

Equity Value

The value of equity shareholders' interest

Exchange ratio

The number of new shares an acquiring firm gives to the target's shareholders for each outstanding share of the acquired firm

F

Fairness Opinion

A third party valuation issued by an independent investment bank in an M&A transaction

FCFF

Stands for Free Cash Flow to the total Firm. Measures excess cash available to the firm after expenses and reinvestments

Financial Buyer

Financial entity which buys a company and tries to create value by taking on additional debt (leverage) while using the cash flows of the acquired business to pay down the debt in the near term

Friendly transaction

A takeover attempt that has the support and backing of the target's board of directors

···································· **G** ····································

Going Private Transaction

A transaction which results in a public company becoming a private one, often in the context of an LBO

···································· **H** ····································

Hostile transaction

An unsolicited takeover attempt that is not welcomed and strongly resisted by the target's board of directors

Hurdle Rate

The rate of return needed to induce investors or companies to invest in something

···································· **I** ····································

Identifiable intangible assets

Intangible assets that provide a benefit for an acquiring company and can be assigned a fair value

Intrinsic value

A theoretical value of a company determined by the present value of its future cash flows

IPO

Initial Public Offering. A transaction in which a company sells its shares to the public for the first time; subsequent transactions are called secondary offerings

IPO prospectus

Registration statement to sell shares to the public for the first time

Internal Rate of Return (IRR)

The return on an investment given an initial investment and a series of positive cash inflows in future periods

···································· **L** ····································

Liquidation

The sale of a terminated or bankrupted business' assets. Proceeds of the sale are used to pay creditors. Any leftovers are distributed to shareholders

League Tables
A ranking of lenders and advisors according to the underwriting (both debt and equity) and advisory mandates

Leverage
The use of various financial instruments or borrowed capital, such as margin, to increase the potential return of an investment

Leveraged Buyout (LBO)
Acquisitions led by financial buyers (sponsors) and primarily funded with debt

Leverage Ratio (or coverage ratio)
A measure of a company's ability to meet interest payments, usually expressed in terms of a measure of profitability over interest expense such as EBITDA / Gross Interest Expense

M

Margins
A measure of profitability expressed as a percentage of a given metric divided by revenue; for example: EBITDA margin = EBITDA / Revenue

M&A
An abbreviation for the term Mergers & Acquisitions

MD&A
An abbreviation for a title in a section of the 10-K called Management's Discussion and Analysis

Middle Market Firms
Boutique financial advisory firms which specialize in providing advisory services to clients which are either private, or have a smaller market capitalization then what the bulge bracket banks target

Merger Proxy / S-4
Document used to solicit shareholder votes regarding a proposed takeover. Serves as a registration statement if securities are issued as part of the deal

Multiple Expansion
The sale of a business at a higher multiple than was originally paid for it

N

Net Debt

Total Debt less Cash & Equivalents. Assumes that an acquirer can reduce debt dollar for dollar using the target company's cash on hand

Net identifiable assets

A company's net assets (assets – liabilities) less its existing goodwill

Non-cash item

An item that is recognized as an expense (income) from an accrual accounting standpoint, but does not generate an actual cash outflow (inflow)

Noncontrolling Interest

Outside ownership of a parent's subsidiary that is consolidated for reporting purposes (often called minority interest).

O

Option

A contract giving an investor (usually an employee, manager or insider of the company) a right to buy a fixed amount of shares of stock at a specified price within a limited time period

P

Preferred Stock

A security giving the holder a claim, prior to the claim of common stockholders, on the earnings and assets of a company in the event of its liquidation

Principal

The amount borrowed or the amount still owed on a loan, separate from interest

Pro Forma

Latin for "as a matter of form." Commonly refers to the presentation of a financial statistic or analysis which reflects the effect of a potential change or transaction, such as estimated EPS resulting from a proposed acquisition. In this example, the "pro-forma" EPS is the EPS the company would be expected to generate if the transaction actually occurred

Proprietary Trading

When a firm trades for direct gain instead of commission dollars. Essentially, the firm has decided to profit from the market rather than commissions from processing trades

Proxy statement

Notification of a shareholders' meeting and matters to be voted on at that meeting (filed with the SEC)

························· **R** ·························

(ROIC) Return On Invested Capital

A measure of the efficiency of a company's use of capital; there are more than a few calculations of this metric, but generally it is expressed as After-Tax Operating Profit / Total Capital

Rollover Equity

In certain LBO transactions, the equity stake that sellers retain in the new firm

························· **S** ·························

S-4

See merger proxy

Schedule TO

An SEC filing which announces the launch of a tender offer – an offer to purchase some or all of the target shareholders' shares.

Secured Debt

Debt backed or secured by collateral to reduce the risk associated with lending. Holders of this type of debt have first claim on specified assets in the event of default

Senior debt

Debt which entitles its holders to a priority claim over other debt holders and claimants of the company in the event of a bankruptcy or liquidation. Typically comprised of a revolving credit facility and a series of bank term loans bought by commercial and investment banks as well as institutional investors such as pension funds and insurance companies. Much like a credit card for an individual, a revolving credit facility allows the company to draw down (borrow) on the facility when needed and pay off the balance with any excess cash flow. Like a traditional home mortgage, a bank term loan has scheduled interest and principal payments

SG&A

Stands for Selling, General and Administrative. Usually the second main expense line item on an income statement

Sponsor's equity
The amount of capital a financial buyer invests in a transaction

Steady state
A condition in which a company's cash flows can be "sustained into perpetuity" (stable growth). Generally, the growth of a company in steady state is estimated not to exceed the general economy's growth rate

Strategic Buyer
A potential acquirer, typically with a competing or complementary line of business, which is interested in the long-term investment prospects of a target company

Strike Price
The price at which an option holder can "exercise" their option to buy or sell a security

Subordinated debt
Debt which entitles its holders to a claim on assets which is below the claim of senior debt holders in terms of liquidation preference. Typically bought by hedge funds, high yield funds, merchant banks, and insurance companies. Because of its higher risk, subordinated debt instruments typically carry a higher coupon

Synergies
Increases in cash flow usually achieved by combining the operations of two companies; the largest expected benefits usually result from cost savings realized by reducing overlapping (redundant) expenses

T

Tax Shield
A benefit from a reduction in taxable income achieved by claiming tax-deductible expenses (e.g. interest payments on borrowed capital)

Total potential shares
A conservative estimate used to determine the total value of all equity holders' claims on a company's assets. Calculated as: basic shares outstanding + in-the-money options + shares from in-the-money convertible securities

U

Underwriting

The process by which investment bankers raise investment capital from investors on behalf of corporations and governments that are issuing securities (both equity and debt)

Unlevered Free Cash Flows (UFCF)

Cash flows that are independent of capital structure; that is, cash flows before principal and interest payments to debt holders or dividend payments to equity holders. The word free means that this cash flow has already covered capital expenditures, working capital and investment needs of the business. Therefore, it is available to all capital holders

W

Weighted Average Cost of Capital (WACC)

A discount rate used to calculate the present value of a company's future cash flows. It can be thought of as the required rate of return for both equity and debt investors (assuming there are no other claimants, such as preferred stock holders)

Warrants

Options to purchase equity in a company typically granted to outside investors

Working capital

Current assets minus current liabilities. Measures the amount of liquid assets a company has available to build its business

Write Up

An increase in the book value of an asset which reflects current, fair market value

APPENDIX:
Real World Case Study

In the earlier part of this book, we discussed many of the primary valuation methods most commonly employed by valuation practitioners—from investment bankers and financial analysts to corporate managers and stock market investors. One of the best ways to illustrate and help reinforce the valuation techniques is to walk through a simulation of valuing a company.

The following is a real world valuation exercise involving actual financial disclosure as well as sample financial models that are typically used by professionals.

HERSHEY CASE STUDY PART ONE:

Imagine that you are a financial analyst trying to get a broad sense of Hershey Foods Corporation's valuation and financial performance.

Hershey Foods Corporation is engaged in the manufacture, distribution and sale of consumer food products. Hershey produces and distributes a broad line of chocolate and non-chocolate confectionery and grocery products.

On May 15, 2002, Hershey was trading at $68.40. The company had 139.069 million diluted shares outstanding.

Exercise

What was the Equity Value for Hershey on May 15, 2002?

Hershey Share Price	
x Diluted Shares Outstanding	
= Equity Value	million

Answer:

Hershey Share Price	$68.40
x Diluted Shares Outstanding	139.069
= Equity Value	**$9,512.3** million

Below is the most recent balance sheet prior to the stock price date for Hershey.

HERSHEY FOODS CORPORATION CONSOLIDATED BALANCE SHEETS
March 31, 2002
(in thousands of dollars)

ASSETS	3/31/02
Current Assets:	
Cash and cash equivalents	$220,026
Accounts receivable – trade	292,226
Inventories	559,556
Deferred income taxes	83,198
Prepaid expenses and other	90,670
Total current assets	1,245,676
Property, plant and equipment, at cost	2,896,366
Less-accumulated depreciation and amortization	(1,383,869)
Net property, plant and equipment	1,512,497
Goodwill	388,691
Other intangibles	40,298
Other assets	137,382
Total assets	$3,324,544

LIABILITIES AND STOCKHOLDERS' EQUITY	
Current Liabilities:	
Accounts payable	$162,332
Accrued liabilities	372,495
Accrued income taxes	32,397
Short-term debt	7,045
Current portion of long-term debt	739
Total current liabilities	575,008
Long-term debt	876,979
Other long-term liabilities	347,529
Deferred income taxes	266,112
Total liabilities	2,065,628
Stockholders' Equity:	
Preferred stock, shares issued:	------
Common stock, shares issued: 149,517,064 in 2002	149,516
Class B common stock, shares issued: 30,433,808 in 2002	30,434
Additional paid-in capital	(2,686)
Unearned ESOP compensation	(15,169)
Retained earnings	2,801,878
Treasury-Common Stock shares at cost: 43,525,109 in 2002	(1,656,391)
Accumulated other comprehensive loss	(48,666)
Total stockholders' equity	1,258,916
Total liabilities and stockholders' equity	$3,324,544

Exercise

Please determine Hershey's Enterprise Value? Please input your answers in $ millions.

Equity Value of Hershey	**$9,512.3 million**
+ Short-term Debt	
+ Current portion of Long-term Debt	
+ Long-term Debt	
– Cash and Cash Equivalents	
= Enterprise Value of Hershey	**million**

Answer:

Equity Value of Hershey	**$9,512.3 million**
+ Short-term Debt	7.045
+ Current portion of Long-term Debt	0.739
+ Long-term Debt	876.979
– Cash and Cash Equivalents	(220.026)
= Enterprise Value of Hershey	**$10,177.1 million**

After getting a sense of Hershey's valuation, you are now analyzing Hershey's financials. Below is a partial 2001 income statement for Hershey.

Hershey Income Statement

($ in thousands)

	12/31/01
Sales	$4,557,241
Cost of Sales	2,665,566
Gross Profit	1,891,675
SG&A Expense*	1,254,664
Business Realignment and Asset Impairments	228,314
Gain on Sale of Business	(19,237)
Income before Interest and Income Taxes	**427,934**
Interest Expense, net	69,093
Income before Taxes	**358,841**
Provision for Income Taxes	136,385
Net Income	**$222,456**

*SG&A expense adjusted for $15.3 million of goodwill amortization. Under current accounting standards, goodwill is not amortized.

What is the closest line item to EBIT? Please identify the line item.

Answer: "Income before Interest and Income Taxes" of $427,934.

What are some items on the income statement that appear to be non-recurring? Please circle any relevant line items.

Answer: "Business Realignment and Asset Impairments" of $228,314 and "Gain on Sale of Business" of ($19,237).

In analyzing the annual report you find the following footnote regarding Business Realignment Initiatives (partial footnote shown).

> *Business Realignment Initiatives*
>
> *In late October 2001, the Corporation's Board of Directors approved a plan to improve the efficiency and profitability of the Corporation's operations. The plan included asset management improvements, product line rationalization, supply chain efficiency improvements and a voluntary work force reduction program. The major components of the plan will be completed by the fourth quarter of 2002.*
>
> *During the fourth quarter of 2001, a charge to cost of sales and a business realignment and asset impairment charge were recorded totaling $278.4 million before tax ($171.9 million after tax or $1.25 per share-diluted). The total charges included a charge to cost of sales of $ 50.1 million associated with raw material inventory reductions and a business realignment and asset impairment charge of $228.3 million (collectively, "the business realignment initiatives").*

Notice that there is a $50.1 million charge to cost of sales. If you are trying to normalize cost of sales for the $50.1 million raw material inventory reductions, the question you should ask yourself is "would you addback the item to or subtract the item from reported cost of sales?"

To normalize cost of sales correctly, you would subtract the item from reported cost of sales because the reported cost of sales is over-stated by the $50.1 million charge. An alternative approach would be to simply "add back" the $50.1 million to reported EBIT, since that number is understated by $50.1 million.

Exercise

Given that the normalized depreciation and amortization for the year was $175.194 million (adjusted for goodwill amortization of $15.3 million), please calculate normalized EBIT and EBITDA.

Reported EBIT	**$427.934** million
+ Raw Material Inventory Reductions	
+ Business Realignment and Asset Impairments	
– Gain on Sale of Business	
= Normalized EBIT	million
+ Normalized Depreciation & Amortization	175.194
Normalized EBITDA	million

Answer:

Reported EBIT	**$427.934** million
+ Raw Material Inventory Reductions	50.100
+ Business Realignment and Asset Impairments	228.314
– Gain on Sale of Business	(19.237)
= Normalized EBIT	**$687.111** million
+ Normalized Depreciation & Amortization	175.194
Normalized EBITDA	**$862.305** million

HERSHEY CASE STUDY PART TWO:

In the last section, we examined the equity value, enterprise value and a normalized income statement. Now, the analysis of Hershey can go deeper through the calculation of multiples.

Recall that on May 15, 2002, Hershey was trading at $68.40. With the Treasury Stock Method, you will now be able to derive Hershey's fully diluted shares from the basic share count.

From Hershey's 2001 annual report's footnotes, you find the following information about options:

	2001	
	Shares	**Weighted - Average Exercise Price**
Outstanding at end of year	**8,006,561**	**$46.39**

Are these options in-the-money? How do you know?

Answer: Yes, these options are in-the-money. The reason is that the weighted average exercise price of $46.39 is LESS than the stock price of $68.40.

What is assumed that a rational option holder do with an option with a strike of $46.39?

Answer: In a hypothetical sense, the Treasury Stock Method would assume that a rational option holder would exercise the option by paying the strike price, receiving the share and selling it in the open market.

The next set of questions assumes that you are using the Treasury Stock Method.

Exercise

What are the option proceeds to Hershey? Note: please use the exact number of options when calculating.

Exercise Price	
x Options Outstanding	
= Option Proceeds	**million**

Answer:

Exercise Price	$46.39
x Options Outstanding	8.006561
= Option Proceeds	**$371.4** million

How many shares are repurchased?

Option Proceeds	million
/ Current Stock Price	
= Shares Repurchased	**million**

Answer:

Option Proceeds	$371.4 million
/ Current Stock Price	$68.40
= Shares Repurchased	**5.430181** million

Assuming that Hershey has 136.492939 million basic shares outstanding, what is the diluted share count?

Basic Shares	136.492939	million
+ Options In-the-money		
– Shares Repurchased under TSM		
= Diluted Shares Outstanding		**million**

Answer:

Basic Shares	136.492939	million
+ Options In-the-money	8.006561	
– Shares Repurchased under TSM	(5.430181)	
= Diluted Shares Outstanding	**139.069319**	million

Given the stock price of $68.40, what is the equity value for Hershey?

Diluted Shares Outstanding		million
x Current Stock Price	$68.40	
= Equity Value		**million**

Answer:

Diluted Shares Outstanding	139.069319	million
x Current Stock Price	$68.40	
= Equity Value	**$9,512.3**	**million**

From this moment on, use the rounded number of $9,512.3 million as the equity value.

Remember from the prior analysis of Hershey, the enterprise value was derived from the equity value.

Equity Value of Hershey	$9,512.3	**million**
+ Short-term Debt	7.0	
+ Current portion of Long-term Debt	0.7	
+ Long-term Debt	877.0	
– Cash and Cash Equivalents	(220.0)	
= Enterprise Value of Hershey	**$10,177.1**	**million**

The next step in getting to a multiple of equity value and enterprise value is to calculate the latest twelve months (LTM) for the income statement information.

Exercise

The following is an income statement for the 2001 fiscal year and the 1st quarter ending March 31, 2002 and the 1st quarter ending April 1, 2001. Please note that the income statement is normalized and adjustments have been made that may influence the rounding of values.

INCOME STATEMENT ($ in millions)	Yr. Ended 12/31/01	1 Quarter Ended		LTM	
		3/31/02	4/1/01		
Total revenues, net	$4,557.2	$988.5	$988.0	[_____]	million
Cost of goods sold (before D&A)	2,425.0	578.2	591.1		
Gross profit	2,132.2	410.3	396.9		
SG&A expense	1,270.0	202.7	205.9		
EBITDA	862.2	207.6	191.0	[_____]	
Depreciation & amortization	175.2	45.6	43.6		
EBIT	687.0	162.0	147.4	[_____]	
Interest expense	71.5	16.2	18.3		
Interest (income)	(2.4)	(0.8)	(1.0)		
Other non-operating items	0.0	0.0	0.0		
Pre-tax income	617.9	146.6	130.1		
Reported taxes	136.4	50.5	48.0		
Tax adjustments for non-recurring items	88.4	3.3	0.0		
Net income	$393.1	$92.8	$82.1	[_____]	million

Answer:

INCOME STATEMENT ($ in millions)	Yr. Ended 12/31/01	1 Quarter Ended		LTM	
		3/31/02	4/1/01		
Total revenues, net	$4,557.2	$988.5	$988.0	$4,557.7	million
Cost of goods sold (before D&A)	2,425.0	578.2	591.1		
Gross profit	2,132.2	410.3	396.9		
SG&A expense	1,270.0	202.7	205.9		
EBITDA	862.2	207.6	191.0	878.8	
Depreciation & amortization	175.2	45.6	43.6		
EBIT	687.0	162.0	147.4	701.6	
Interest expense	71.5	16.2	18.3		
Interest (income)	(2.4)	(0.8)	(1.0)		
Other non-operating items	0.0	0.0	0.0		
Pre-tax income	617.9	146.6	130.1		
Reported taxes	136.4	50.5	48.0		
Tax adjustments for non-recurring items	88.4	3.3	0.0		
Net income	$393.1	$92.8	$82.1	$403.8	million

Exercise

With the LTM information calculated for the relevant statistics, the next part is to calculate equity value and enterprise value multiples. *Use the rounded equity value of $9,512.3 million and enterprise value of $10,177.1 million.*

Equity Value	$9,512.3
Enterprise Value	$10,177.1

	LTM	Multiples
EBITDA		
Net Income		

Answer:

Equity Value	$9,512.3
Enterprise Value	$10,177.1

	LTM	Multiples
EBITDA	$878.8	11.6x
Net Income	$403.8	23.6x

The following is the public comparables analysis for Hershey:

Public Comparables Analysis of Selected Food and Beverage Companies

($ in millions, except for share data)

Company	Stock Price as of 5/12/02	Market Value of Equity	Enterprise Value (a)	Enterprise Value as a Multiple of: LTM EBITDA	LTM EBITDA Margin	Total Debt/ EBITDA	Proj. 5 Yr EPS Gr. Rate
Cadbury Schweppes plc (b)	$30.55	$15,841	$18,635	11.9x	19.8%	1.9x	8.5%
Campbell Soup Co.	27.67	11,370	15,148	11.3	19.5%	2.8	7.7%
Kraft Foods Inc.	41.21	71,711	87,531	13.0	19.8%	2.4	14.0%
Tootsie Roll Industries, Inc.	47.05	2,431	2,298	20.4	26.4%	0.1	NA
Wm. Wrigley Jr. Company	56.60	12,815	12,504	21.0	24.0%	0.0	11.2%
High				21.0x	26.4%	2.8x	14.0%
Average				15.5	21.9%	1.4	10.4%
Median				13.0	19.8%	1.9	9.9%
Low				11.3	19.5%	0.0	7.7%
Hershey Foods Corp.	$68.40	$9,512	$10,177	11.6x	19.3%	1.0x	10.0%

(a) Calculated as Market Value of Equity plus total debt, noncontrolling interest and preferred stock, less cash & equivalents.
(b) Converted to US $ from British £ at an exchange rate of 1.44 US $ per British £

What factor is primarily driving Tootsie Roll and Wrigley's high multiple?

- Size
- Risk
- Growth

Answer: Risk – both of these companies have higher EBITDA margins than their competitors, and are virtually debt free.

Do you think that Tootsie Roll and Wrigley deserve to be trading at a premium?

Answer: There is nothing notable about their size (market value), but they have higher margins compared to their peers (low operational risk) and very little/no debt (low credit risk). But, the magnitude of this difference is subjective. One can argue that they may be slightly overvalued.

At 11.6x Enterprise Value/LTM EBITDA, is Hershey fairly valued? Yes or no?

Answer: Yes. They do not deserve Tootsie Roll or Wrigley's multiples because Hershey does not have similar margins/leverage as those companies. One can also argue that Hershey also does not deserve Kraft's multiple because Kraft's larger size and higher expected growth. Hershey trades in line with Cadbury and Campbell, which both possess similar margins.

Given the public comparables analysis, what is a reasonable multiple range to expect for Hershey (e.g., 7.0x to 9.0x)? Feel free to round the range. Note, you do not need to use all of the comparables…some are trading at a premium or discount to Hershey for a reason.

Answer: Given that Hershey is fairly valued, you can imply a range close to where they are currently trading. Somewhere around 11.0x to 12.5x would be reasonable (rounding down from Campbell to 11.0x and just 0.5x less than Kraft recognizing a potential size advantage for Kraft). What is the appropriate/justifiable range? This is the ART portion of valuation, which is subjective in nature.

HERSHEY CASE STUDY PART THREE:

We have done most of preliminary valuation. Now, we will discuss merger analysis.

Let's assume that on May 16, 2002, Wrigley makes an $89.00 per share bid for Hershey.

Here are the relevant facts you will need for the following exercises:

Offer Price	$89.00
Current Share Price	$68.40
Options Outstanding	8.007
Average Exercise Price	$46.39
Basic Shares	136.493
Net Debt	$664.7

Exercise

What is the implied premium?

Offer Price	
− Current Share Price	
= **$ Premium**	
/ Current Share Price	
= **% Premium**	

Answer:

Offer Price	$89.00
− Current Share Price	$68.40
= **$ Premium**	**$20.60**
/ Current Share Price	$68.40
= **% Premium**	**30.1%**

Exercise

What is the Offer Value at $89.00 per share?

Basic Shares		
+ Options In The Money		(see above)
= **Total Shares Outstanding**		**million**
Exercise Price		
x Options Outstanding		
= **Option Proceeds**		**million**
Total Shares Outstanding		**million**
x Offer Price		
		million
− Option Proceeds		
= **Offer Value**		**million**

Answer:

Basic Shares	136.493
+ Options In The Money	8.007
= Total Shares Outstanding	**144.500** million

Exercise Price	$46.39
x Options Outstanding	8.007
= Option Proceeds	**$371.4** million

Total Shares Outstanding	**144.500** million
x Offer Price	$89.00
	$12,860.5 million
– Option Proceeds	(371.4)
= Offer Value	**$12,489.1** million

Exercise:

What is the implied Transaction Value at $89.00 per share?

Offer Value	$12,489.1 **million**
+ Net Debt	(see p.13 for Net Debt)
= Transaction Value	**million**

Answer:

Offer Value	$12,489.1 **million**
+ Net Debt	664.7
= Transaction Value	**$13,153.8** million

In Part 2 of the case study, we calculated Hershey's normalized LTM Revenues, EBITDA, EBIT and Net Income. See p. 10 & 11 for LTM calculations.

Exercise

What are the implied LTM EBITDA and net income multiples?

Offer Value	**$12,489.1**
Transaction Value	**$13,153.8**

	LTM	Multiples
EBITDA		
Net Income		

Answer:

Offer Value	**$12,489.1**
Transaction Value	**$13,153.8**

	LTM	Multiples
EBITDA	$878.8	15.0x
Net Income	$403.8	30.9x

Exercise

A research analyst expects a 14.0x EBITDA multiple based on similar transactions. What is the implied offer value and net income multiple? Please assume the following:

EBITDA multiple	14.0x	
Net Debt	$664.7	million
LTM EBITDA	$878.8	million
LTM Net Income	$403.8	million

EBITDA multiple		
x LTM EBITDA		million
= Implied Transaction Value		million
– Net Debt		million
= Implied Offer Value		**million**
/ LTM Net Income		million
= Implied Net Income Multiple		

Answer:

EBITDA multiple	14.0x	
x LTM EBITDA	$878.8	million
= Implied Transaction Value	$12,303.2	million
– Net Debt	(664.7)	million
= Implied Offer Value	**11,638.5**	**million**
/ LTM Net Income	403.8	million
= Implied Net Income Multiple	**28.8x**	

The following is a deal list of food and beverage transactions:

Selected Food and Beverage Transactions

($ in millions, except for share data)

Target/Acquirer	Date Announced	Offer Value of Equity	Transaction Value (a)	LTM EBITDA	PRE-SYNERGIES: Transaction Value/ LTM Sales	LTM EBITDA Margin	Announced Synergies	Synergies as % of Target Sales	POST-SYNERGIES: TV/ Adjusted EBITDA
Ralston Purina Co. / Nestle S.A.	1/16/01	$10,101	$10,310	15.7x	3.73x	23.8%	$260	9.4%	11.2x
Quaker Oats Co. / PepsiCo.	11/02/00	13,542	14,066	15.6	2.82	18.0%	400	8.0%	10.8
Keebler Foods Co. / Kellogg Co.	10/26/00	3,853	4,553	11.3	1.67	14.8%	170	6.2%	7.9
Pillsbury / General Mills	7/17/00	5,358	10,500	11.1	1.73	15.6%	400	6.6%	7.8
Nabisco Holdings Corp. / Phillip Morris	6/25/00	14,934	18,934	13.6	2.23	16.4%	600	7.1%	9.5
Bestfoods / Unilever PLC	6/06/00	20,895	23,535	14.6	2.72	18.6%	750	8.7%	10.0
	High			15.7x	3.73x	23.8%		9.4%	11.2x
	Average			13.9	2.41	17.2%		7.7%	9.5
	Median			14.6	2.23	16.4%		7.5%	9.7
	Low			11.1	1.67	13.0%		6.2%	7.8

(a) Calculated as Market Value of Equity plus total debt, noncontrolling interest and preferred stock, less cash & equivalents.

Why do you think Keebler's EBITDA multiple is on the low end of the range?

A) Lower EBITDA margins and higher relative synergy potential
B) Lower EBITDA margins and lower relative synergy potential
C) Higher EBITDA margins and higher relative synergy potential
D) Higher EBITDA margins and lower relative synergy potential

Answer: **B** – Lower EBITDA margins and lower relative synergy potential

Why do you think the Quaker Oats EBITDA multiple exceeded the Bestfoods multiple?

A) Size
B) Risk (operating efficiency)
C) Synergy potential
D) Other deal factors not shown above (growth, deal dynamics)

Answer: **D** – By process of elimination, other deal factors. Quaker Oats is a smaller company than Bestfoods, has lower EBITDA margins and a lower relative synergy potential. But, Quaker Oats owned Gatorade, the dominant sports beverage drink (over 80% market share in North America in 2000) with expected growth rates in the 7-10% range. Additionally, Coca-Cola was another bidder for Quaker Oats, making the strategic imperative higher for Pepsi to keep a prized asset out of the competition's hands. The growth potential and competitive deal dynamics were important to fuel this higher multiple, emphasizing again how important it is to know the transaction!

What is a reasonable EBITDA multiple range to expect for Hershey (e.g., 7.0x to 9.0x)? Feel free to round the range. Note, you do not need to use all of the deals... some were done at a premium or discount for a reason.

Recall as of May 15, 2002, Hershey's information:

- ◆ Market Value = $9,512.3 million
- ◆ Enterprise Value = $10,177.1 million
- ◆ LTM EBITDA = $878.8 million
- ◆ LTM EBITDA margin =19.3%

Answer: Probably somewhere in the 12.5x/13.0x to 14.5x EBITDA range. Hershey is trading at 11.6x EBITDA, so the Keebler and Pillsbury multiples are too low. Even a small premium would probably make the low end of the expected range 12.5x to 13.0x. At the high end, Ralston Purina is probably not a good data point given the stronger margins relative to Hershey. Quaker Oats growth prospects also probably make their 15.6x too high for Hershey. The Nabisco (13.6x) and Bestfoods (14.6x) transactions also point to 14.0x–14.5x EBITDA.

HERSHEY CASE STUDY PART FOUR:

Imagine that you are a financial analyst trying to value Hershey Foods Corporation using a discounted cash flow analysis.

On May 15, 2002, Hershey was trading at $68.40.

Assumptions:

Risk Free Rate	5.1%	
Market Risk Premium	7.4%	
Marginal Tax Rate	38.0%	
Cost of Debt	7.3%	
Levered Beta	0.44	
		% of total
Market Value of Debt	$884.8	8.5%
Market Value of Equity	9,512.3	91.5%
Total Capitalization	$10,397.1	100%

Exercise

Please calculate the Cost of Equity utilizing the CAPM formula.

Risk Free Rate	
+ Beta x Market Risk Premium	
= Cost of Equity	

Answer:

Risk Free Rate	5.1%
+ Beta x Market Risk Premium	3.3%
= Cost of Equity	**8.4%**

Exercise

Next, calculate the WACC for Hershey. Remember to use the after-tax cost of debt.

	Cost	Weighting		Weighted Avg. Cost
Equity		x	=	
Debt		x	=	
			WACC:	

Answer:

	Cost		Weighting			Weighted Avg. Cost
Equity	8.4%	x	91.5%	=		7.6%
Debt	4.5%	x	8.5%	=		0.4%
					WACC:	8.0%

Assume the following unlevered free cash flow model for Hershey:

	Projected FYE December 31				
	2002	2003	2004	2005	2006
Sales	$4,739.5	$4,929.1	$5,126.3	$5,331.3	$5,544.6
EBITDA	900.5	951.0	1,004.0	1,059.8	1,118.5
Less: Depreciation & Amortization	(180.0)	(185.0)	(190.0)	(195.0)	(200.0)
EBIT	720.0	766.0	814.0	864.8	918.0
Less: Taxes @ 38.0%	(273.8)	(291.1)	(309.3)	(328.6)	(349.0)
Tax-Effected EBIT	446.7	474.9	504.7	536.2	569.5
Plus: Depreciation & Amortization	180.0	185.0	190.0	195.0	200.0
Less: Capital Expenditures & Software Additions	(200.0)	(200.0)	(200.0)	(200.0)	(200.0)
Less: Changes in Working Capital	(15.0)	(15.0)	(15.0)	(15.0)	(15.0)
Unlevered Free Cash Flow	**$411.7**	**$444.9**	**$479.7**	**$516.2**	**$554.5**

Exercise

Assuming an 8.0% WACC, please calculate the present value of the unlevered free cash flows.

Answer:

Present Value of Unlevered Free Cash Flow
= $411.7 / (1+0.08)^1 + $444.9 / (1+0.08)^2 + ... $554.5 / (1+0.08)^5
= $1,900.2 million

Exercise

Assuming an 11.0x EBITDA exit multiple, calculate the present value of the terminal value.

WACC:	8.0%
Multiple:	11.0x
Year 5 EBITDA	_____ million
Year 5 Terminal Value	_____ million
/ 5 years discount factor	1.469 = (1+8.0%)^5
Present Value of Terminal Value	_____ million

Answer:

Discount rate:	8.0%
Multiple:	11.0x

Year 5 EBITDA	$1,118.5 million
Year 5 Terminal Value	$12,303.5 million
/ 5 years discount factor	1.469 = (1 + 8.0%)^5
Present Value of Terminal Value	**$8,373.6** million

Exercise

Assuming net debt of $664.7 million and 139.069 million diluted shares, please calculate enterprise value, equity value and equity value per share.

Present Value of the Cash Flows		million
+ Present Value of Terminal Value		
Enterprise Value		**million**

Enterprise Value		million
– Net Debt		
Equity Value		**million**

Equity Value		million
/ Diluted Shares Outstanding		
Equity Value Per Share		

Answer:

Present Value of the Cash Flows	$1,900.2	million
+ Present Value of Terminal Value	8,373.6	
Enterprise Value	**$10,273.8**	**million**

Enterprise Value	$10,273.8	million
– Net Debt	(664.7)	
Equity Value	**$9,609.1**	**million**

Equity Value	9,609.1	million
/ Diluted Shares Outstanding	139.069	
Equity Value Per Share	**$69.10**	

As of May 15, 2002, Hershey was trading at $68.40, so the resulting DCF value you get should be very close to the stock price (see Excel for solution). The DCF value per share is typically expressed as a range of values. For training purposes, let's simplify and say that the value is between $65.00 and $74.00, depending on assumptions and other factors. (An 8.5% WACC and 10.5x EBITDA exit multiple yields $64.86; a 7.5% WACC and 11.5x exit yields $73.50. Test yourself and recreate those answers!)

From earlier parts, we have already performed the public comparables analysis and the acquisition comparables analysis. Recall that from the public comparables, we valued Hershey at approximately 11.0x to 12.5x LTM EBITDA. From our acquisition comparables, let's assume that the valuation range is between 12.0x to 15.0x LTM EBITDA.

Exercise

Assuming net debt of $664.7 million, LTM EBITDA of $878.8 million and 139.069 million diluted shares, please calculate the equity value per share for the ranges of the public and acquisition comparables analysis.

Public Comparables	MIN	MAX
Multiples	11.0x	12.5x
x LTM EBITDA		
= Implied Enterprise Value		
– Net Debt		
= Implied Equity Value		
/ Diluted Shares Outstanding		
= Implied Equity Value Per Share		

Acquisition Comparables	MIN	MAX
Multiples	12.0x	15.0x
x LTM EBITDA		
= Implied Transaction Value		
– Net Debt		
= Implied Offer Value		
/ Diluted Shares Outstanding		
= Implied Offer Value Per Share		

Note: All dollar amounts and shares are in millions, except for per share values. Also assume share count remains the same for public and acquisition comparables. This is for illustrative purposes only.

Answer:

Public Comparables	MIN	MAX
Multiples	11.0x	12.5x
x LTM EBITDA	$878.8	$878.8
= Implied Enterprise Value	$9,666.8	$10,985.0
– Net Debt	(664.7)	(664.7)
= Implied Equity Value	$9,002.1	$10,320.3
/ Diluted Shares Outstanding	139.069	139.069
= Implied Equity Value per Share	$64.73	$74.21

Acquisition Comparables	MIN	MAX
Multiples	12.0x	15.0x
x LTM EBITDA	$878.8	$878.8
= Implied Transaction Value	$10,545.6	$13,182.0
– Net Debt	(664.7)	(664.7)
= Implied Offer Value	$9,880.9	$12,517.3
/ Diluted Shares Outstanding	139.069	139.069
= **Implied Offer Value per Share**	**$71.05**	**$90.01**

Exercise

Examine the following graph to see how we mapped out the equity value per share under a DCF, public comparables and acquisition comparables analyses.

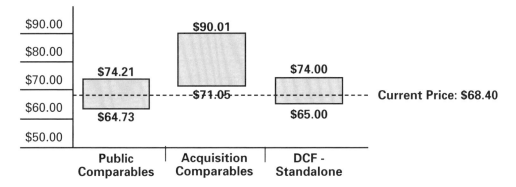

Given that Hershey is trading at $68.40, what conclusions can you make about the standalone valuation?

Answer: The DCF analysis and the public comparables analysis broadly overlap, which either means the public comparables are fairly valued or the DCF is using somewhat reasonable assumptions given current market conditions. The current stock price is comfortably within both the public comparables and DCF analyses ranges, indicating the stock is probably fairly valued.

Due to a necessary control premium and expected synergies from combining with another food company, an acquisition of Hershey would probably be in the high $70's or even well over $80.00 per share. We would need to evaluate what a potential buyer could afford to pay—the focus of the "Merger Consequences" chapter.

HERSHEY CASE STUDY PART FIVE:

In this section, we are going to go deeper into the merger analysis. Here is a little background information.

Wm. Wrigley Jr. Corp. (Wrigley) is a manufacturer of confectionery goods such as gum and mints. Imagine that you are representing Wrigley as their financial advisor, and they have requested that you analyze a potential acquisition of Hershey Foods. Hypothetically, Wrigley is considering making a move to become a major player in the manufacturing of chocolate and feel that this would complement their product offering in the confectionery goods industry.

After evaluating the situation (and analyzing the acquisition comparables and performing a discounted cash flow analysis), you have recommended that they make a bid of $89.00. Wrigley is trading at a premium compared to its peers on the basis of its price to earnings per share multiple. Therefore, the value of the stock as acquisition currency could potentially be high. Your preliminary analysis begins with a **70% stock / 30% cash** bid. At $89.00, what is the pro forma impact on EPS and leverage ratio?

Exercise

Assume the following:

Acquirer: Wrigley*	
Current Share Price	$56.60
Total Assets	$1,837.4
Total Liabilities	$533.1
Existing Goodwill	$0.0
Net Income	$398.3
Diluted Shares Outstanding	225.000
EPS	$1.77
EBITDA	$635.0
Existing Total Debt	$0.0
Tax Rate	31.1%
Interest on New Debt	6.5%

Target: Hershey*	
Current Share Price	$68.40
Total Assets	$3,324.5
Total Liabilities	$2,065.6
Existing Goodwill	$429.0
Net Income	$423.1
Diluted Shares Outstanding	139.069
EPS	$3.04
EBITDA	$915.4
Existing Total Debt	$884.9
Offer Price (per Share)	$89.00

* Dollars and shares in millions, except per share data.

The first step is to figure how much the offer value is. How much is Wrigley paying in aggregate for the equity of Hershey?

Diluted Shares Outstanding*
x Offer Price
= **Offer Value**

Answer:

Diluted Shares Outstanding	139.069
x Offer Price	$89.00
= Offer Value	**$12,377.1**

Exercise

Assuming no write-ups of Hershey's net assets, how much goodwill would be created?

Assets		Offer Value	
– Existing Goodwill		– Net Identifiable Assets	
– Liabilities		**=Goodwill**	
= Net Identifiable Assets			

Answer:

Assets	$3,324.5	Offer Value	$12,377.1
– Existing Goodwill	(429.0)	– Net Identifiable Assets	(829.9)
– Liabilities	(2,065.6)	**=Goodwill**	**$11,547.2**
= Net Identifiable Assets	**$829.9**		

Since it is a partial stock deal, the exchange ratio is important. Wrigley wants to know how many shares it will be issuing on a per share basis. Or, in other words, Wrigley wants to know how much value is being paid relative to its own stock value.

What is the exchange ratio?

Offer Price		
/ Acquirer Price		
= Exchange Ratio		at 100.0%
= Exchange Ratio		at 70.0%

Answer:

Offer Price	$89.00	
/ Acquirer Price	$56.60	
= Exchange Ratio	1.572	at 100.0%
= Exchange Ratio	1.101	at 70.0%

That means for every share of Hershey owned Wrigley will be issuing 1.101 shares of their own stock. Notice that the exchange ratio factors the % stock consideration in the transaction.

Exercise

Now that you know how many shares of the acquirer are issued per target share, please calculate the aggregate number of shares issued to Hershey.

Exchange Ratio	
x Target Shares Outstanding	
= New Shares Issued	

Answer:

Exchange Ratio	1.101	actual
x Target Shares Outstanding	139.069	
= New Shares Issued	**153.074**	

*Please note, the solution is using the actual exchange ratio instead of a rounded value. Therefore, you may be slightly off

Exercise

What would be the implied pro forma ownership?

Wrigley Shares		
+ New Shares Issued		
= Pro Forma Shares Outstanding		

Answer:

	actual	
Wrigley Shares	225.000	59.5%
+ New Shares Issued	153.074	40.5%
= Pro Forma Shares Outstanding	**378.074**	**100.0%**

Hershey shareholders would own 40.5% of the combined equity under the proposed structure.

Exercise

Let's turn our attention to leverage. How much debt is being raised? Assume that all cash paid in the transaction is 100% debt financed.

Offer Value	
x Percentage of Debt Issued	
= New Debt Issued	

Answer:

Offer Value	$12,377.1
x Percentage of Debt Issued	30.0%
= New Debt Issued	**$3,713.1**

Relative to the amount of debt Wrigley had before this transaction, is this a material amount?

Answer: Absolutely! Wrigley had no debt before this transaction. This transaction would add approximately $3.7 billion of new debt, in addition to Hershey's existing debt.

Exercise

The $3.7 billion represents the amount of new debt on the balance sheet. What is the impact of the debt on net income? In other words, what is the after-tax interest expense?

New Debt Issued	
x Interest on New Debt	
x (1 –Tax Rate)	
= After-tax Interest Expense	

Answer:

New Debt Issued	$3,713.1
x Interest on New Debt	6.5%
x (1 –Tax Rate)	68.9%
= After-tax Interest Expense	**$166.3**

Exercise

Given the level of interest expense that they will have to pay and the new shares issued, Wrigley has noted concern about the accretion/dilution levels of the transaction. In order to analyze accretion/dilution, please calculate the pro forma EPS before any synergies.

Answer:

Acquirer Net Income + Target Net Income +/– Adjustments
= Pro Forma Net Income
$398.3 million + $423.1 million + ($166.3) million = $655.1 million

Acquirer Shares Outstanding + New Shares Issued
= Pro Forma Shares Outstanding
225.000 million + 153.074 million = 378.074 million

Pro Forma Net Income/Pro Forma Shares Outstanding
= Pro Forma EPS
$655.1 / 378.074 = $1.73

The only *"adjustment"* here would be the after-tax interest expense.

Exercise

Is this deal accretive or dilutive? Please indicate accretion/dilution per share and percentage.

Pro forma EPS	
– Acquirer's Standalone EPS	
= Accretion / (Dilution) per share	

Accretion / (Dilution) per share	
/ Acquirer's Standalone EPS	
= Accretion / (Dilution) Percentage	

Answer:

Pro forma EPS	$1.73
– Acquirer's Standalone EPS	($1.77)
= Accretion / (Dilution) per share	**($0.04)**

Accretion / (Dilution) per share	$0.04
/ Acquirer's Standalone EPS	$1.77
= Accretion / (Dilution) Percentage	**(2.3%)**

Exercise

Given that this deal is dilutive, what are the pre-tax synergies to breakeven? Use the rounded dilution of $0.04 from the previous calculation.

Accretion / (Dilution) per Share	
x Pro Forma Shares Outstanding	
= After-tax Synergies Needed	
/ (1–tax rate)	
= Pre-tax Synergies Needed	

Answer:

Accretion / (Dilution) per Share	$0.04
x Pro Forma Shares Outstanding	378.074
= After-tax Synergies Needed	$15.1
/ (1–tax rate)	68.9%
= Pre-tax Synergies Needed	$21.9

So, if Wrigley believes it can generate at least $21.9 million in pre-tax synergies in any Hershey acquisition, it will be at a breakeven point (pro forma EPS versus standalone Wrigley EPS).

Exercise

But affordability is not just based on accretion / dilution on the income statement. Affordability is also driven by balance sheet constraints. Specifically, Wrigley had indicated that they are focused on their pro-forma debt / pro forma EBITDA credit statistic. They would like to maintain a multiple of 3.0x Debt/EBITDA or less. What is their pro forma debt / pro forma EBITDA ratio if Wrigley assumes all of Hershey's existing debt and before any synergies?

Wrigley's Existing Debt			Wrigley's EBITDA	
+ Hershey's Existing Debt			+ Hershey's EBITDA	
+ New Debt Issued in Transaction			= **Pro Forma EBITDA**	
= **Pro Forma debt**				

$$\frac{\text{Pro Forma Debt}}{\text{Pro Forma EBITDA}} = ?$$

Answer:

Wrigley's Existing Debt	$0.0		Wrigley's EBITDA	$635.0
+ Hershey's Existing Debt	884.9		+ Hershey's EBITDA	915.4
+ New Debt Issued in Transaction	3,713.1		= **Pro Forma EBITDA**	$1,550.4
= **Pro Forma debt**	$4,598.0			

$$\frac{\text{Pro Forma Debt}}{\text{Pro Forma EBITDA}} = 3.0x$$

What conclusions can you make about this proposed transaction? Can they afford to pay $89.00 per share with a 70% stock / 30% cash mix?

It seems like they can. Before synergies, the deal is slightly dilutive, but $21.9 million in synergies is only 0.5% of Hershey's sales; based on precedent transactions, synergies in the range of 5-8% (see p. 15) of target's sales is probably attainable. In terms of leverage, the pro forma Debt / EBITDA is right at 3.0x. A 30% cash mix would be the maximum amount of cash consideration that Wrigley could offer, assuming an offer price of $89.00 per share.

HERSHEY CASE STUDY PART SIX:

Imagine that you are trying to evaluate whether or not an LBO transaction of Hershey Foods is feasible.

On May 15, 2002, Hershey was trading at $68.40. As a simplification, we are going to assume that the LBO transaction will be analyzed using the financial data as of the end of 2001.

From this basic knowledge only, would Hershey seem like a good LBO candidate?

Answer: From the earlier discussion, a good LBO candidate is a company that has stable cash flows, operates in a mature industry and does not require huge research and development costs (like a biotech firm).

Hershey seems to fit that profile. The confectionery and food products industry is very mature. Given the type of industry Hershey operates in, there seems to be a steady cash flow stream. Seems like a good candidate, right? But, another key criteria for an LBO candidate is that it is undervalued.

Recall from our earlier analysis (p. 11) that Hershey was trading at 11.6x LTM EBITDA. Is that too expensive for a financial sponsor?

We are going to investigate and address the following two questions:

1) Can an LBO be done for HSY at the current stock price?
2) If not, what would be the feasible price?

Let's first check the feasibility at the current share price.

Exercise

Assume the following for Hershey and the LBO transaction:

1) 2001 EBITDA of $847.0 million
2) Existing debt of $884.9 million
3) 139.069 million diluted shares outstanding

What is the total enterprise value?

Refinancing of Debt	
+ Purchase of Equity	
= Implied Total Enterprise Value	

Answer:

Refinancing of Debt	$884.9
+ Purchase of Equity	9,512.3
= Implied Total Enterprise Value	**$10,397.2**

Exercise

Assuming that the lenders (both senior and subordinated) are willing to lend up to 5.0x total debt to EBITDA, what is the maximum amount of debt that the financial buyer can raise?

Maximum Leverage Multiple	
x 2001 EBITDA	
= Total Debt Capacity	

Answer:

Maximum Leverage Multiple	5.0x
x 2001 EBITDA	$847.0
= Total Debt Capacity	**$4,235.0**

How much would that represent as a % of the total enterprise value?

Total Debt Capacity	
/ Total Enterprise Value	
= % Debt Contribution	

Answer:

Total Debt Capacity	$4,235.0
/ Total Enterprise Value	$10,397.2
= % Debt Contribution	**40.7%**

Exercise

Assuming the remaining amount would be financed with financial buyer's equity contribution, what is the dollar amount of that equity investment? How much of the total enterprise value does that represent?

Total Enterprise Value		% Equity Contribution	
– Total Debt Capacity			
= Total Equity Contribution			

Answer:

Total Enterprise Value	$10,397.2	% Equity Contribution	59.3%
– Total Debt Capacity	4,235.0		
= Total Equity Contribution	**$6,162.2**		

Assume that the financial buyer only wants to make a 30% equity contribution, will this deal structure work? How do the other two parties feel about the transaction structure?

Answer: This would nearly double the financial buyer's maximum equity contribution! Clearly, the financial sponsor would not be happy with this.

In terms of the selling party, Hershey is a publicly traded company. A buyout at the current stock price of $68.40 would represent a 0% premium. It is highly unlikely that Hershey shareholders would accept this as a fair price.

The amount of money the lenders also provide a limitation in this structure. A maximum leverage of 5.0x debt / EBITDA limits the purchase price. Presumably they would not be willing to lend more due to the perceived risk of such a highly levered capital structure.

In conclusion, with a maximum leverage of 5.0x total debt to EBITDA, an LBO does not work at $68.40.

Let us work backwards and figure out at what price an LBO transaction could happen for Hershey. The best place to start is with the funding of the transaction. Afterwards, we will examine the IRR.

Recall that the maximum amount of debt in this transaction is:

Total Debt Capacity = 5.0 x $847.0 million
                    = $4,235.0 million

Exercise

Working backwards from the equity contribution percentage of 30%, what is the enterprise value? Equity contribution? Enterprise Value / EBITDA buyout multiple from this structure?

Total Debt Capacity	
/ (1 –Equity Contribution %)	
= Maximum Purchase Price	
Maximum Purchase Price	
– Total Debt Capacity	
= Total Equity Contribution	
Maximum Purchase Price	
/ LTM EBITDA	
= Implied Buyout Multiple	

Answer:

Total Debt Capacity	$4,235.0
/ (1 –Equity Contribution %)	70.0%
= Maximum Purchase Price	$6,050.0
Maximum Purchase Price	$6,050.0
– Total Debt Capacity	4,235.0
= Total Equity Contribution	$1,815.0
Maximum Purchase Price	$6,050.0
/ LTM EBITDA	847.0
= Implied Buyout Multiple	**7.143x**

Exercise

Let's calculate the financial buyer's IRR.

Typically, you would need to forecast the cash flows and debt repayments in the future periods. In our model, we have forecasted that EBITDA in projected year 5 is $1,118.5 million and that net debt is $2,400.0 million. Assuming a no multiple expansion situation, what is the IRR to the financial buyer?

Total Equity Contribution		or "Initial Investment"
Future Residual Equity Value		= (Projected EBITDA * Exit Multiple) – Net Debt
Number of Periods	5.0	

= Implied Investment IRR

Answer:

Total Equity Contribution	$1,815.0	or "Initial Investment"
Future Residual Equity Value	$5,589.3	= ($1,118.5 * 7.143x) – $2,400.0
Number of Periods	5.0	

= Implied Investment IRR **25.2%**

$$IRR = \left[\frac{\$5,589.3}{\$1,815.0} \right]^{(1/5)} - 1 = 25.2\%$$

Leverage is reasonable at 5.0x total debt / EBITDA. The IRR is good. But remember that an LBO transaction only happens when all three parties are satisfied.

The selling shareholders would definitely NOT be happy with a below market price offer price.

Exercise

Assuming:
1) Refinancing of existing debt $884.9 million
2) 139.069 million diluted shares outstanding

Based off of the $6,050.0 million enterprise value and the assumptions above, what is the implied purchase of equity per share?

Total Enterprise Value	
– Refinancing Debt	
= Purchase of Equity	
/ Diluted Shares Outstanding	
= Equity Value per Share	

Answer:

Total Enterprise Value	$6,050.0
– Refinancing Debt	(884.9)
= Purchase of Equity	$5,165.1
/ Diluted Shares Outstanding	139.069
= Equity Value per Share	**$37.14**

A $37.14 offer price is a 46% discount compared to the original price of $68.40! Clearly the sellers would not agree to this.

CONCLUSION
What comes next?

After completing this book, we hope that you feel more confident in understanding and utilizing the valuation techniques that practitioners use.

A common phrase that you hear practitioners use is, "valuation is not rocket science." The techniques are straight forward and somewhat intuitive. Half of the learning process is picking up the terminology or jargon. Also, valuation is sometimes more ART than SCIENCE. Speaking in general terms, most people have access to the same knowledge and information. But, people will differ in their interpretation of that data.

Anyway, there may be some questions on your mind such as:

"How do I get more practice?"

"What comes next?"

We believe that the best way to get more practice is through real world examples. We will continually update our case study packages and utilize real companies with real financial disclosure.

In terms of what comes next, please check our website at **www.trainingthestreet.com** for advanced valuation and modeling topics.